Masks and Mirrors

Other Books by Bernard Carl Rosen

Adolescence and Religion

Achievement in American Society (coeditor)

The Industrial Connection

Aspettative di Istruzione e Occupazione Nei Giovani (coauthor)

Women, Work, and Achievement

Winners and Losers of the Information Revolution

Masks and Mirrors

Generation X and the Chameleon Personality

BERNARD CARL ROSEN

Westport, Connecticut
London

Library of Congress Cataloging-in-Publication Data

Rosen, Bernard Carl.
    Masks and mirrors : Generation X and the chameleon personality /
    Bernard Carl Rosen.
       p.   cm.
    Includes bibliographical references and index.
    ISBN 0–275–97325–5 (alk. paper)
    1. Generation X—United States.   2. Elite (Social sciences)—United States.
    3. Social change—United States—Psychological aspects.   4. Defense
    mechanisms (Psychology)   I. Title.
    HQ799.7.R67   2001
    305.242'0973—dc21   00–069863

British Library Cataloguing in Publication Data is available.

Library of Congress Catalog Card Number: 00–069863
ISBN: 0–275–97325–5

First published in 2001

Praeger Publishers, 88 Post Road West, Westport, CT 06881
An imprint of Greenwood Publishing Group, Inc.
www.praeger.com

Printed in the United States of America

∞™

The paper used in this book complies with the
Permanent Paper Standard issued by the National
Information Standards Organization (Z39.48–1984).

10 9 8 7 6 5 4 3 2

To the memory of my great-grandfather
who built the mill

Deceit has a thousand masks.
—Montaigne

Contents

Acknowledgments

Over the time it took me to research and write this book, I was fortunate to have family and friends who put up with me during the book's sometimes difficult gestation. My thanks to them all. I am greatly indebted to my editors: Acquisition Editor, Suzanne Staszak-Silva; Copyeditor, Pelham Boyer; and Production Editor, Nicole Cournoyer. They moved the book through all its stages, and each one improved it along the way. My special thanks to the reference librarians of Cornell University's superb libraries. They were unfailingly friendly and helpful. To all of these people, I am deeply grateful.

1

Generation X

In the 1990s America entered a new gilded age. Not since the late nineteenth century has the pace of getting and spending been so hectic and passionate. Conspicuous consumption, castigated by Thorstein Veblen a century ago, has lost its taint. A new elite, eager to enjoy its success, unembarrassed by charges of shameless bad taste and arrogantly indifferent to the angry stares of envious losers, has gone on a spending spree, seeking legitimacy through possession and display.[1]

Across the country, people who have only recently grown rich in the burgeoning information economy are living the American Dream. In the city, they live in well-appointed apartments or town houses located in safe, carefully policed areas. Prudently, they avoid public transportation, stay clear of lower-class environs, and give city parks a wide berth. For neighbors they seek out people much like themselves: successful, discerning strivers obsessed with self-improvement, with being lean and trim, with eating the latest nutritionally approved foods and drinking designer water, with staying on top of the latest fads in clothes, art, and music, with being eternally sexually attractive. None of this comes cheap.

Many who can do so escape the city altogether. Some build mansions in the country, palazzos that would have caught the admiring attention of a Frick or a Morgan or a Carnegie. No expense is spared. Nestled on estates sprawling over many acres, these big, elegant homes possess every convenience money can buy and architectural

ingenuity can conceive: rooms wired with state-of-the art electronic
wizardry, kitchens equipped with fiery Viking ranges, temperature-
and-humidity-controlled wine cellars stocked with bottles of vintage Bordeaux and Burgundy, garages gorged with Lamborghini
Diablos or Ferraris, elaborate lawns and gardens, intimate theaters,
pools, and much more.

Away from home, the new elites do not hesitate to indulge themselves. They dine in the best restaurants and jet first class to Marbella
and St. Barts and other playgrounds of the rich to sample the erotic
tidbits that new climes and surroundings afford. They stay at elegant hotels, golf on exquisitely tailored greens, and dance the night
away to the music of native bands dressed in colorful costumes. All
in all, as in a dream, they are living a life previously available only to
princes, industrial tycoons, and movie stars.[2]

This spending frenzy has been fueled by an unusually sustained
period of high national economic growth. For about a decade the
good times rolled.[3] Inflation was tamed and all but banished; unemployment was the lowest in three decades; credit was easy. The result
of this confluence of positive forces was the longest boom in American history. Information-age companies exploded in a frenzy of
speculative expansion and wealth creation. The boom of the 1990s
added more than five trillion dollars of new financial wealth to the
national kitty. True, the figure was cut by $1.6 trillion in 2000-2001
when the new economy stock bubble burst and the old economy
slowed to a crawl. Even so, the total number of American millionaires now stands at eight million, not including 275,000 fortunate
souls worth more than 10 million, and a new batch of billionaires.[4]

WHO ARE THESE ELITES?

Most of them are successful Baby Boomers, an aging cohort now
securely established in positions of power and wealth. But there is
another group nipping at their heels: young meritocrats at the leading edge of Generation X. This was originally the name of a British
punk band; only later was it applied to an entire generation, by novelist Douglas Coupland. I shall call them Xers, to save ink. A short-
hand way of distinguishing between the two groups is to follow the
guidelines of William Strauss and Neil Howe, who were among the
first to compare the Boomers with the Xers. "The Boomers," they
wrote, "were too young to remember Roosevelt dying, while the
[Xers] were too young to remember Kennedy's assassination."[5] Like

their predecessors, some Xers have become rich; others are well on their way; still others, though just getting started, appear determined to knock the Boomers off their comfortable perches and make it big whatever the cost.

Born in the 20-year period from 1965 through 1984, the Xer generation numbers about 80 million souls, a number slightly larger than that of the Baby Boomers.[6] Slowly, Generation X has emerged as a recognizable group with distinct attitudes, values, quirks, fidgets, and personality traits that set it apart from earlier generations. The elite of the Xer generation—about 15 percent of the entire age cohort—shares many of the values of its age group. But its members have also been exposed to certain meritocratically influenced experiences that set them apart from their entire age cohort.

This book is about elite Xers: their triumphs and travails, their worries and hang-ups, and their misadventures and good fortune in a nation that is changing with bewildering cyberspeed. It examines their struggle to succeed in a skeptical world that is leery of their motives and not inclined to give them much slack. More specifically, it explores the way Xers handle the anxieties and fears that intense competition in a cutthroat market economy inevitably produces. In their urgent quest for success, many elite Xers fall prey to acute anxiety when faced with pitiless competition. Frightened that challengers may be getting the upper hand, they don masks to hide their intentions, adjust mirrors to distort reality, and pretend to be what they are not. I call this response to danger chameleonism, and it is upon chameleonism that much of this book focuses.

THE ELITE XERS

Elite Xers are a diverse group. Some are computer nerds, geeky wizards of the new technologies based on digital compression and high-speed data transmission. Others are money managers and investment experts, wizards of financial dealings. Still others are designers of innovative devices and consumer products. Many are journalists and editors, artists and creative people in publishing, television, motion pictures, and the theater. Adding color to the group are gobs of publicity spin-doctors and other image makers, a few dabs of ambitious entrepreneurial wannabees, a passel of would-be entertainment celebrities, and a scattering of just plain eccentric exhibitionists driven by a hunger for fame and fortune. This list is not meant to be exhaustive; it is meant simply to illustrate the range of jobs held by elite Xers.

But common to all elite Xers is the unforgiving nature of the realms they populate: they move in circles that laud winners but have no place for losers. And bear this in mind: above all, Xers want to be winners. They will do whatever is necessary to stay ahead of the pack: work hard, dream not a little, and scheme relentlessly. As a result, successful Xers are beginning to fill important slots in the financial and entertainment industries, advertising and publishing circles, government and private foundations, and other sectors of the society.

Having grown up with the new information technology, elite Xers easily mastered the art of generating and analyzing facts and figures. They are adept at identifying and solving problems and at formulating and merchandising ideas. By organizing and manipulating information, they create ideas and images, they rearrange words, sound bites, and pictures all of which inform, influence, and amuse audiences. They interpret events and history, help set the standards for music, dance, fashion, and beauty, and disseminate dreams and fantasies. They show us how to make more money and run businesses more efficiently, how to lose weight and make love, how to live longer and more successfully. They also teach us how to have more fun—which is not the least of their contributions, because, perversely, the world goes to great lengths to frustrate our legitimate right to live well at small expense and with minimum effort.

Using a panoply of special knowledge and skills, and frequently employing tools difficult for the layman to grasp—technical jargon, scientific, financial and legal expertise—they shape the nation's perception of itself, expand its range of options, and assist in its evaluation of choices. For good or ill, we cannot escape their influence. The cars we buy, the food we eat, the clothes we wear, the movies we see, and the tunes we dance to are influenced by the work of Xers, who cleverly weave together fabric and fashion, ideas and skills, to produce new goods and services that give concrete form to our fantasies and hopes and dreams. Their skills have made them the newest mandarins of the Information Society.

Xers have an asset older generations lack—youth. Today, youth is cool. Twenty-somethings fresh out of college bring to the market place firsthand knowledge about their cohort: the latest sounds, the catchiest phrases, and the most exciting images. They know what is likely to capture the attention of the hugely profitable youth market.

With this asset to their credit, they not only help decide what is correct in dress and dance and demeanor but influence what will sell and stay stylish, and what will drift off the screen of the national consciousness.

Youth is especially critical to a high-tech economy, because modern telecommunications tends to be a young person's game. Advancing age, it is thought, causes one to fall behind the leading edge of technological change. Age deadens the appreciation of the money-making potential of zany fads and wildly fluctuating fashion, and it eventually dulls the zest for the competitive fray—all serious handicaps in arenas where the scramble for money and power is furious and unending. If winning is your aim, youth is no small asset.

MAKING IT TODAY

Although they often complain about the niggardly way the world treats them, elite Xers are among the best paid and most cosseted people in the country—and for good reason. Working at the leading edge of the techno-service society, using state-of-the-art techniques, and allocating resources in ways that save precious time and energy, Xers sit in the catbird's seat.

Nowhere is this more apparent than in the arcane world of international finance. Positioned before computer terminals, with a few taps on a computer keyboard elite Xers send mind-boggling amounts of dollars, euros, marks, pounds, francs, and yen streaming around the globe. Buying and selling stocks, bonds, and currencies, 25 year-old traders with nerves of steel and ice-water in their veins make and lose vast sums in a few minutes on bets made with other Xer speculators located in cities thousands of miles away.

Operating beyond the control of governments, Xer traders bind the world of finance together in an electronic network that transcends national boundaries and parochial interests, evaluating economic performance, depressing or elevating the value of national banknotes at international currency exchanges in Tokyo, Frankfurt, London, and New York. Traders exchange about a trillion or more dollar's worth of currency each day. They are putting at naught the efforts of central bankers to control the value of the world's money. In the course of their work Xer traders loosen or tighten the flow of money available for investment, ultimately touching the lives of almost everyone.

Manipulating currency is not by any means the only Xer game. They are moving into many other spheres. For example, Xers are at the forefront of e-commerce. Seeking entrepreneurial outlets for their talents in the exploding domain of the Internet, young people are changing the nature of retailing and commerce. Their dot-com companies have sometimes achieved spectacular results. Take the case of David Filo and Jerry Yang, both still in their twenties, who in the spring of 1996 founded Yahoo!, the Internet's most popular portal site, an enterprise that promptly made them multimillionaires. After obtaining some modest start-up capital, they started the company and then offered their stock to the public at $4.33 a share, split adjusted. At the end of the first day, the stock had risen 154 percent. Filo and Yang, who wisely retained 31 percent of the stock, quickly became seriously rich, with a combined worth in the millions, only a brief stop on the way to the stratosphere.

Filo and Yang are not the only Xers to have made it big in the Internet world. Take for instance, Stanford University pals Larry Page and Sergey Brin. While still in their twenties, they put together Google, the Web's largest and fastest search engine. In just two years it gained a reputation for speed and accuracy that may make them billionaires.[7]

Needless to say, not all Xer ventures are this successful. Relatively few have made their founders millionaires overnight. Most ambitious Xers are still struggling to make their way to the top of the slippery pole of success, eager to become rich and important, doggedly fighting to get their shares, even when the threat of failure dogs their footsteps. Indeed, more than a few Xer entrepreneurs have failed. This is an especially devastating prospect, one that haunts their every dream. For although failure is always heartbreaking, in America it is also a sin.

THE PRESSURE COOKER

But why are so many elite Xers worried about failure? After all, they have a lot going for them. It is, in part, because they believe that the pressures of the competitive world in which they live and work are threatening to reduce them to pulp. The pressures are manifold. For one thing, the world is changing in ways they cannot control or entirely understand. A new order—the information economy—has arisen, to which they are committed but whose functioning seems chaotic and out of their control. And nothing worries Xers more than the sense that things are veering inexplicably out of control. Ironically, although the new order is their own darling, many Xers feel unloved, adrift, confused, not knowing what to expect, where to fit in, or how. In this unfathomable world, unpredictable and without firm guidelines, dealing with events and people becomes an ordeal, a game based on guesswork—and all too often the guesses turn out to be wrong.

For another thing, the hustle to win, the fierce scramble for recognition and reward, the hunger for status and security, is being exacerbated by competition from a frightening array of new contestants. These are people who in the past had never dreamed of entering the competitive ring but now clamor to get in. Women, minorities, immigrants, once excluded from the big races for wealth, power, and status, stridently demand the opportunity to compete with privileged white males for the glittering prizes that success brings. In some cases they insist that valued jobs and promotions are due them, merited or not, to compensate for past discrimination—and their claims for preferences have occasionally been validated by the state. As a result, a furious gyre of competition has erupted without parallel anywhere, prompting a pervasive anxiety that is fueled by envy, anger, uncertainty, and the fear of failure.

Who exactly is responsible for this mischief? As the Xers see it, troublemakers abound. Political panders, envious rivals, and ruthless competitors, at home and abroad, threaten to undermine their positions, ignore their legitimate rights, trash their values, and disparage their identity—in effect, to push them aside. Xers are finding that making one's way up the corporate ladders of the competitive hierarchies in which they move is daunting. It is all too easy to lose one's balance and fall. Frightened Xers believe they could be forced out of the running, pushed over precipices, and permanently doomed to be losers. This is an especially terrifying prospect to elite Xers, who have little time for losers.

Their fears are exacerbated by the status confusion and disarray the information revolution has produced. Xers must relentlessly jostle each other for the attention of their bosses, colleagues, and the public. But who among them will be noticed? Who is entitled to respect? Who can be casually pushed aside? Whose calls must be returned? These are important questions, at least to Xers, for the answers will affect their chances to be winners.

Xers could use help. At the very least, they need an explanation of what is happening to them. But uniquely in the nation's history, they are a generation without a paradigm to guide them. The ideology that sustained their predecessors, the dream of endless progress, has been abandoned. A dreary Darwinian, survival-of-the-fittest, social-evolutionist ideology has taken its place. Unfortunately, no comfort can be found there. Elite Xers are having to live with an explanatory ideology that is making them nervous—for who knows when the evolutionary process, impersonal and relentless, will push them aside?

To sum up, brisk and unremitting competition, galloping social and economic change, and a grim philosophy of life have all combined to quicken and enlarge the anxieties that torment elite Xers.

STRATEGIES OF DEFENSE

What is to be done? How to fight off unfriendly competitors, some of whom work in offices down the hall? How to protect oneself against the depredations of unscrupulous strangers bent upon seizing treasured prizes? The situation is dangerous but not hopeless. There are things Xers can do, limited, it is true, but not insignificant. What are these things? For one thing, they can fight—struggle and maneuver openly for advantage. But this time-honored response to danger, still valued in some circles, has in recent times come to be frowned upon. Fighting is considered disruptive and unproductive, gross, detrimental to success in a corporate world obsessed with consensus building and team spirit. To illustrate, candidates for positions at Goldman Sachs, deemed by M.B.A. students to be the most desirable place to work in America, are asked by recruiters, "Are you a team player?" At Goldman the team player is admired and the individualist disparaged.[8]

Many organizations, not just upper-level brokerage firms, discourage open fighting for advancement and denounce displays of individualistic ambition as detrimental to the firm. But individualism is pronounced among elite Xers—too pronounced, say managers, who accuse their Xer underlings of viscerally rejecting authority. Xers seem indifferent to the needs of the organization, hating orders, wanting to have everything their own way. Not at all the way Xers see it, of course. Individualism seems to them a sign of inner strength, not mere truculent defiance.

If fighting must be eschewed and ambition muted, the threatened Xer may decide to run away. Flight seems the better part of valor. But apart from being humiliating, flight means abandoning the goal of success—an idea abhorrent to meritocratic Xers. However, in some circumstances flight appears to make good sense, even if to others it will surely look like cowardice; some Xers take this route, as we shall see in a later chapter.

Of course, there is always submission. When fighting is frowned upon and flight is not possible or acceptable, one can give in. Of the choices mentioned so far, this one is the least acceptable to the elite Xer. Basically hostile towards authority, rebellious, reluctant to take orders of any kind, most Xers find the very idea of submission totally repulsive. What appears to others as sensible accommodation seems to many Xers nothing more than spineless conformity, the mark of a weak spirit. And so they look about them for an alternative way to cope with anxiety-inducing competition.

There is, it turns out, a fourth way. Xers may respond to the challenge of dangerous competition by pretending to be like their adversaries. Appearances in this case are meant to be deceiving. These Xers profess to hold the values and goals of their opponents. They seem docile and unthreatening. But in fact the struggle continues under cover, a surreptitious battle fought with devious techniques. Though apparently content to go along rather than fight, beleaguered Xer's may in fact privately pursue their own objectives, covering their tracks and making their plans as they go along. By cleverly lulling their competitors into a false sense of security, they position unwary opponents for drubbings when circumstances permit. I call this strategy chameleonism.

FROM STRATEGY TO PERSONALITY

Of course, fighting, fleeing, submitting, and pretending are responses to danger almost everyone employs at some time or other, depending on the circumstances. But for some people one or another of these strategies becomes dominant. Used over and over again, even when some other response might be equally appropriate or even more successful, it becomes a part of their personalities, a predisposition to respond to challenge or danger in a certain way. For instance, when someone habitually attacks the source of a threat, it seems fair to infer predisposition to aggressiveness. Similarly, if another's response to danger is a rigid pattern of flight or submission, that person may be said to have acquired a personality predisposing him or her to flee or to comply. Finally, if an individual's response to threat is unreflective dissembling, a fixed tendency to conceal his or her true self, that person may be said to have a predisposition to be a chameleon—that he or she has a chameleon personality.

Developed early in life, products of our efforts to cope with the world, these predispositions—to fight, fly, submit, pretend—become unconscious defenses against danger. Acting defensively, the individual interprets every threat within the framework of earlier experiences and responds in a predisposed way. But the interpretation may be mistaken and the response self-defeating, in which case the individual will suffer as a result. Nonetheless, once incorporated into the personality, a defense mechanism is relatively enduring and resistant to disconfirming evidence. Personality, though not necessarily fixed for all time, generally abhors change.

National surveys and clinical interviews, described later, suggest that many elite Xers possess the personality trait I call chameleonism. Moreover, in addition to empirical evidence, there are good theoretical reasons for believing this trait exists among Xers. Theory suggests that chameleonism tends to develop in people who grew up in troubled families, who fear losing status, who work in anxiety-creating circumstances, and who want desperately to control the events affecting their lives—and in fact, many elite Xers possess these characteristics. They tend to come from fractured homes, they usually work in nerve-racking situations, and they desperately want to control the forces that act upon them. In these circumstances, if they have decided that fighting is useless, submission intolerable, and escape impossible, chameleonism offers their only chance for protection.

There are, of course, problems with being a chameleon. For one, its emotional cost is high. Being unmasked and consequently disgraced and rejected is always possible. For another, managing impressions and pretending to be what one is not is a perilous affair. The public role, initially assumed purely for pragmatic purposes, may override the private inner identity, creating confusion about who one truly is and what one truly believes. In short, the chameleon's lot is not an easy one. Nor is the role of a chameleon a snap to play: it is hard work, the payoff is not guaranteed, and the risk of being unmasked is great.

Nonetheless, many elite Xers choose to play this game. Explaining why they do so and with what consequences is the task I have set for myself in this book. My approach, please note, is primarily social-psychological and closely tied to the present. But from time to time I must place the Xers' present condition within the broader context of history, for large and lofty changes have often their origins in ancient circumstances. Also, though the past never repeats itself in every detail, a knowledge of history alerts us to look for patterns in human experience. It warns us that change and anxiety are not unique to our times. This is useful for everyone to know, especially Xers.

Even so, explorations of history tend to make Xers restive. They seem to feel that the scroll of time began with them; consequently they see no point in ransacking the musty records of the past for explanations of the present—one reason why they view their present predicament as uniquely and darkly inexplicable. But they are mistaken. In one respect, Xers are no different from the rest of us. Like everyone else, their lives are rooted in the great social transformations that have shaken this country over the past century. Whether they are aware of this or not, they are caught in the loop of history's tempered coils, from which there is no escaping.

I believe their current anxieties and misgivings will come into sharper focus when we understand the record of the past, which will emerge as the book progresses. But first let us begin by examining the structure of chameleonism, the technique many Xers use to help them fend off competitors and to cope with anxiety.

2

The Structure of Chameleonism

On graduating from college and going out to work, ambitious young people today discover that youthful utopianism has gone out of fashion. It is not enough to be well-meaning and idealistic: performance also counts. And so pragmatism, not idealism, becomes their major preoccupation. With survival and success their goal, they must immerse themselves in a Darwinian world that continuously culls the weak from the strong, a brutally competitive arena where an unremitting struggle for wealth, status, and power generates deep insecurity in most contestants. In this dog-eat-dog world winners are celebrated, but losers tend to be dismissed out of hand and subjected to the hurt of having been found wanting.

To success-hungry people who work in challenging, rapidly changing, highly unpredictable environments where worry awaits and humiliation and betrayal stalk the unwary and insecure, the world seems dangerous and hostile, populated with predators who seek to pull them down. Losing is always a terrifying possibility. Feeling beleaguered, they fall victim to loneliness and a sense of helplessness. They believe themselves the prey of enemies out to abuse, cheat, and defeat them, and feeling endangered they can become disabled by anxiety. To prevent this calamity, some of them (even figuratively) take refuge in chameleonism.

Human chameleons, like their reptilian counterparts, ward off danger by assuming a protective coloration whenever danger arises. Not willing to run away, not wanting to put up their fists (even figuratively), reluctant to give in, chameleons take cover. Deception is their game. They pretend to be what they are not. They spread smoke to hide their actions, skillfully arrange mirrors to confuse the enemy, and don masks to conceal their true faces, hiding their real intentions and designs from envious competitors and implacable enemies. Although chameleonism begins as a deliberate attempt to fend off competitors and to guard self-esteem, in time and with practice it becomes automatic, a mostly unconscious way of ensuring personal safety. When it works properly, chameleonism helps win over needed clients and friends, and protects self-regard from the appraisals and actions of fierce rivals. With training it becomes a tool in the struggle for success, an invaluable aid in the struggle to keep from falling behind in a ferociously competitive world.

In general, chameleons try to please whomever they are with—adversaries, neutrals, and friends alike—hoping in this way to blend inconspicuously in the group. Their ability to take on outward appearances congenial to others, much as a ship (to change our metaphor) hoists acceptable colors in order to attach itself to a convoy navigating dangerous waters, helps assure survival in a unfriendly world, though much depends, of course, on choosing the right convoy, on identifying the winning side. Another way of looking at chameleons is to think of them as salesmen whose principal item of sale is themselves. In Erich Fromm's terminology, chameleons are people with a marketing personality. To the chameleon, other people are merely customers. Making the sale counts above all else, and to clinch the sale chameleons will do almost anything that—to paraphrase Richard Stengel's comment about flattery—"advances self-interest while concealing it at the same time."[1] Since chameleons regard the customer as expendable, someone to be abandoned when circumstances change and the connection proves unprofitable, they studiously avoid establishing relationships that would tie them down. Only a superficial bond, strong enough to sustain the wear and tear of business, is considered useful.

Chameleons are skilled at sensing changes in their environment and quickly adjust their behavior to suit the expectations of others. Impression management is their forte. Seeking to blend safely into hazardous surroundings, they behave congenially, ingratiating themselves with superiors and doing as little as possible to arouse suspicion or attack. Candor in response to danger, the chameleon believes, would be foolish to the point of folly; flimflam, humbug, hustle, and hype take the place of honest exchange. With luck, no one notices the fraud, no one is the wiser.

Needless to say, chameleonism is not unique to our times. It has been noted in many places and in many times. For instance, by one account Lucius Sergius Catalina (Cicero's Cataline) was a master chameleon. A patrician, a governor of Africa, a murderer, Catalina could mingle in the highest circles with ease, not least because he was a master of dissimulation, which enabled him to assume any character and deceive all but the sharpest eyes. As early as the fifteenth century, Pico delle Mirandola, an influential writer, used the term "chameleon" to describe humanity, citing as his authority Asclepius of Athens, who believed people are able to transform their natures whenever the occasion requires. Philip Dormer Stanhope, Lord Chesterfield, the fourth earl of Chesterfield, admitted to being a chameleon. "With all men I was a Proteus," he wrote in a letter to his son, "and assumed every shape to please them all: among the gay, I was the gayest; among the grave, the gravest."[2]

Nor is chameleonism in today's America limited to any one group. Chameleons can be found in diverse racial and ethnic groups, in all social classes, in all age categories, and in both sexes. Surely everyone at some time or other has played the chameleon. It is a price we pay for getting along with others. But for some people, it is only a temporary expedient. It does not become embedded in the personality, as it does with chameleons, who engage in deception as a matter of course whenever danger threatens them.

It is easy to view chameleonism with distaste, and this would be warranted if chameleonism were always a calculated and devious ploy, steeped in insincerity, basically manipulative, designed to deceive others for personal gain. In fact it often is not. It begins, true enough, as a response to danger, as a deliberate practice to be used and dropped when the occasion requires. Yet in time, after repeated use, it becomes a deeply embedded personality trait, the existence of which the chameleon may be unaware.

This tendency of repeated actions, though practiced originally for pragmatic reasons, to become part of one's belief system was recognized by the Jesuits centuries ago and became an element of their famously effective educational practice. In 1890, William James, in his seminal work *Principles of Psychology*, recognized that habituated action can be internalized and become an unconscious part of personality. That explains why chameleons can deny without qualm or guilt that they are dissemblers, two-faced, underhanded, and dishonest. Not all chameleons are unaware of what they are doing, of course. Some know very well what they are up to and are unfazed. It is not deceit that bothers them; it is the possibility of being found out and disgraced.

But chameleonism is more than a habitual response to danger, more than the concealment of one's true identity and the pragmatic assumption of a useful disguise, a mask to be assumed or removed as the occasion requires. It is a trait to which the individual can become strongly attached, one not easily abandoned, and though it is costly, its cost is not obvious, at least to the chameleon. Moreover chameleonism has several advantages. For example, chameleons can move easily in and out of relationships as their situation requires, without emotional turmoil and regret, and this gives them a significant advantage over people who lack this flexibility.

Being a successful chameleon is not easy. It takes concentration and luck, because a chameleon's path is strewn with mines. One misstep and all is over. Chameleons are always at risk. They cannot afford to lower their guard, even for a second. Skeptical adversaries may at any moment rip off their masks; a slip of the tongue may reveal their true intentions; someone may call the chameleon's bluff, and suddenly the game is up. The chameleon lives, therefore, in constant fear of being found out and unmasked. Yet unmasking a chameleon is not as easy as most people think. They imagine they can spot a chameleon at a glance, and sometimes they are right, though often they are wrong. Chameleonism well done is difficult to discern. Even chameleons are often deceived by their own facades: they begin by fooling others and end up fooling themselves.

In the beginning, when they are aware of what they are doing, chameleons realize they are acting in ways deeply at odds with what they truly believe. But they think they can live with this. After all, the human mind can hold absurdly contradictory points of view at the same time, and it is not uncommon for people to act in ways distinctly opposed to their private views. Moreover, various psychological defenses—compartmentalization, denial, cognitive dissonance reduction—help keep the chameleon mostly unaware of, or indifferent to, personal inconsistencies.[3]

But to believe that contradictory attitudes and behavior can be permanently sealed in neat compartments without causing confusion and anxiety is to expect too much of human nature. Inevitably the chameleon pays a price for acceptance bought with counterfeit coins, for safety obtained under false pretenses. The price is a profound confusion about one's identity, a pervasive anxiety about what to believe and whom to trust. As Nietzsche wrote, "Whenever a man strives long and persistently to appear someone else, he ends up finding it difficult to be himself again."[4]

ANXIETY AND FEAR

With the danger of inadvertent self-revelation or spiteful betrayal always present, and confusion about identity a possible problem, the chameleon cannot help being anxious and fearful. Both anxiety and fear are painful, of course, and yet of the two, anxiety is by far the more complex and in some ways the more disabling. Though unpleasant, to say the least, fear can be recognized and faced, and because it can be faced it can be overcome. Moreover, fear has its uses. Fear is a rational response to an objective threat, and as such it sensitizes the individual to danger, focuses attention on the problem, and helps mobilize energy to deal with it.

Anxiety, on the other hand, has quite the opposite effect. As a diffuse feeling of discomfort, often without specific content, anxiety mixes anticipation of punishment with a sense of impending doom; it confuses the victim, distracting attention from the true cause of pain, thus making effective remedial action all the more difficult. Nor should anxiety be dismissed as a trivial distemper, a mysterious mood change that emerges out of nowhere for no particular reason, a momentary disturbance to be treated with soothing words. Anxiety is a fever, and like any fever it should be seen as a symptom of an underlying malady of which the cause may be obscure.

Anxiety deserves a better press and more attention. Anxiety is often the result of conflict, internal or external, and popular opinion condemns conflict and extols harmony. But anxiety and conflict, within bounds, are not necessarily signs of sickness; they may also be signs of health. Indeed, conflict is natural in every society, the inevitable result of a struggle between individuals and groups for a share of always-limited resources. In this conflict lie the seeds of change. Conflict can be a sign of vigor and life; the absence of all social conflict and anxiety usually indicates the existence of stagnation, lassitude, indifference, widespread withdrawal into private concerns at the expense of the public interest. Only the community of the dead, safely planted in a cemetery, is without conflict.

Identifying the true cause of personal anxiety, however, may not be easy, because anxious people often do not know what is bothering them. They feel troubled and angry, and in their anger they may strike out at the presumed causes of their distress. But since they often misjudge the situations, mistaking particularly disagreeable people or groups for the real source of their misery, they may attack the wrong target. Sometimes, in an ironic twist of fate, the mistaken target of their hostility is themselves. In such cases people unconsciously blame themselves for their misery and turn their anger against themselves.

How can we locate the true causes of anxiety? Who will help us separate the wheat from the chaff and get to the kernel of the matter? Fortunately or not, there is no shortage of explicators of anxiety.[5] Let us consider just a few of the best known and see what can be learned from them. The focus will be on the work of Sigmund Freud and his followers. Others have speculated about anxiety, of course, but in my judgment none have done so as systematically and fruitfully as the psychoanalysis-oriented theorists.

Freud believed that anxiety is triggered when instinctual needs—principally the needs for sexual satisfaction and the expression of aggression—run up against society's rules forbidding their expression except in sharply limited ways and situations. The inner conflict this engenders, the clash it creates between instinctual drives and internalized social norms inevitably generates anxiety.[6] Unfortunately, Sigmund Freud's theory of anxiety, though certainly insightful, seems not especially useful for an understanding of anxiety today. Where is the repression of sex and aggression that Freud thought so important to the development of anxiety? It would be hard to show that prohibitions against the expression of sexual and aggressive needs greatly shackle contemporary young people. On the contrary, the sexual revolution has introduced an anything-goes ethic that has made sexual expression far easier than it was in Freud's day.

As for aggression, the let-it-all-hang-out attitude of contemporary popular culture has made it much easier to display anger and even to resort to aggression if the need arises. Indeed, these days some therapists urge people to enroll in courses that teach self-assertiveness, how to give vent to formerly repressed fury, on the assumption that anger unexpressed eats away at mental health. In sum, whatever his value as a guide for other areas of life and however accurate his observations may have been for his times, Freud will not be of direct help to us here.

Theorists influenced by Freud focused on the damage society and personal experience inflict on the individual's sense of self-worth. Freud's disciples, Harry Stack Sullivan, Alfred Adler, and Karen Horney (or to be more precise, former disciples—to some degree they all broke with the master), speak directly to our concerns. Though differing from each other in some respects their analyses of anxiety have a common theme: the troubled self responding to a stubbornly unfriendly world. As they see it, the damaged self, under pressure from a hostile environment, reacts with resentment and anxiety, and will seek relief and safety through accommodation. This idea permeates the present book and will serve as a guide throughout my presentation.

Briefly, Harry Stack Sullivan thought anxiety occurs when experience is discrepant with self-expectations and self-picture, a most infuriating condition that occurs when fractious people refuse to act in accordance with our dearest hopes and demands.[7] This frustrating situation, always difficult to endure, develops out of the parataxic distortions that creep into our perceptions of ourselves and others. Misjudging others, misperceiving what they think of us, and miscalculating what we can rightly expect of them, we act inappropriately, bringing down on our heads disapproval and rejection. The result is painful anxiety.

Alfred Adler also believed anxiety to be the product of living in a frustrating world that ignores our basic hopes and needs, that holds us in low esteem, and thus that makes us feel insignificant and helpless.[8] Adler believed these frustrations generate, as a compensation, a need to be superior (or at least to feel superior) to other human beings. All too often this need is frustrated; all too often we encounter indifference or rejection when we expected admiration and love; all too often we cannot convince others of our superiority. The need to be superior, he argued, is especially pronounced among people whose sense of self-worth has been damaged in the merciless competition for advancement that is characteristic of capitalist societies. Made to feel inferior, hurt, angry, and anxious, seeking to alleviate their pain and to prove their adversaries wrong, some anxiety-ridden persons may go to extraordinary lengths to prove their superiority. If luck and talent are with them, they demonstrate their superiority by becoming famous and rich. Success becomes for them, or so they hope, the royal road to a life free of anxiety.

In the absence of objective accomplishment, the wounded ego must do something. What it often does is to compensate for failure by making extravagant claims of superiority, even though to an impartial observer no basis for this self-assessment objectively exists. And yet bogus though it is, this bizarre but psychologically comprehensible defense mechanism magically bolsters self-esteem. For real or imaginary, a feeling of superiority can help reduce anxiety to somewhat more manageable levels. The danger, of course, is that a spurious sense of superiority is an unreliable defense against the attacks of a skeptical world, which is not always willing to take assertions of superiority for the real thing. Called to demonstrate their superiority, to put up or shut up, the superiority-fantasist may become overwhelmed by anxiety, which negates the fantasy's value.

Horney took a somewhat different tack. She granted the importance of superiority (perfection, in her schema) to the anxious person, but she thought the hunger for approval and acceptance was a more basic need. In her theory, it is the frustration of this need that produces crippling anxiety.[9] Unfortunately, frustration is inescapable in a competitive world that is pitiless in its evaluation of people, and very sparing in its approval. In fact, sad to say, acceptance in contemporary America can seldom be taken for granted: it is often up for grabs. The possibility of rejection looms before almost everyone. The result is devouring anxiety and, in its wake, a corrosive hostility toward self and others, the consequence of anxiety that is not recognized and dealt with.

THE VICIOUS CIRCLE

When anxiety cannot be acknowledged or hostility expressed, as is often the case, they must be denied, suppressed, hidden, repressed. But this only increases their power and makes them more dangerous, for recognized or not, they are still in place, doing their nasty work. Willy-nilly, the anxious individual becomes tangled in a vicious circle. As Horney sees it, the circle starts with anxiety. Naturally, this creates a need for reassurance, and inordinate demands are made for approval and affection. When, as often happens, these demands are not met, the individual feels unfairly rebuffed and reacts with rage, which must be repressed for fear of retaliation. But, as we know, repressing rage only increases anxiety.

In despair, eager to break free from this malignant bind, determined to be rid of the incubus of anxiety, the individual (the process is the same for both sexes) projects his fear and anger onto the outside world. Unfortunately, this only compounds the problem, for it convinces him that the world is indeed as dangerous as he feared. Whereupon he becomes even more anxious and angry. But since this anger cannot be safely expressed, it remains bottled up and thus a generator of more gnawing anxiety. And so the circle continues.

Horney considered several ways one may escape from this cruel trap.[10] Withdrawal is one: the individual may simply abandon any effort to win over the enemy and leave the field. This drastic solution is sometimes effective, at least for a time, but it is not available to everyone: there may be no where to go. Or he may instead gather enough power to himself to overwhelm his enemies, and coerce their approval and affection, reducing in this way their potential for harm. But since hostile people lack trust, acceptance attained through force will seem counterfeit, and enforced goodwill will make no lasting dent on his anxiety and hostility.

Or he may submit to his enemies and comply with their demands, ingratiating himself with them by smiles and nods of agreement, and become one of the group. When this submission is genuine (as it is not with the chameleon), the acceptance that follows may be authentic and reliable. Unfortunately, acceptance bought with affidavits of friendship proffered under pressure often proves worthless in the long run. The compliant person cannot be sure, when the time comes for payment, that these dearly bought certificates of acceptance will be honored. Moreover, submission to a foe requires an erasure of self that violates personal integrity, which to some people is an unacceptably high price for approval and safety.

There is another response to threat and anxiety, one that Horney and the other Freudian analysts do not mention, though it can be deduced from their theories: the individual may *pretend* to comply— that is, he can become a chameleon. He *seems* to all intents and purposes like his dangerous rivals. He talks and acts like them; he belittles any difference between himself and them; he seeks to disarm them with expressions of loyalty and affection. He hopes in this way to win them over and defuse the threat of attack. Underlying this ploy is the unspoken assumption: "If I seem like them, they won't hurt me." Insincere he may be, but he is simply trying to find safety and bring his anxiety under control.

Paradoxically, chameleonism, developed as a way of coping with anxiety, is itself a source of anxiety, because the price the chameleon pays for acceptance is exorbitant. In the process of ingratiating themselves with rivals, chameleons tend to develop traits that eventually make foes of friends and turn foes into even more envenomed opponents, thus endangering the very safety they so desperately seek. For instance, expert interpersonal skills and critical intelligence, the very things that make for successful chameleonship, may eventually boomerang against the dissembler. These qualities, although usually acceptable in most circumstances, may come across as arrogance when the chameleon seeks to manipulate others.

In addition, a skill at handling people can easily degenerate into cynical manipulation for personal gain. The need to control the impressions of others, the very essence of chameleonism, can develop into an obsession with dominating them. It is an easy step from domination to exploitation and not surprisingly the chameleon often becomes the sort of person who uses people. When this is discovered the injured party may react punitively, the very thing the chameleon most wants to avoid.

But nothing jeopardizes the chameleons' safety more than their unrelenting drive to prove their superiority over friend and foe alike. It is not enough for them to know they are superior; they must get others to admit it. Almost every encounter chameleons have with others involves an effort to demonstrate their superiority in some activity, by witty wordplay, erudite knowledge, business enterprise, creative artistry, and the like. Often a chameleon's superiority is a fact, for intelligence and interpersonal skill chameleons usually have in goodly measure; without these qualities no one can become a successful chameleon. Chameleons daily demonstrate their cleverness by bamboozling other people, controlling them, getting them to buy the phony pictures of themselves they offer to the world. Given such success in flim-flammery, it is not surprising that a sense of superiority comes easily to chameleons.

Eventually,this imperious urge toward superiority, this need to be wonderful in their own eyes and in the estimation of others, gets chameleons into trouble. For they have difficulty concealing their contempt for the inferior people they manipulate. That they are superior to others seems obvious to them. What else would explain the ease with which they gull their marks? But when this sense of superiority impels them to try constantly to impress others, to win them over, to exact from them admissions of their brilliance and the singularity of their accomplishments, they are asking for trouble. It is, to say the least, incautious of anyone who is also seeking to be inconspicuous among rivals and possible detractors.

Still, chameleons have little choice in the matter, since in large part their self-esteem rests on being in control, on being respected, on being admired. Nevertheless, excessive need for control and admiration jeopardizes every relationship chameleons have with other people, even those they consider friends. Chameleons feel humiliated when control vanishes and admiration is not forthcoming. Their reaction to humiliation is devouring fury. But this must be concealed, lest it brings down on their heads retributive ire. It is this fear of reprisal and the concealment of fury that keeps the chameleon entrapped in the vicious circle of anxiety.

THE SUCCESSFUL CHAMELEON

Above all, what chameleons want is safety: it is this need, in part, that drives them, without letups, to pursue success. But since they live in a fiercely competitive world and are exposed to assault from many hostile forces, they know that safety may elude them, and this understandably feeds their anxiety. To help keep this hungry monster at bay, they become adept at recognizing danger from any quarter. They learn to keep their radar well tuned to pick up the slightest signals of trouble ahead. By watching the horizon for the smallest cloud and scanning faces of friends and foes for the slightest variation in mood, they quickly recognize changes in what others expect of them and quickly adapt to new conditions. Nevertheless, since circumstances can change abruptly, and since the discovery of the hoax they are visiting upon others is always a chilling possibility, chameleons cannot afford to let their guard down; they must remain alert at all times. Absent-mindedness and overconfidence are their worst enemies.

In order to adapt successfully to the game of life, chameleons must be able to understand intuitively what others think and why they behave as they do. They must recognize the other players' values and adjust to them, or at least conceal disagreement. And it is essential that chameleons have enough insight into themselves to hide any personal quirk that could damage a relationship. In short, a skill at psyching out opponents is something the chameleon must develop and continually hone. None of this is easy. But then, managing impressions and projecting friendliness are chameleon fortes, learned early and practiced often.

To survive in a rapidly changing world, chameleons must be flexible, able to break away from the established ties of family and community, prepared to adopt new practices, ready to about-face when the need arises. Above all, they must be able to recognize the true direction of change, fit into each new situation as it develops, and not let fixed principles get in the way. Their enemies call this insincerity, but to chameleons it just seems like good sense. "Change or die" is their code.

On the positive side, chameleons possess qualities that commend them to other people. They are bright, often charming and resourceful, and, since they like to enjoy themselves, fun to be with. Sadly, though, all this may work against them, because not surprisingly, given their sense of superiority and with these admirable qualities, chameleons tend to have exceedingly high opinions of themselves. Time and again this gets them into trouble. Enamored with their own brilliance and charm, they may slip into self-congratulation and openly wallow in the joys of concinnity and superiority. Such blatant narcissism offends most people, of course, and smart chameleons try to conceal it. But it is a difficult matter to hide, in part because they are mostly unaware of its existence, in part because they have no control over it, and in part because they cannot bear to part with it.

Unfortunately, despite his genuine assets, numerous and admirable, the chameleon's narcissism is based in large part upon delusion. He imagines himself to be far more clever, more resourceful, more attractive and sexually irresistible, more upright and deserving of respect and deference, than any objective evaluation of his character would justify. To make matters worse, his unrealistically high self-evaluation often coexists with deep-seated doubts of this true worth, nagging suspicions that the real self and imagined self are worlds apart. But then, self-doubt is unavoidable, because the chameleon's narcissism is based upon expectations so out of touch with reality that they cannot possibly be satisfied. At bottom, narcissists want to be accepted on their own terms; they demand that the world unconditionally acknowledge their superiority. Needless to say, a coldly indifferent world will inevitably reject such demands. The unavoidable reaction to rejection, as we know, is rage and hatred, directed against both self and society.

Finally, chameleonism is riddled with contradictions. On the one hand, chameleons want to be inconspicuously embedded within their milieu; they seek to mask their superiority under the pretense of ordinariness. On the other, chameleons are convinced of their own personal superiority and want it publicly acknowledged. They exude friendliness and openness but beneath this facade is contempt for a credulous public that accepts the fictious character they have created for their own benefit and to the detriment of others. They must project a personae of unsullied sincerity, even though they believe that only by duping others can acceptance be found. And to add to their troubles, they want to have a good time but must move carefully so as not to arouse envy.

In sum, chameleons are beset by contrieties, torn by inner conflicts, and pulled in opposite directions. They treasure independence but want to blend into the group; they cultivate self-detachment but seek to convey an impression of genial collegiality; they present an inviting facade but at heart want to keep people at a distance; they pretend to be part of the group but are reluctant to establish enduring relationships with anyone. In fact, they want to go their own way. They view dependency as a weakness and avoid true intimacy as a trap. They want to be free to break old ties and to make new ones whenever their interests require. They believe a commitment to anyone or to anything inevitably inhibits their freedom of action and hinders their chances to get ahead.

THE OTHER-DIRECTED PERSONALITY

In some ways, the chameleon resembles the other-directed personality of David Riesman's typology. Both the chameleon and the other-directed personality display tendencies toward ingratiation; both seek to win acceptance by reducing the visible differences between themselves and others.[11] Nevertheless, there are important differences between the two types, differences that merit examination.

To begin with, while it is true that other-directed people, like chameleons, constantly orient themselves toward the expectations of others, in the case of other-directed people this is because they lack strong personal identities and convictions of their own. They have no firm beliefs. They want only to know *what* to believe; they are seeking direction. Above all, they want satisfying identities, and they believe acceptance by the group will give this to them. Chameleons, on the other hand, resist abandoning their private identity to the group. They may appear to be doing so, but this is a ploy. They will adopt the group's identity only so long as it enhances personal safety and advantage. Nor do they necessarily lack convictions. They may, in fact, hold strong opinions. But knowing when it is not expedient to express them, they go along in order to get along.

For another thing, other-directed persons are passionately committed to their peer groups, and conformity becomes an end in itself.

Pretense plays no role, disguise and dissimulation no part, in their efforts to be accepted. Other-directed people truly want to be integrated into the groups in which they seek membership. They search for compatible groups, and gaining acceptance becomes their overriding objective in life.

Consequently, other-directed people have few defenses against the demands of their peers. As Riesman put it, "The peer group becomes the measure of all things."[12] The individual feels "powerless, safe only when performing a ritual in approving company."[13] In time, sensitivity to peer group expectations becomes an obsession. Readily shifting their positions to align themselves with the group and waffling when no one signal dominates the screen, other-directed people appear passive and indecisive. In time, their sensitivity to the opinions of others develops into an insatiable need for approval: their self-esteem comes to hinge entirely on what other people think of them. It is to peers that other-directed persons turn, automatically and almost indiscriminately, for validation of their success, attractiveness, sexual appeal, intelligence, and moral stature.

Other-directed people tend to stay put. Once acceptance by the group has been won, they seldom wander away. But immobility is a price they willingly pay for acceptance. Immersion in the group and acceptance of its demands becomes a comfortable way of life worth almost any sacrifice, including abandoning all efforts for personal advancement, if doing so would mean the loss of peer acceptance.

In contrast, chameleons are nothing if not flexible and mobile. They are willing to seek out any change that will enhance their security, even at the risk of alienating friends. Indeed, chameleons are rarely emotionally at peace with peers, though they will seek to hide this fact. They know that the pursuit of personal advantage excites suspicion and envy, yet they are perfectly ready to risk disapproval, though disapproval worries them, if advantage beckons and success seems a good possibility. Still, chameleons much prefer to avoid open breaks. They will, when necessary, disguise their intentions from peers, try to keep the peace, and stay safely put—until, that is, it becomes advantageous to move on.

Chameleons are always prepared to change groups if this helps get them where they want to go. This is the beauty of chameleonism: it predisposes the individual to move on when change becomes profitable. As long as chameleons know what they are doing, this flexibility can be useful. But as already noted, in the long run chameleonism tends to become so embedded in the personality that it becomes a force of its own, and then it may move the chameleon in directions not consciously selected and in ways not in the individual's best interest, and toward dubious goals.

The internal structure of chameleonism is a marvelously complex thing, far more intricate than I have managed to convey in this brief chapter. No one, myself included, fully understands this under-researched topic. More of this personality trait's complexity and exquisite variety, of its many functions and manifestations, will become clearer in later chapters. But first let us look at the forces that incline elite Xers to become chameleons.

3

The Xer Chameleon

Elite Xers will some day inherit the country—a rich prize, a cornucopia of money, power, and position, a legacy that is the envy of much of the world. As computer-savvy experts running the information system of a superpower, elite Xers are guaranteed privileged places in the world labor market. As long as the information economy thrives, there will always be employment for them, secure and well-paying jobs, interesting work with high prestige and pull. You might think they would be bubbling with confidence and joy. But this is not the case.

In fact, despite their growing influence and affluence, many elite Xers appear to be not at all at ease. They seem worried and uncertain, fearful that events, unknown and unforeseeable, may write finis to all their hopes and plans. The world cannot be trusted, they say. It has let them down, treats them less well than they deserve, and threatens them with unmerited punishment. Indeed, many Xers think that whatever they already have achieved—far less than they hope to one day—may at any moment be taken from them. Nothing pleasant in their future can be taken for granted.

After struggling so hard to make their way—against the wishes, it must be added, of a grudging society—elite Xers feel they cannot afford to stop and enjoy the fruits of their achievements, even when success seems within their grasp. A pause might be refreshing, but the price is a loss of momentum, and after all they have been through, this would be tragic. The climb up the slippery slope was steep, each step perilous, a misstep always possible, and a crash to smithereens a sure result of any carelessness. To relax and lose one's footing at this point would be calamitous. Small wonder many elite Xers appear obsessed with a fear of falling, a dread of losing status—the quintessential angst of the middle-class arriviste.

Is it surprising, then, that many elite Xers resort to chameleonism to protect themselves? Not all do, of course; some choose other ways to defend themselves. Nevertheless, it seems reasonable to infer from the work they do, the nature of their childhood experiences, and the things they say about themselves and their peers that chameleonism is common among elite Xers. Indeed, some observers have charged that Xers use what I call chameleonism as a tool for personal advancement, as well as a way of coping with stress when things go badly and a fall from the ladder of success seems imminent. Thus J. Walker Smith and Ann Clurman in their generally sympathetic portrait of Xers, based on observation and longitudinal survey data, assert that in today's rapidly moving world Xers have no choice but to live a "chameleon-like life," constantly changing, always cautious about becoming involved, and avoiding commitment whenever possible.[1]

That living at the leading edge of a rapidly changing, intensely competitive society could predispose Xers to become chameleons may seem obvious enough. But the question remains: how precisely does social change generate Xer chameleonism? For in truth, the specific link between the current spasm of social change and chameleonism is not fully understood—a glaring gap in our understanding of change, and one that deserves far more attention than it has to date received. I propose in this chapter to make a modest start at filling this lacuna. Let us begin with a look at the nature of the changes with which Xers must cope.

THE RITALIN AGE

For good or ill, Xers live in interesting times. Change is everywhere, unpredictable and seemingly chaotic. With rapid change comes social dislocation: the trashing of traditional norms and customs, the cacophony of conflicting demands and expectations, the mind-numbing effects of technological mutation and confusion—more than enough to upset most Xers and make them jittery.

But, it will be said, rapid change is nothing new. It has been a characteristic of Western industrial life for more than a century, as numerous monographs and books well document. Nevertheless, something new has happened. Not only has the pace of change accelerated but a new social entity has emerged out of the chaos of change—the information revolution.[2] It is this revolution that is responsible in large part for the growth of anxiety and chameleonism among elite members of Generation X.

Horribly complex and dynamic, the information revolution could do with far more analysis than it has so far received. But even at this point, its outlines are fairly clear.[3] It is a market-driven convulsion brought about by numerous breathtaking improvements in telecommunications: for example, the cell phone, the fax machine, the computer, and the Internet. To the delight of experts and the consternation of neophytes, these devices never stand still, changing almost from day to day, continually providing new ways to collect, analyze, and disseminate information.

In this realm of electronic wizardry, where youth reputedly rules, even Xers may suffer nausea from riding the technological roller coaster. As Xer author Douglas Rushkoff argues, modern inventions overload the mind: there are simply too many things to do, too many decisions to make, too many skills to acquire. The ubiquitous pocket-sized cell phone/pager/organizer, and the fax machine, modem, Internet, and World Wide Web have collectively flooded the world with more data and ideas than most people can comprehend, burdening elite Xers with mountains of information and tons of trivia.[4] And to worsen matters, this torrent has made some skills, acquired after much study, useless overnight. Equipment maintenance and operation have become increasingly complicated, causing endless muddle and eating up precious time and energy. Even nimble elite Xers are finding it difficult to cope with the effects of rapid technological innovation.

Time is a problem. There is never enough of it; too much is expected too quickly; almost no space is allowed for thought or regret. As Malcolm Gladwell put it, people have become "addicted to speed—to cellular phones and beepers and faxes and overnight mail and computers with powerful chips and hard-driving rock music and television shows that splice together images at hundredth-of-a-second intervals."[5] Nothing seems to stand still; speed has become the measure of most things.[6] The result is widespread Ritalin-like hyperactivity that only accentuates a deep-seated Xer insecurity about staying ahead of the pack.

WE HAVE BEEN THERE BEFORE

Not that pandemic anxiety is anything new in America. George M. Beard observed it full blown in late-nineteenth-century America. Beard was a neurologist, a Fellow of the New York Academy of Medicine and a member of other scientific organizations. Writing in 1881, he expressed alarm at the steep rise in sick headache, hypochondria, nervous exhaustion, insomnia, hysteria, nervous dyspepsia, and other symptoms of neurasthenia among people in the upper strata of society. These emotional ailments he attributed to industrialization—or as he put it, to modern civilization.

The pace of modern life, he concluded, was too hectic for the emotional well-being of Americans. They had become addicted to work. They were compulsive watchers of clocks and slaves to punctuality—and "punctuality is the thief of nervous force."[7] The immediate cause of this malady was not hard to find. He believed one needed look no further than the modern city, which shut people up in crowded streets and neighborhoods, pummeled them with incessant noise, subjected them to intense competition, and afflicted them with information overload. There were, he felt, just too many actors on the stage of modern life, just too may people confronting one another in closely packed scenes where people got emotionally hurt.

Beard singled out the telegraph as the villain of the piece. Telegraphy put people under constant strain, bombarding them with more information than they could handle and swiftly transmitting in minutes news that had once taken weeks to travel, overloading the mind. Businessmen were the telegraph's most pathetic victims. By transmitting the prices of goods immediately across the globe and requiring responses to information before it could be digested and reflected upon, the telegraph kept merchants in a constant state of apprehension. "This continual fluctuation of values, and the knowledge of those fluctuations in every part of the world, are the scourges of business men, the tyrants of trade—every cut in prices in wholesale lines in the smallest of any of the Western cities, becomes known in less than an hour all over the Union; thus competition is both diffused and intensified."[8]

Beard was not, of course, the first to recognize the effects of technology on the emotional state of people.[9] The Luddites—eighteenth-century British workmen who destroyed modern machinery in protest against the changes it was bringing—among others, had dilated on this topic before him. But though he was clearly concerned about the impact of too much information on people's peace of mind, Beard was no Luddite. He never talked about turning the clock back. Good American that he was, he took technological innovation for granted, not least in the distribution of information. What he would think of the computer and the Internet, we can only guess, but were he alive today, he would surely be struck by the competitiveness of contemporary life. Given his predilection to link anxiety to the rapidity with which communication occurs, he would no doubt see a connection between the computer, the fax machine, the cellular telephone, and the corroding anxiety in evidence among Xer elites.

WORKING UNDER PRESSURE

It is not, of course, simply the need to cope with a complex technology and with information surfeit that makes the Xer elite especially vulnerable to anxiety. The nature of their work is also a factor. Typically, they work in an exacting arena that offers little room for error. A mistake that might be bearable in other endeavors can be ruinous in the fast-moving, high-risk environments of speculative finance and cutthroat capitalism, in the worlds of fashion design and theatrical production, telecommunications, publishing, and advertising in which many Xers move.

Elite Xers know they can expect almost no toleration for failure. A misjudgment of public taste, a slackening of creativity, a slowness in decision making will cost them or their employers fabulous amounts of money and every scrap of personal influence and power. Bosses and clients are seldom forgiving when Xers fail to deliver the goods, and failure tags them as losers. That is not something easily shrugged off, for as we know, the consequences of losing are often devastating.

Losing in elite Xer circles is treated like a social disease, a communicable one; losers tend to be avoided for fear of contagion. Friends and former associates, leery of infection, wonder whether the loser's bad luck is catching and prudently put distance between themselves and the loser. A sort of *cordon sanitaire* subtly emerges; it may be smoothed over, but perfunctory expressions of sympathy do not really hide the chasm that now separates the loser from the winner. Not infrequently, aggression soon replaces sympathy, and the hapless loser soon becomes a target of nastiness. Winners discover they can safely vent their frustrations on the poor wretches who have been shown not to have the right stuff. Slights of all kinds, snide re-

marks, knowing winks and nods, all of which are satisfying to winners, communicate to losers the true significance of their falls.

It does not help matters that elite Xers are often required to work
with other Xers, some of whom eventually turn out to be competitors as well as colleagues. This can be tricky. As members of teams
that meet to tackle certain problems and then disperse, elite Xers
must be able to mix smoothly with people they hardly know, an important item in their toolkit of skills. They must appear friendly,
open to the give-and-take of sharing information, and sensitive to
the reactions of others in the group. Flexibility and image management are essential if the job is to be done properly, because their
knowledge, even though their stock-in-trade, will not count for
much unless it can be communicated. For this to happen in situations where information is transmitted as advice rather than as orders, as is often the case, elite Xers must understand the needs and
personality quirks of the people they work with. They must recognize that information arrogantly presented may die still-born, ignored and unused, even by clients who would have welcomed help
had it been offered in an acceptable way.

As though this were not enough, their jobs often require elite Xers
to provide services to impatient and demanding clients and
co-workers in nerve-racking face-to-face situations. They must appear helpful even when they feel out of sorts, courteous even when
provoked by a client's nastiness, able to make a client feel at ease
even when circumstances upset them. In short, they must be individualistic yet cooperative, approachable yet detached, open yet impersonal, friendly and at the same time emotionally uninvolved in
the lives of their clients. None of this is easy to manage; all of it is
emotionally draining.

To put it another way: they must be masters of dissimulation, ap-
pearing to be what they are not, manipulating others in ways not
necessarily in the client's best interest. Although pulling this off is no
easy task, the chances for success improve if the Xer is a skillful chameleon. Even then, mistakes happen, and colleagues and bosses may
become irritated or totally alienated. When this happens, Xers can
find themselves in deep trouble, prey to enervating confusion and
anxiety—the loser's lot.

STATUS ANXIETY

Elite Xers stand to lose a lot when things go sour. Money, good
food and sumptuous lodging, a safe environment for themselves

and their families, all fall away. But something far more precious may be lost: self-respect and the respect of others. This is a hard loss indeed for narcissistic Xers, who have built their self-regard on a foundation of success. On what will Xers base their self-esteem when success slips away?

This is not to disparage money and various forms of real property. They are important contributors to self-esteem, of course, and it would hurt to lose them. But material assets can be won and lost, even frivolously scattered and miraculously recouped, without permanent damage to self-regard. Donald Trump, the ubiquitous real estate developer, exemplifies the speed, indeed regularity, with which tangible wealth can be squandered and then recaptured. Like a phoenix he repeatedly rises out of the ashes of investment conflagrations, only to soar to new heights. But the phoenix is a rare bird, not one to be depended upon, as Xers undoubtedly know.

Status once lost is not easily restored. Intangible and subjective, evanescent and ephemeral, status is prone to evaporate just when one needs it most. It is unsafe to lean on in troubled times. In truth, because it exists only in the eye of the beholder, status needs constant repair and replenishment; it can never be taken for granted. Even when carefully nourished, status is, in Andrew Sullivan's words, "nerve-rackingly fragile, a source of simmering anxiety."[10] This is understandable, because social status—evidenced by the respect with which one is treated—is excruciatingly difficult to assess. In some circles, social standing may be measured by such criteria as the number of telephone calls not returned and appointments safely canceled, by the admiration and emulation one's clothes, cars, clubs, and academic degrees elicit. But evidence for any of this is hard to collect and evaluate.

Another factor complicating the evaluation of status is its wildly fluid, wobbly character. In contemporary America a person's social position may fluctuate with dismaying frequency, ultimately crashing into flinders in a shatteringly brief period of time. For in America prestige is often linked to membership in a group, and this panache is not necessarily transportable. To illustrate: top golfer-hood in a high-status club may not carry any weight in a locker room of handball addicts; expertise in medieval French literature could very well elicit polite yawns among philatelists; the awe inspired by old-stock family ties, the foundation on which status once rested, has all but eroded away. In meritocratic circles, genteel breeding carries little weight.

Of course, having beneficent parents still helps. So do unlimited charge-card privileges and a BMW for one's 16th birthday. But these alone will not automatically confer status: one must work and be good at it. As one young woman, a graduate of a private Manhattan school, recently told *New York Times* journalist Monique P. Yazigi, "It's unacceptable to say you don't work. Work is the definition of how you spend your time. If you don't work and don't have to work, you eventually look like a dummy who lunches." Bluntly put, status in contemporary America can seldom be inherited; it must in most cases be earned. Moreover, it must be earned in a peculiarly American way—through successful achievement in a competitive sphere. Status is the reward of enterprise, hard work, skill, acumen, resourcefulness, and brains. Even with these splendid assets to one's credit, however, staying successful in America is not a sure thing. Hence the fear of falling, the terror of losing status, that afflicts elite Xers.

That elite Xers feel apprehensive and unappreciated, constantly worrying about their status, is not as peculiar as it may seem. True, that young people, usually footloose and just getting started, might be preoccupied with their social standing may strike an older person as ludicrous, even paranoid, but Xers correctly recognize status for what it is: a tender plant, always in jeopardy and needing constant nourishment. Considering the way status affects how seriously one is taken, this concern makes good sense. Keep in mind, elite Xers mean to be taken seriously—and their worries about personal standing are not irrational or unfounded. Xers have reason to believe that society respects them little and treats them less well than it did their predecessors. In fact, the oft-voiced Xer complaint that the Boomers were better rewarded at a similar age turns out to be more than just generational moaning. A Current Population Survey published in 1998 found that Xers were receiving less money, as measured by median real income, in the labor market than did Boomers at a comparable age: Xers earn 15 percent less than did their predecessors.[11]

But even granting this discrepancy in rewards, the reader may ask, what is really going on here? Why do so many elite Xers paint so bleak a picture of their status and their prospects for advancement when the evidence shows that all things considered, they are doing remarkably well? Why do so many of these highly intelligent manipulators of knowledge, upon whom society smiles so benignly, appear anxious and frightened? Why do they see themselves as victims of hostile forces determined to grind them down? Why is the worm of worry eating away at their souls?

One answer comes quickly to mind: that the frantic rate of social change associated with modernity is causing enormous personal disorientation. Surprisingly, its impact on Xers has either been overlooked or underrated. And yet its effects are there for all to see. When we look closely at the elite Xers we find, for one thing, that Xers are exceptionally sensitive to stress. When asked about their problems they are quick to complain about the tensions in their lives. Thus, a 1997 national survey found that 75 percent of the Xers in the sample felt the need to reduce the stress under which they worked and lived. "People feel they are living stress-filled lives because they are overloaded . . . too many responsibilities, too many decisions, too many choices."[12] Xers say life has become too complicated and overstretched, muddied with problems not of their making and for which they have no solutions. It is no coincidence that authors David Lipsky and Alexander Abrams, themselves Xers, describe Xers as "nail-biters and champion worrywarts," caught up in a competitive frenzy, frantic to become secure through piling up money. [13]

XERS AND GLOBALIZATION

Perhaps most important of all, many Xers feel they are losing control over their lives. Why is that? Is it only because the pitiless competitive milieu in which they work, its hectic pace of life, its buzzing, strepitious clamor, is making elite Xers anxious? This surely adds to the Xers' sense of a world careening out of control. But there is another factor: the economy has undergone fundamental change—it has become global—and this is complicating the Xers' lives. No generation before the Xers knew with such thundering explicitness that America was dependent upon the good will, resources, and trade of other countries. No other generation was so "globalized," was so exposed to the competition, moods, mistakes, demands, and follies of other nations.

In a word, America is no longer autarchic. Its economy is interdependent with the rest of the world. Elite Xers are keenly aware of this. Their work often brings them into competition with highly skilled technicians living and working in foreign countries, information specialists like themselves who do good work and often for much less pay. These competitors write software in Bombay and Tel Aviv, analyze data in Milan and Montreal, keep accounts in Dublin and Liverpool—all for client companies in the United States. With the pool of people with whom Xers must compete increasing exponentially in the last decade, Xers are learning that they cannot depend on always winning. They must live with that fact, with all its stresses and anxieties.

Of course, America became interdependent with foreign countries, dependent upon their good will and resources, several generations ago. But the degree of this dependence did not become frighteningly clear to the general public until the 1970s, during the oil crisis. The Organization of Petroleum Exporting Countries, a cartel largely composed of Middle Eastern countries, turned off the oil spigot in 1973 in retaliation for America's support of Israel in the Yom Kippur War. In the period 1973 to 1974 the price of oil quadrupled, and in 1979, egged on by Iran's Ayatollah Ruhollah Khomeini, the cartel drove up the price of crude oil to unprecedented heights. The price of crude oil in 1979 rose to about 40 dollars a barrel, a stunning increase for a commodity that for decades had hovered around four dollars a barrel. The result was long lines at the gas pumps, angry motorists, spiraling inflation, and an alarmed public facing unaccustomed high energy prices.

Responsible leaders, including the president, warned that something had to be done. In a televised address, Jimmy Carter cautioned the public that economic drift, stagnation, and eventual paralysis were inevitable unless Americans curbed their appetite for oil.[14] The oil crisis then afflicting the country, he said, was not merely annoying; it imperiled the nation's security. Bold steps must be taken: restrictions had to be placed on foreign oil imports, new energy sources had to be developed, and most important of all, energy had to be conserved—in the factory, on the road, and in the home. In the nation's interest, citizens were asked to turn down their thermostats at home, drive to work in car pools, and leave family cars at home one day a week. These were personal sacrifices, admittedly modest ones given the nature of the crisis, but the times and the problem called for sacrifice.

Initially, the public's response to the call for austerity was positive. Then a reaction set in; some editorialists and other critics complained that the politicians were unfairly blaming the victim. The fault was not that of the long-suffering public, they said, but of the country's lackluster leadership, the cowardly politicians who lacked the backbone to tackle the nation's serious energy problem.

With remarkable ease, the public came around to this point of view. After all, no one likes to be scolded, called self-indulgent, and admonished to mend one's ways. This sort of rhetoric seldom wins friends and influences people. Smart politicians, if they wish to be elected or stay in office, know this and studiously avoid commenting on the character flaws of their constituents. Because in the popular estimation politicians are seldom as good as they ought to be, usually much worse, sermons from them, except perhaps in time of war, do not sit well. The public does not care to be blamed for the nation's troubles and becomes restive and resentful when lectured. Politicians who engage in this sort of thing are asking for trouble. Eventually, the admonitions from politicians were dismissed as misguided directions from questionable sources on a topic few wanted to think about.

The oil crisis of the late 1970s had no lasting effect on oil consumption. After cautiously experimenting with lowered house lights and briefly flirting with car-pooling and tiny, gas-efficient cars, Americans returned to their profligate ways. Sitting in dimly lit rooms and wearing heavy sweaters indoors never really caught on, and the attraction of small cars proved temporary. Large gas-guzzlers regained their popularity, and drivers once again returned to their earlier carefree habit of racing on the nation's highways, paying speed limits little mind. (Note the popularity of gas-guzzling SUVs among Xers today.) As a result, after a brief dip, energy consumption returned to previous levels, and America's dependence on imported oil continued unabated. Foreign oil as a proportion of oil consumed in the United States rose from one-third to one-half, its present level.

History has something to teach us here. The oil crisis of the 1970s should interest more people than antiquarians. Although few Xers have any memory of the 1970s oil crisis, it holds a cautionary lesson for today. For in the year 2000, once again, OPEC curtailed production to increase the income of the cartel's members, and once again crude oil prices soared to nearly 40 dollars a barrel, its 1970s high, and gasoline prices at the service station rose correspondingly. Oil prices in the 1970s kindled inflation; interest rates rose to protect the currency; as a result, purchases of homes and cars declined; a nasty recession followed. Such a sorry scenario could happen again, but this time its principal victim would be the Xers. They have not known anything like the inflation of the 1970s, nor have they experienced a recession in more than a decade. They are not prepared, most of them, either financially or emotionally, for the turmoil that an economic slowdown would bring. Its effects upon them could be severe, even demoralizing. It is something Xers may be thinking about.

GLOBAL FINANCIAL TURMOIL

In addition to having to cope with foreign competitors and turbulent global events, Xers have to deal with unexpected market tailspins. A cautionary example of the damage that global financial turmoil can leave in its wake is the fate of people associated with Long Term Capital Management, a hedge fund that specialized in bond trading. John Meriwether and Hans Hufschmid, middle-aged senior partners, ran the show and set the firm's policy. Much of the day-to-day trading was in the hands of bright young Xers, guided by a congery of Boomer economists, including two Nobel laureates in economics. These eminent experts had developed a mathematical model of bond trading based upon identifying tiny differences in bond prices and then profiting from these discrepancies. Assuming that others would behave equally rationally, they thought they had figured out a sure-fire way to make a bundle of money.

So it seemed for a time. In the beginning, things went splendidly. Huge profits were made, and the reputation of the company soared on Wall Street. Then, in the summer of 1998, speculators attacked the currencies of several wobbly economies in Southeast Asia. To protect itself, Thailand devalued its currency, quickly followed by Indonesia, Malaysia, and then the Philippines and South Korea. Finally, with the currency markets in turmoil and the ruble in free fall, Russia defaulted on its debts.

The financial markets panicked. Almost everyone tried to get out of bonds at the same time, and prices dropped disastrously. Long Term Capital Management, which had not figured on irrational herdlike behavior of Wall Street investors in a time of great stress, lost more than four billion dollars in six weeks. Its 16 senior partners, who had invested $1.9 billion of their own money, saw it all go down the drain. What the junior staff, which included many Xers, lost has never been reported. Only quick action by the Federal Reserve, which persuaded (some say strong-armed) several private banks to assume Long Term's debt in exchange for equity, saved the company and perhaps the bond market from going under.[15]

Usually the damage caused by economic dislocation is less sudden and dramatic than the disaster that overtook Long Term Capital Management. For most employees, the fallout of economic downturn feels more like slow Chinese water torture than the swift, sharp bite of an executioner's sword. But the malaise that enveloped the New York financial district during the Asian economic crisis and the Russian default spread quickly. Its cumulative effects were devastating. Brokerage firms ruthlessly pruned their workforces. Merrill Lynch laid off 3,400 workers, including many junior analysts, many of them elite Xers. As time went on, other companies followed suit. Eventually, a slew of Wall Street jobs dissolved like snow under the fiery afternoon sun.

For many elite Xers, this could hardly have happened at a worse time. Psychologically speaking, they had not yet recovered from the 1990–1991 recession, a worldwide slowdown that, though mercifully brief, had threatened for a time to abort their careers permanently. Abruptly, with no warning, elite Xers found themselves jobless and burdened with onerous college loans and other obligations optimistically assumed in the good times, debts that urgently needed to be repaid. Broke and out of work, many Xers moved in with their parents, a humiliating defeat for a generation determined to succeed on its own, to be beholden to no one, least of all to their parents. Elite Xers, who had been confidently riding the buoyant waves of an expanding information economy, found unemployment a blow hard to handle.

Needless to say, when disaster strikes, belt-tightening becomes unavoidable. Apartments have to be sold, kids taken out of private schools, college loans defaulted, vacation plans abandoned, friends avoided for fear of embarrassing questions about being sacked. Self-esteem takes a terrible beating. Extravagant rewards, not dismissal, had been the Xers' usual experience. The market had showered them with big bonuses, praise, vacation apartments in Europe and the Caribbean, planes to jet them here and there, and not least, options to buy expensive stock at low prices. Now it coolly and without ceremony buried them in contempt, speedily stopped all benefits and showed the poor miscreants the door. They had failed to deliver the goods. Lured to Wall Street like moths to a flame, they were burned to a crisp.[16]

These setbacks, denounced as the ruinous work of corporate mismanagement, tricks, and foolishness, frightened the wits out of many an Xer, who even now wonders if it could happen again—as it probably could. Not only did Xer confidence take a beating in this brief but painful economic tailspin, but a palpable distrust of the economy was imprinted on their impressionable minds. Even now, relatively few Xers feel relaxed about the present; even fewer take future prosperity for granted. This may seem paradoxical, because elite Xers are often accused of being cocky, too sure of themselves, too certain that things will come their way—rational exuberance, Xer author Meredith Bagby has called it. But this is mostly for show. Insecurity lurks beneath their confident facade, the nagging worry that disaster may occur at any time.

Furthermore, the Xers' insistent need to be in charge of their lives, to take control of events that jeopardize their security, cannot help but generate continuous friction with peers, parents, and superiors. In a changing world where the rules governing the legitimate lines of authority are under attack, it is not always clear who should be in charge and what should be done when things go awry and decisions must be made. The struggle for power that frequently develops in such circumstances must inevitably heighten Xer insecurity and anxiety—and in this fertile compost of anxiety, chameleonism flourishes.

FAMILY TROUBLES

As though all this were not enough, many Xers have to live with the effects of troubled upbringing that have left them confused and filled with resentment. Life in their families, they say, was anything but idyllic. According to their reports, relatively few elite Xers grew up in stable and nurturing families. Their parents were distracted and inattentive, everyday life was fractured by parental squabbles and bickering that often ended in separation or divorce. Not surprisingly, elite Xers tend to blame many of their problems on family instability and breakup. As they see it, their parents made them apprehensive and distrustful, complicating their adjustment to life.

Here is what many elite Xers say. As the children of professional and business parents whose work required them to change locales, Xers were frequently on the move. Perforce they had to change schools, leave friends behind, and make their way into new peer circles; they found developing an enduring sense of community and connection with peers exceedingly difficult. Nor was this all. Even when their parents stayed put, they spent too little time at home, or at least not as much as their children would have liked. All too often their parents were busy at work and could give the child only tiny packets of "quality time," a poor substitute for reliable, sustained attention. Ignored, required to fend for themselves, Xer children felt neglected and alone.

Even as adults, many Elite Xers report feeling isolated. Isolation is not what they want, they say. "We don't seek isolation; we come from it," said one Xer author, Bruce Tulgan, in response to complaints that Xers are distant and unapproachable.[17] Remember, he reminded managers in his book *Managing Generation X*, "Xers are latchkey kids," victims of parental absence, forced to manage on their own. No wonder they are independent, Tulgan says; how else would they have survived? Other Xer authors tell the same story. For instance, David Lipsky and Alexander Abrams, in their book *Late Bloomers*, lament the Xers' bad luck in having been born just as the family in America was falling apart.

This is what happened. In the mid-seventies the economy stagnated, and some mothers who had been content to be full-time homemakers reluctantly took outside jobs to make ends meet. Other mothers, restive at home, sought self-realization in the work- force. From 1960 to 1980 the number of working mothers with children under five more than doubled—from 20 percent to 47 percent.[18] With both parents working, the kids were left alone a good deal of the time. When school let out each day, no one was waiting at home, no one bustled about in the kitchen with milk and cookies, no one kept loneliness away. A sibling (if there was one—families were small) was more likely to be someone to take care of rather than a companion. Watching The Brady Bunch, a TV fantasy of familial togetherness, was no compensation; it only emphasized that something quite delightful was missing in their lives.

More traumatic was family breakup: many Xers are children of divorce. Broken families are, of course, nothing new in America. Divorce has been on the rise for well over a century. [19] Even so, in the 1960s, when the Xer generation first came upon the scene, the rate of divorce reached a new high, nearly tripling between 1960 and 1979, from nine per thousand per year to nearly 23. By 1986, it was the highest in the Western world.[20] Xers show this trend clearly. In about half of the cases, parents divorced when the Xers were still quite young. Xer author Steven Gibbs has said, "Perhaps our single most common characteristic is our nearly universal exposure to divorce. We have a general lack of models to teach us the grace of marriage."[21]

For its impact to be felt, divorce need not have been experienced personally. Divorce was in the air everywhere, among relatives and teachers, among schoolmates, as the kids listened to gossip and consoled friends whose parents had split. The effect was inescapable and depressing, often devastating. Karen Ritchie, a mother and keen observer of Xers, has written "Divorce occurred on a scale large enough to be disruptive to the security of the entire generation, and to help form their earliest opinions about marriage, family, and trust." [22]

Still quite young, these children of divorced parents were forced to take care of themselves, to work out things alone, and to grow up a lot faster than they had expected or wanted. They had to learn to feed themselves, shop for groceries, care for younger siblings, vacuum the rugs, scrub the bathroom floor, heat up leftovers, change diapers, organize car pools, and feed the dog. They had to adjust to a constant stream of new baby-sitters, listen to neighbor's complaints, let the plumber in when the toilet overflowed, and cope with self-absorbed parents too preoccupied with their own problems to notice their kids' bewildered resentment.

Divorce can be hard on kids in other ways as well. When parents quarrel, children get caught in the middle. They are dragged into fights not of their own making or even accessible to their comprehension. Sometimes parents tell spiteful stories about each other and ask children to take sides. Pressed to become the confidants of distressed adults, even consulted as to what action to take, a heavy responsibility for a child, they feel overwhelmed. A typical reaction of the young Xer caught in this trap is to dream of escape. As one young woman says, "I mostly wanted to grow up, get out, make a life for myself that was more predictable."[23]

Even after a divorce, the child may continue to feel conflicted, torn by opposing loyalties. Visiting a divorced parent can be agony; saying hello and good-bye to an increasingly remote parent is painful, to say the least. Often money becomes scarcer, and hard times becomes the lot of children used to an easier life. Now as they look back, many Xers feel exploited and exhausted, cheated of the stable and carefree childhood they believe other generations had enjoyed. Says one young Xer, age 27, who feels too much surrogate parenting was required of her, "And now I'm just tired . . . just tired. I want to play in the sandbox. I want to sit on the couch and toss bonbons in my mouth. Like retired people when they move down to Florida."[24]

Could a divorce have been at least in part the child's fault? Surely, few parents would so argue. But some children wonder whether they could have done something to keep their families intact: perhaps behaved better, cleaned their rooms more frequently, been more loving. Children who believe this self-destructive fantasy live with nagging feelings of inadequacy and a persistent doubt about being able to rise to the next crisis.

That divorce hurt some Xers in childhood is well documented. For example, Kristi Lockhart Keil, a therapist and lecturer in psychology at an Ivy League university, found the effects of divorce on her students damaging and lasting. In her study of 164 Xers enrolled in college, she discovered that students from divorced families tended to suffer from depression, eating disorders, and substance abuse. Of course, the children of divorced parents were not the only ones to be so affected, but they were twice as likely to be depressed than those from intact families. Keil found that many of the Xers in her classes were having difficulty establishing relationships with peers. Parental divorce had shattered their faith in people: they expected others to let them down just as their parents had.[25]

In many cases, Keil discovered, even when the parents had not divorced, their single-minded pursuit of self-realization had caused them to skimp on time with their children. These parents justified this neglect by saying they wanted their children to become self-reliant and independent. But could it be that what they really wanted was to be free to enjoy life unencumbered by the responsibilities of parenthood? Perhaps this explains why many Xers now put off getting hitched. They tend to marry later than their Boomer predecessors. In 1997, the median age at the time of first marriage for Xer women was 25 years and 26.8 for men. In contrast, the median age for marriage for Boomer women in 1970 was 20.8 years, for men 23.2 years.

Deprived of consistent parental nurturance, shunted into the care of nannies and day-care centers, many of today's elite Xers have developed a deep reluctance to depend upon others, coupled with a dark distrust of all but a few friends, and sometimes even these. Xers in Keil's study said they saw dependency as a personality flaw, a sign of weakness. Xers believe that personal fulfillment must be achieved on one's own, without the help of family or friends, however well meaning others profess to be. Many Xers believe that professions of good will cannot be taken at face value: a 1994 national survey found that 67 percent of Xers, age 18 to 24, thought "one can't be too careful in dealing with people."[26] Xer author David Leavit put it succinctly in an *Esquire* essay: "We trust ourselves and money, period."[27] This determination to go it alone, this belief in self-reliance, this distrust of others, may be what Boomer managers have in mind when they accuse their Xer subordinates of being standoffish and difficult to deal with.

An insistence on independence can have a downside: a pervasive feeling of alienation. Xers whose parents divorced, or who were simply emancipated too early, feel alone. Keil writes, "Many Gen Xers don't feel they have a safe harbor of loved ones they can pull into when life's storms blow. . . . There may be a house, but no home."[28] Small wonder many Xers believe they have no safe place to rest their anxious heads. A childhood in troubled families has bred into them deep-rooted insecurity and an insatiable hunger for stability and control.

I am not suggesting that troubled relationships with parents fully explain Xer anxiety and chameleonism. Certainly, other people besides their parents have influenced the way Xers think and act: the Boomer generation, members of the opposite sex, and immigrants entering the workplace. In order to understand the prevalence of anxiety among Xers we must assess their relationships to these people. But first we need to examine, albeit briefly, the social transformations that have changed America in the last hundred years. For in changing the world in which Xers live, these transformations changed the Xers and their relationships with other people, among them Boomers, members of the opposite sex, and immigrants.

4

The Great Transformations

Since America's founding as a republic, three huge waves of change have hit it. Each wave changed how goods and services were produced, how people viewed themselves and the world, and how they associated with one another. Inevitably, each wave altered the relationships between groups, including the ties between generations, thus transforming the entire society over which it swept. These were hideously complex phenomena, and examining their social characteristics in detail is beyond the scope of this book. Fortunately, there is no need for an in-depth analysis here, since much is already known about them. Their structures have been amply described elsewhere.[1]

Even so, something should be said about their social psychological effects—the changes in values and attitudes, in hopes and aspirations, in frustrations and targets of anger that always follow massive structural change. This chapter explores the way massive social change brought about change in culture and personality, and in doing so influenced intergenerational relationships in the nineteenth and twentieth centuries, and how they continue to do so in the twenty-first century. The focus will be on generational stereotypes, the way they corroded intergenerational connections—and still do. For generational stereotypes rarely die or fade entirely away; they find new lives as new generations appear on the scene. Predictably, stereotyping is very much at work today, envenoming the relationships between Xers and Boomers.

FROM COTTAGE TO FACTORY

The first wave, or transformation, got under way in the late nineteenth century, when the industrial manufacturing system, an impersonal and efficient process, finally put an end to traditional methods of production. The old system was based on cottage industry and the "putting out" system, a decentralized and leisurely manner of doing business that had for centuries been the dominant way of producing and distributing goods. Although the old system had begun to falter by the early nineteenth century, it was not until a new system emerged to take its place that this tenacious relic finally died.[2]

In the new system, capital invested in machines became the prime generator of wealth. Human skill, expressed through craftsmanship in the home and in the shop, was replaced by machines. Handicraft, the fruit of centuries of dedicated labor, went into decline, and much work was divided into simple tasks that required no special skill. Production was separated from marketing, and salesmanship emerged as an important economic function. Based on private property and profit, richly competitive and relatively open to innovations that increased production, the industrial system rewarded efficiency and prized individual merit. It increased productivity and spurred unprecedented economic growth—and in the process generated exceptional personal wealth. By bringing together machine production, capital, and competitive marketing methods, the new manufacturing system eventually attained extraordinary economic power and influence.

The keystone of the new system was the factory, a large, noisy, and noisome structure built to house expensive machines and cheap labor. It brought together ordinary wage laborers and forced them to work together in tandem with machines, under strict supervision, according to a set schedule. It also confined them to a workplace many workers loathed. Crowded and impersonal, the factory seemed to them not unlike a slave pen, and they voiced this view loudly and often. Nevertheless, despite worker resistance, the industrial factory system took hold and ultimately won out.

But to achieve its goals the industrial system required new kinds of people. It needed entrepreneurs willing to invest money, eager to exploit natural resources, and ready to take risks. Equally important, it wanted a different type of worker, a disciplined and self-reliant machine operator, punctual and orderly and amenable to regimentation. The industrial entrepreneur and the factory worker were breeds different from those that had preceded them, in a number of ways. First, they valued rewards based upon individual merit; second, they viewed the pursuit of success as commendable and natural; and third, they accepted distinctions between people based upon training and technical competence.

Even so, adapting to the demands of an industrial system was not easy. In America, most entrepreneurs found getting adequate capital difficult, in many cases impossible. The banks and individual lenders were reluctant to support risky ventures, and correctly so, for the risks were great. In its early years the technologies of manufacturing were crude and unreliable, and the markets were uncertain and often unprofitable. Many businesses failed; their workers lost their jobs, and the owners lost their shirts. But some entrepreneurs persevered and became successful, and in the process of becoming rich they changed the structure of the economy.

As for becoming an industrial worker, this too was difficult. Not only was the factory a repellent place in which to work and the work itself repetitious, but many of the new factory workers were migrants from rural areas who found the transition from farm life to industry deeply disorienting. Annoyed by the clangor of machines, put off by tight work schedules, confused by new rules, and offended by peremptory orders from impersonal bosses, they became unhappy and sometimes expressed their anger by absenteeism and by sabotaging machines.

But despite the sporadic resistance of disgruntled workers, the hostility of established agricultural factions in the South (which disliked the manufacturers' protective tariffs), and the foot-dragging of reactionary commercial elements in the North, this first transforming wave could not be stopped. A torrent of industrial change inundated the nation, and manufacturing became America's dominant economic enterprise. A country that had been largely agricultural at mid-nineteenth century became in two generations predominantly industrial, a manufacturing giant without peer. The United States in the year before the Great War of 1914–18 produced as many manufactured goods as its three nearest competitors—Great Britain, France, and Germany—combined. Manufacturing became the nation's premier employer, replacing agriculture.[3]

As agriculture declined, the country became increasingly urban; people left the village and moved to the city, where work could be found. The magnitude of this change in residence was breathtaking. When the Civil War broke out, only one in five Americans lived in an urban area; when the century ended, the proportion of urbanites had radically increased; and by the second decade of the twentieth century, the rural-urban balance had tipped in favor of the city— 51 percent of the population were urban dwellers. America had become a nation of city people.[4]

Industrialization and urbanization greatly changed the ties between generations. These ties had been based primarily on family affection and shared work, and both grew weaker in the industrial city. The family, particularly in its extended form, had never been as strong as sometimes believed, lost many of its functions, fragmented into disenchanted parts, and much of its appeal evaporated. Outside of the home, most work became individuated, specialized, and impersonal. The city's large size, its competitiveness, and the diversity of its inhabitants hindered the development of a strong sense of community. The end result was an enfeeblement of the mutual interests and emotional links that heretofore had bound the generations together.[5]

The first transformation also made social relations between generations more difficult than they had been, by creating differences in the core character and culture of each generation. People have always been shaped by the needs of the economy of their times. In the case of the older generation during the U.S. Industrial Revolution, it had been the demands of a largely agricultural economy; in the new generation, the requirements of the manufacturing system were paramount. As the two economies were different, so were their workers: the older generation was family-oriented and conservative, the younger individuated and open to change. Friction between the two was only natural, for as the economy took a new direction, the older generation lagged behind the times. Inevitably, its grasp on power weakened, and the younger group sought to take charge. The result was acrimony between generations, as they battled to keep or impose their holds on society.

To complicate matters, sharp differences in viewpoints and interests between city residents and rural folk muddied the relationship between generations. These differences—over politics, school districting, union legislation, and prices—grew larger as manufacturing prospered while agriculture declined. A division of interest between the two groups developed. Farmers wanted higher prices for their products; city folk angrily resented having to pay more for bread and milk. Workers wanted higher wages; farmers were indifferent or openly unsympathetic to workers' petitions. Each group seemed coldly indifferent to the needs of the other.

In their defense, each group had serious problems of its own. Life in the early years of this first transformation was hard for many farmers. Drought and low prices for their crops drove many of them into bankruptcy, and those who survived, particularly in the rain-scarce prairies, were often driven to ruinous desperation, condemned to a hardscrabble life by credit-stingy city banks and exploitative railroads. In contrast, city people looked prosperous; booming factories, plentiful jobs, and lots of exciting things to do made city life seem easy. But in fact city people had much to complain of. Factory workers were generally overworked and badly paid: 10-to-12 hour days were common, and pay of a dollar or two a day was considered munificent. Unemployment and malnutrition were endemic, and slum housing and disease poisoned countless lives. Many city folk felt mistreated, and they put some of the blame on the farmer. They resented the farmers' over-representation in the state legislatures, their enmity toward labor unions, their support of capital punishment, and their efforts to impose limits on alcohol use.

All this—the clash of interests and the indifference to each other's plight—may seem like more than enough to explain the dislike rural and urban populations felt for each other. But in fact this was not the entire story. A more subtle force was stirring up dissension between farmers and city folk: the irritations of intergenerational differences. Beneath the din of clashing rural-urban interests could be heard the rumble of anger, the muted whine of people of different ages rubbing each other the wrong way. The friction was aggravated by a difference, on average, between the ages of city people and those in the country. City people tended to be younger than the inhabitants of the village.

The city was a magnet that drew into its field ambitious and adventurous youths, many of them from rural areas, seeking work and opportunity for advancement. Those left behind on the farm tended to be disproportionately middle-aged or elderly. As is often the case, the older age groups were more set in their ways and more likely to be suspicious of change, whereas the young welcomed it. Given these different points of view, clashes between generations were only to be expected. Of course, generational differences were not the whole story, but they contributed significantly to urban-rural antipathy, revealed particularly in the ugly stereotypes farmers and urbanites had of each other.

RURAL–URBAN STEREOTYPES

In the rural dweller's minds, city folk were money-mad adventurers, often absurdly young, who had grown rich manipulating money, generally at farmers' expense. Worse yet, city people lived riotously, flaunting their ill-earned riches without embarrassment or conscience. They dressed in deluxe clothes, enjoyed life in glittering theaters and restaurants, and carried on in licentious ways. Clearly, such people were not to be trusted. Their tricky methods of doing business, their loose morals, and their free-and-easy spending habits were sure signs of wickedness. But then, what else could be expected of people who lived in a city? To villagers, particularly those bred in the Calvinist tradition, the city was a den of iniquity. Wicked things went on there: drinking, card playing, dancing, and prostitution. City women were reported to be as depraved as their men. In short, as the farmer saw it, city people were sensualists, freebooters, rootless drifters who cared only for fun, food, and frolic. Interestingly enough, this rural assessment of urbanites resembles in many respects the picture Boomers tend to have of the Xer generation.

City people had their own stereotypes of the villager. The farmer was a yokel, a straw-mouthed slow-wit, a hayseed out of touch with the latest developments in music and dance, a mossback tied to fashions and ideas long out of style. In the urbanites' view, rural people were hypocrites. Rural men, even the older ones, wenched and drank and sought their pleasure whenever they could get away with it, and yet they wanted to stamp out fun among the young denizens of the city. This stereotype eerily resembles the perception Xers have of their own immediate predecessors, the middle-aged Boomers. To youthful eyes, the Boomers appear to be faux moralists, all too willing to impose their own rules on the younger generation and yet obsessively eager to seek personal fulfillment in self-indulgent pleasure.

City folk and farmers alike found much to complain about in the behavior of the young people around them. City people, perhaps because they tended to be more educated, could express their antagonism to the younger generation in print and were more likely to have it noticed. Cornelia A. P. Comer, fortyish and urbane, in a now-classic article published in the *Atlantic Monthly* of February 1911, accused the youth of her time of being oafs, addicted to pleasure, and inclined to cut corners when expedience beckoned. Young people suffered from "mental rickets and curvature of the soul." They were, she went on, "thirstily avid for pleasure [,] . . . so selfish and so hard."

She was not alone, of course; there were many others in her generation of a similar persuasion.[6]

THE RISE OF THE SERVICE ECONOMY

Even as the manufacturing system reached the peak of its power and influence—that is, during World War II, when every sinew was strained to harness the nation's resources to the war effort—a second transformation was under way, the triumph of the service sector. At the war's end about as many people were employed in providing services as in manufacturing. But numbers do not tell the whole story. In fact, the service sector had become the most dynamic force in the economy, destined to demote manufacturing to second place.[7]

As the second transformation progressed, the percentage of the labor force employed in manufacturing declined steadily. By 1970, the proportion of Americans working in manufacturing had fallen to 27 percent; it fell to 16 percent by 1993 and now stands at about 15 percent. In contrast, the service economy boomed. More than half of all paid employees, 58 percent, worked in the service sector in 1960, 67 percent in 1980, and 78 percent in 1994, approximately where things stand now. Services now contribute more to the gross domestic product than any other sector, 72 percent; manufacturing's share has fallen to 23 percent. The United States is dependent upon the service sector to provide new jobs for its people and to help keep its trade in balance. Service exports are in surplus, while merchandise exports are chronically in the red.[8]

The manufacturing sector concerns itself primarily with making tangible goods: tractors, cars, airplanes, washing machines, refrigerators, bicycles, and other articles that can be put in crates and trucked to distant markets, things that can be handled lovingly or smashed to smithereens when careless hands abuse them. Of course, services like advertising, sales, and customer relations are attached to manufacturing's main body, but they are considered secondary to the central task of making touchable products.

Manufacturing rewards people at the factory-floor level for their skill at handling things, not at dealing with people. Factory workers pride themselves on their manual dexterity, on their capacity to stand for hours at a machine making objects to factory specifications. Even at elite levels—for example, managerial engineers—advancement often goes to persons with competence in manipulating solid goods or in organizing the production of tangible gear. (Charles

Wilson, formerly president of General Motors, was not called "Engine Charley" for no reason.) From its beginning the manufacturing economy required, and in the main received, a workforce that was disciplined and self-reliant, willing to accommodate itself to the dictates of an organized work life. In addition, particularly in its expansive early years, the manufacturing sector got as a bonus a population that was generally supportive of the new system and optimistic about the future. Growing up in halcyon years, there was bred into these people a sturdy confidence in themselves, in the country, and in the future. An expanding economy had seen to that.

But in the final stage of its hegemony, the manufacturing system faltered. Calamities not entirely of its own making put the viability of the system in doubt. A great depression in the 1930s threw one-quarter of the labor force out of work—clearly not a confidence-building experience. To make matters worse, World War II, hard on the heels of the Great War of 1914–18, shook the nation to its core. It was in this crucible of economic upheaval and catastrophic war that a new generation was formed. Born between 1920 and the war years, this generation (now called "great" by the Boomers who had rejected them) knew hard times and a plethora of problems too difficult for many of them to understand.

History's contradictions puzzled them. They had been led to believe in the value of hard work, but many of them, though willing to work, suffered prolonged joblessness during the Great Depression. They had been taught to esteem self-denial and duty but saw these qualities put to work in the waging of wars, from which many never returned. They had been told to relax and celebrate their victory over alien tyrannies but soon found themselves asked to endure the burdens of world rehabilitation and the cold war. They had been trained to obey authority but witnessed power being abused by the authorities they most respected: the government, the church, the school. Some were radicalized by these experiences; many became conservative, cautious, and conformist.[9]

The generation that came into power with the triumph of the service economy—the Baby Boomers, people born after the end of World War II through 1964—was a very different breed. It had to be, in order to fit the needs of the new service economy. A service economy requires workers skilled at dealing with people, not at manipulating physical objects; at work requiring people-oriented competence, the Boomers excel. The elite among the Boomers are today highly educated specialists whose talent for dealing with people and analyzing complex problems is essential to the smooth functioning of the new techno-service system. Masters of the art of social relations on which a complex service economy depends, they have become in middle age respected authorities in business and government, prestigious professors in elite universities, masters of creative design in art and theater, well-placed directors in foundations, and powerful figures in publishing and entertainment firms—they rule the roost.

RIDING THE WAVE

The power and affluence the Boomers presently enjoy are not entirely their own doing; they had important help. For the second transformation ushered in a period of extensive prosperity in which elite Boomers had the good fortune to participate fully. When they entered the marketplace, jobs were plentiful, the pay was fine, and chances for advancement were excellent for almost anyone willing to seize the moment and make an effort to get ahead. To their credit, many Boomers made the most of the opportunities the new system afforded them. Their successes were in line with the future that society had foreseen. From childhood on, a good future had been promised the Boomer generation, and for the most part this promise was kept, at least for the progeny of the middle class. Nourished on great expectations and given more opportunities to achieve their dreams than any other generation the twentieth century had known, the Boomers were set for a splendid voyage through life.

This voyage would include a journey in search of the inner self: the essence of one's being, the child within them. With their economic problems apparently solved, the Boomers were given the luxury of devoting much of their time to the deliciously absorbing task of self-discovery. Self-absorption was and is no sin in Boomer eyes. They cannot imagine a topic of greater significance than the self—or, rather, themselves. It is no coincidence that under their aegis a variety of self-fulfillment therapies has flourished, each designed to help the Boomers get in touch with their inner feelings. This self-immersion has caused critics to describe the elite Boomers as narcissistic souls, impatient for personal satisfaction, self-righteous, and intolerantly didactic. That was not at all what their parents had in mind. What happened?

Probably what happened is that from the beginning the Boomers were treated as something quite special. Their parents, determined to spare their children the hardships earlier generations had had to endure, raised them in child-centered households of unprecedented indulgence. This was an untried path in child rearing, it is true, but the parents never lacked for advice on how to travel it. Experts eagerly showered them with instructions on how to produce happy and constructive citizens for the new and improved world to come. Child-rearing experts like Benjamin Spock advised parents to be attentive, solicitous, and reasonably permissive—advice much criticized today but eagerly seized upon at the time. Educational savants created new curricula and classrooms molded to suit the presumed needs of the new generation: a new math to replace old math, new reading methods instead of the old phonic system, new classrooms without partitions instead of the old wall-bound variety—all designed to produce a new generation of creative, spontaneous and democratic citizens. Pampered and spoiled, accustomed to being the centers of attention, the young Boomers "grew up thinking they were something special, destined for a special place in history."[10]

Even as they grew older, Boomer youths never lacked for inspiriting instructions. Gurus, such as marketer Faith Popcorn, who told the young Boomer to teach others about "what is real, what is honest, what is quality, what is valued, what is important" kept the young elite alert to its responsibilities.[11] Boomer-oriented magazines, like, *Rolling Stone*, called upon Boomer youths to "muster the will to remake [themselves] into altruists and ascetics."[12] That was a very large assignment, you might think, but it was one that seemed not at all unreasonable to a generation as cosseted, as praised, and as enveloped in a cloud of libidinous euphoria as the young Boomers.

Wafted by a favoring breeze to giddy heights, exhorted to take on big tasks, entranced by a vision of limitless possibilities, the elite Boomers felt Promethean. They had heroic visions. They would remake society, make it just and equal, unsullied by petty self-interest, closer to what they thought it could become—perfect, like themselves. Seeing themselves as agents of change and willing to disrupt and demonstrate to advance their agenda, they marched noisily down major city thoroughfares, picketed the pentagon, occupied deans' offices or took over entire college buildings, interrupted ministers during religious services, harassed politicians at public rallies. They shook up every major institution they encountered, at little cost to themselves, because their bewildered elders, though occasionally disapproving, seldom questioned the purity of Boomer intentions. But sadly, this was doomed to change. The Boomers were about to encounter a group not at all taken with their charm and claim to exemption from carping criticism.

SOMETHING NEW UNDER THE SUN

Imagine the Boomers' surprise when they encountered the Xer elite. This new elite is the darling of the third transformation—the information revolution. This revolution continued the changes brought about by the previous transformation, and both transformations and their respective elites have been incorporated into the techno-service society. But the Xers are the true masters of the information revolution, because better than anyone else they understand the new electronic technology, the heart of the new information economy.

Using new technology, the Xer elite accelerated the transmission of information, critical to the smooth functioning of the service economy, and introduced new methods of manufacturing and merchandising. In effect, the new Xer elite, like its predecessors, transformed the way things, tangible and intangible, are produced and distributed. But Xers have shown they are better adapted to the new information age and more skilled at using the new technologies than are the Boomers—no small advantage for the Xers and a source of chagrin for the Boomers. Ineptitude in the use of the new information technology is a handicap no ambitious person or group can afford. Whoever masters the tools of data processing, whoever can come up with imaginative ideas for how best to employ the new technologies to solve new problems or perform old tasks more efficiently—that person or group will control the future. With a prize this large at stake, it is only natural that a spirited competition would develop between Boomers and Xers for control of the information revolution.

Mastery of arcane information-age technologies came easily to elite Xers. Their education was visual and high-tech oriented. The TV screen, the computer monitor, the video game—not simply the textbook and the teacher—were their instructors.[13] Xers were the first generation to have grown up with the computer, the first to have color television in their homes and VCRs in their schools, the first to send e-mail, the first to surf the Internet. This mastery has given them an edge in their competition with the Boomers, who have never felt completely at ease with the Internet and its mysterious properties. Awkwardness with the Internet and similar digitized information sources is costing Boomers dearly.

Boomers are not accustomed to being behind the technological curve. Adulation for being at the forefront of change has been the usual response to Boomer expertise; now, in their dealings with Xers, the Boomers meet only contempt. The stereotype Xers hold of the Boomers is of clowns, clumsy with computers and wedded to old-fashioned ideas. Boomer Karen Ritchie, addressing her own cohort, described the Xer image of the Boomers this way: "Our energy is met with apparent numbing lethargy and indifference. Our conviction is matched with impregnable skepticism. Our charm eludes them. They don't get the jokes, they don't take us seriously, and they don't think this is funny." [14] In brief, elite Xers are not at all taken with the Boomers' vision, the Boomers' program, the Boomers' performance. On the contrary: the Xer elite fervently dislikes its Boomer counterpart.

Why is that? There are several reasons. First, bitter clashes of interest and heated exchanges over rival claims for power and status have poisoned the relationship between Xers and Boomers. Second, clashes of personality and culture growing out of differences (and, paradoxically, in some cases similarities) in values and perceptions have made the two generations unintelligible, offensive, and ludicrous to each other. The first reason makes Xers feel anxious, exploited, and betrayed; the second makes Boomers feel misunderstood, unappreciated, and put upon.

The troubled relationship between Xers and Boomers is a complex and involuted business. Understanding it is not easy. I have not covered all of its aspects in this chapter, nor do I pretend to have a complete knowledge of the matter. But perhaps the following analysis will make it somewhat more intelligible. In the next chapter we will examine in more detail the causes of Xer–Boomer antagonism and the mechanisms Xers employ to handle the anxieties caused by this animosity.

5

Make Way for the Xers

Conflict continually vexes relations between Xers and Boomers. They bicker incessantly, complain of bad faith, and harp upon each other's hypocrisy and propensity for betrayal when things go awry. Xers see their predecessors as self-indulgent and incompetent, morally bankrupt, ruthlessly exploitative of the weak. Boomers portray their young detractors as shiftless slackers unwilling to pay their dues, truculent rebels who expect free rides to the good life. In short, they view each other with fulgent dislike. The two generations rub each other the wrong way and make each other anxious.

The root cause of this anxiety is a clash of interests, a war between generations. It is not, as some aver, merely the result of imagined injuries, slights, and hurts, or the jar of different lifestyles that so often mar the relations between age groups. Rather, it reflects a growing competition for power and wealth between Boomers and Xers, a fact many Boomers deny but most Xers stoutly affirm. There is, however, more to it than that: differences in the cultures and core personalities of the two generations also enter the picture. These factors have put them sharply at odds with each other, clouding their perceptions and making it difficult for them to understand each other. The result is a collision that is personal, intense, and pervasive. It would be silly to deny its importance.

Probably few Americans find the idea of intergenerational conflict at all surprising. It seems entirely natural and unavoidable: has not youth always been impatient to enjoy the privileges of seniority?

Since over time differences between generations in attitudes and behavior inevitably creep in, setting everyone's teeth on edge and fueling ill temper, is not conflict inevitable? And to clinch the argument, has not the cause of these differences—rapid social change—always been the hallmark of life everywhere, inexorably replacing established ways of life with newfangled ideas and manners, irritating the previous generation and delighting the young? Isn't this the way it has always been, here and elsewhere?

No. The conflict between generations in America is significantly different today than at any time in the past; it is greater, more complicated and murky, more attenuated and remote, more tension ridden and abrasive. Why is this? As I shall explain in this chapter, the Xer and Boomer generations were shaped by radically different experiences and have been marked by complexly different social forces, which have set them apart and in opposition to each other. This is a more subtle explanation than the one commonly proffered: the idea that the Boomer generation is immensely larger than its Xer competitor and hence the two groups cannot help but be different from each other, since cohort size matters above all else. This statement is wrong, both as empirical fact and as theory.

THERE ARE MORE OF THEM THAN YOU THOUGHT

Whence came the notion that the Boomers are more numerous than the Xers and that this accounts for the differences between the two groups? It very likely arose from the startled reaction of analysts to the Boomers' humongous numbers. Born in the years 1946 through 1964, the Boomer cohort numbers 76 million, about 27 percent of today's estimated 281.4 million Americans—an impressive figure no doubt, too large to be ignored.[1] Boomer numbers reflect the buoyant birth rate of the years immediately following the end of the war; it rose to 3.7 live births per woman in 1957, after having fallen to 2.1 during the years of the Great Depression and the Second World War.[2] Doubtless, it was the Boomer generation's enormous size that caused Landon Y. Jones to write in 1980, "The size of a cohort is the force that shapes it life. . . . The size of a generation is its most crucial characteristic"—a generalization that greatly influenced popular thinking about the Boomer generation.[3]

But this generalization is a gross oversimplification. If cohort size is critical, then the Boomers and Xers ought to be substantially alike—for if the time frame of a generation is taken to be about twenty years (an idea proposed by William Strauss and Neil Howe in their book *Generations*, and followed by many others), the Xer and Boomer cohorts turn out to be somewhat similar in size.[4] In fact, by some estimates the Xers are numerically larger. Born during the years 1965 through 1984, the Xers number 80 million, about 28.4 percent of the population. By 1995 they had become half of the adult population age 18–49, and about 30 percent of adults 25–54. At the end of the second millennium, adult Xers (persons over 18) equaled the number of adult Boomers and will exceed them sometime during the first decade of the twenty-first century.[5]

Marketers are well aware of this fact. To them the Xers are the preeminent target market for their goods. According to Karen Ritchie, a marketing expert, Xers already bought more "disposable diapers, gas ranges, oven cleaners, and electric can openers than Boomers bought in the past twelve months."[6] And as more Xers marry, their new households will require new appliances and furniture, and a host of the other goods that fill stores. Since popular culture has been deeply influenced by Xer tastes, filmmakers, TV producers, clothing manufacturers, music-CD makers, and other purveyors of mass entertainment strive to satisfy the desires of Xer youths—as a brief stroll through a shopping mall, a cursory scroll through Internet offerings, or a visit to the local cinema will quickly show. Storekeepers and Web site owners have learned that Xer tastes are too insistent and Xer numbers too large to be safely ignored.

Still, though Xer numbers are impressive, an emphasis alone on cohort size misses something important: other factors have gone into the formation of Xer attitudes and traits. Not, to repeat, that size is irrelevant; it has, for example, exacerbated the competition for jobs. But a generation is forged not so much by its size as by experiences common to its members—by their exposure to economic ups and downs, by war and social dissension, by pandemic disease and natural catastrophe. Most of these factors are shaped by social forces set in motion by rapid social change. No understanding of Xer character is possible without taking into account the significant social changes that have occurred during the lifetime of this group.

THE ZERO-SUM GAME

Elite Xers and Boomers want the same thing: power and status. But unfortunately these are zero-sum entities; they can only be increased for anyone at someone else's expense. This inevitably pro-

vokes conflict, a clash of interests over something considered a basic
right: the right to decide one's own future. This seems natural
enough in this individualistic era. It is, after all, only a manifestation
of the general right to control one's own life. But the additional claim
to a right to control others is another matter: this cannot help but pro-
voke resentment and conflict. And so it has been with relations between the Xer and Boomer generations.

It is evident to elite Xers that the Boomers run the country and can
do pretty much what they please. It is equally clear that the elite Xers
would dearly love to take their places. This is understandable, of
course, but there is a problem: the Boomers are not ready to go. They
are settled in, comfortable, and totally unwilling to transfer power to
another generation. They are not at all exhausted by their trip to the
top. The Boomers had it easy; they came to power without a fight.
They grew up during a period of remarkable prosperity, and when
they eventually challenged the previous generation, their parents,
who were products of deprivations caused by a great depression
and a world war, these pliant souls were not disposed to deny their
progeny anything. In contrast, the Xers face an opponent, the Boomers, a generation accustomed to getting its own way and not about to
relinquish control to an upstart generation. Xers know this all too
well, and yet they cannot bring themselves to give up their hunger to
control their own lives, the prerequisite for which is power.

The Boomer generation has done nothing to assuage this hunger.
If anything, its actions have only intensified the Xers' appetite, first
by frustrating Xer yearnings and then by scoffing at the very idea. To
the Boomers the Xers' push for power seems like youthful imperti-
nence, a juvenile putsch to be resisted at all costs. This attitude is sea-
soned with a large dollop of disappointment and bitterness: things
are not turning out as the Boomers expected. To a generation determined to stay young forever, middle age has come as something of a
shock. Tragically (to them), the Boomers are aging, and though they
continually redefine the boundaries of life's stages to accommodate
the passage of time (they have decided that they are still young at
fifty and that it is perfectly acceptable for actors in their fifties and
sixties to play romantic roles in films), the tolls of aging are all too
visible. The teeth of time are no respecters of Boomers, however
much their bodies may once have been lithe and lovely.

They are losing their hair, getting fat, and developing unsightly
wrinkles and bulges, despite the best efforts of skilled cosmetic sur-
geons to erase these unwanted blemishes of age. Other disappoint-

ments abound. Perhaps their children are drifters, apathetic and sullen; certainly, their president was impeached; and without doubt, some members of their elite group, caught taking illegal paths to success, have been hauled off to jail. Worst of all, winning no longer seems a sure thing. This is baffling to Boomers, because they have always considered winning as their birthright. Now a specter haunts them: the prospect of ultimate failure. Could it be they will turn out to be losers after all? Nothing could fill them with more dread.

It has occurred to some Boomers, a breed notoriously reluctant to take responsibility for its own actions, that the Xer generation is significantly contributing to their troubles. For the Xers have introduced a scary element of competition for power into a world hitherto under unchallenged Boomer control. That this unexpected threat comes from mere kids, just out of school and barely presentable in polite society, is a fact the Boomers still haven't fully learned how to deal with. Some Boomers refuse to take the Xer challenge seriously. But it would be a mistake for the Boomers to dismiss summarily their young challengers. Elite Xers are occasionally off-putting, it is true; they can get on people's nerves, including the tender sensibilities of other Xers. But they are also smart and energetic, especially skilled in the use of the most advanced technologies of the information age, hungry for advancement, and eager to control the information revolution.

Make no mistake: intense competition between the two generations not only exists; it is growing. Though not evenly matched, both groups have significant assets and handicaps. The elite Boomers still control the levers of economic and political power. They are rich, well connected, wrapped in enviable prestige, and experienced at running the show. But they are slowing down. They were slow to recognize the possibilities that new technologies have opened up. For example, it was only after much foot dragging that Boomer-dominated businesses like Microsoft, Barnes and Noble, Citibank, and Wal-Mart moved into the Internet in a big way. Belatedly recognizing the threat from Xer-controlled companies and determined not to let the Xers take over the new economy, Boomers are currently investing heavily in the Internet. Their logos now adorn the World Wide Web.

Still, the Xers have something important going for them: apart from being young, they have also had a head start. They not only saw the future, they helped bring it about. Bursting with youthful energy, nimble, computer savvy, willing to take great risks, they are perhaps the most entrepreneurial generation in this century. Xers pioneered advances in computer design, software development, and the Internet. It should come as no surprise that the founders of the eBays and many other dealers in electronic commerce are Xers.

Economic slowdown early in 2000 caused many dot-com enterprises to founder. Poorly conceived and badly managed, they went under as cash melted away and credit vanished. Their demise sent a wave of anxiety throughout the Internet community. But there were survivors, some of whom, barely out of their teens, have become fabulously rich. It is only a matter of time before they translate their wealth into political, economic, and cultural clout. Everything we know about the Xers suggest that the struggle for power will be a no-holds-barred, give-no-quarter, take-no-prisoners contest. The Boomers may fare badly in this contest, as many of them have begun to suspect will be the case.

The Xer challenge currently in progress to Boomer hegemony is a battle for control of the information revolution. Its outcome is up for grabs, and this uncertainty is generating intense anxiety among both Boomers and Xers. The outcome cannot be taken for granted. The Boomers are without doubt formidable opponents. But then Elite Xers are no pushovers either, though to be sure they are young and inexperienced. Still, it takes a lot of work, serious commitment, and a gutsy tolerance for stress to do battle with the Boomers. Not all Xers are convinced that winning the battle is worth the hassle, the stress, the self-denial that victory in a drawn-out war with the Boomers would require. The temptation to withdraw and call it quits lurks in many an elite Xer mind. Battles are not won by people who feel this way.

BOOMER FAULTS, XER WOES

The Boomers came upon the national scene chanting slogans about their right to do their own thing, to make the rules and break them at will and not be punished, to embrace the unconventional, to experiment with drugs, and to blur gender lines. In short, they demanded to be free and in control, as is only fitting for an idealistic generation destined for great things. But more than that, they believed in their right to hegemony over not only their own lives but also over the lives of others. And why not? Who, in the Boomers' estimation, is as qualified as they to be on top and in charge? Who is more gifted and brighter, armed with higher principles and better equipped to take the country into a brighter future? Who has the country's best interests more at heart? These questions answer themselves. Clearly, not only do they know what is best for themselves, the Boomers also know what is best for others—the Xers included, of course.

Xers see things quite differently: they believe themselves perfectly capable of running their own lives. They had expected to be allowed to control their own fates, to pursue their own dreams, as they believed their elders had done. But control perversely eludes them. This discrepancy between expectation and reality, between being in charge and having to take orders, generates consternation, disappointment, disgust, and pervasive anxiety in the Xer soul, as Harry Stack Sullivan's theory predicted it would. Disappointment is never much fun; in this case, it is made all the less tolerable because fate has put Xers in the hands of people who do not have Xer interests at heart—the Boomer generation.

Overshadowed by the Boomers, watched by condescending and critical elders who cursorily dismiss its accomplishments and magnify its shortcomings, the Xer elite feels unappreciated and abused. Obviously, no one would enjoy such treatment, but it is particularly detestable to elite Xers because it comes from Boomers, a generation in which Xers have no confidence whatsoever. What scares Xers is the Boomers' propensity for self-indulgence and self-absorption, their mania for grandiose ideas in which they soon lose interest, their proven record of mismanaging every project. These traits, as Xers see it, have caused great harm to the country in the past and could easily inflict even greater damage in the future, not least upon the Xers, who await anxiously the fallout from future Boomer debacles.

These are heavy charges indeed. Ann Clurman summed them up succinctly: "Forget what the idealistic boomers intended and look at what they actually did: Divorce. Latchkey kids. Homelessness. Soaring national debt. Bankrupt Social Security. Holes in the ozone layer. Crack. Downsizing and layoffs. Urban deterioration. Gangs. Junk bonds."[7] Xers believe they have been saddled with the thankless job of repairing the damage done by Boomer excesses and neglect. "Our job," wrote Meredith Bagley, an Xer author, "is to make order out of chaos—to resurrect America from the ashes of burning draft cards, and bras, from the humiliation of public betrayal, from the rubble of riots, from the shells of cities rotted by crime and despair."[8] Jonathan Karl, a CNN correspondent, sees the Xer task this way: "The biggest challenge for our generation will be cleaning up the messes left by the short-sighted, instant gratification tendencies of the previous generation."[9] No doubt to most Boomers these charges sound like adolescent whining, but they deserve to be taken seriously; they reflect a genuine sense of grievance—the Xer resentment of Boomer rule.

If the Xers' charges are true the Boomers are in trouble; but the Xers are not worried about the Boomers' fate. Why should they be? They have troubles enough of their own. As they see it, their lives have been plagued with disasters not of their making. First there were, as already noted, parental divorces—rents in family fabric that have never been fully repaired. Then they found the educational establishment beset by traumatic change: conventional pedagogy was under attack, instruction was substandard, school was boring. Furthermore, just as they grew old enough to drive the family car, the gasoline supply dried up: OPEC had turned off the faucet. When they entered college, financial aid became hard to find, and when they graduated, jobs were scarce. Starting out, many of them had to settle for McJobs in junk-food emporiums instead of filling the fine positions for which they had been trained—another Boomer promise broken.

Xers grew up in a time of scandal and disillusionment. Politicians were caught in flagrante with prostitutes or other ladies of easy virtue, betraying their constituents, selling favors for money. Advertising was misleading, all hype, not to be taken seriously. Celebrity icons, once adored and emulated, proved to be dishonest, flogging products of dubious value. Greedy businesses, after buying immunity from governmental prosecution with under-the-table campaign contributions, contaminated rivers with industrial poisons, filled the air with noxious fumes, and despoiled virgin woods, clear-cutting in days forests that had taken nature centuries to create. No one, it turned out, could be trusted.

Even the environment had let the Xers down. Annually, floods and droughts, tornadoes and hurricanes, hammered the suffering earth, and as Xers watched helplessly, topsoil disappeared and coastlines eroded. To compound their anxieties, scryers of gloom, confidently prophetic, foresee yet more calamities to come: nuclear winter, global warming, melting ice caps, widening holes in the ozone layer, population explosion, asteroid impacts. Even the sexual revolution turned out to be a bust: AIDS appeared just as Xers entered puberty, and the unspoiled sexual pleasures their Boomer predecessors had enjoyed were denied them.

With all this to contend with, Xers think they have reason enough to complain, and they would like speedy redress of their grievances. But with the Boomers running the show, they believe no notice will be paid to their wishes and needs. Things might improve if the Boomers would only go away, retire to enjoy their easily gotten gains, get out of the Xers' way. But this the Xer knows is highly unlikely: the Boomer establishment shows no sign of ever wanting to relinquish control.

The problem, Xers say, is not merely that the Boomers want to hang on to power; the problem is that they are doing a rotten job. The Boomers have made a mess of things. Apart from the fact, already mentioned and all too obvious, that pollution is rampant, politics a joke, and the welfare net in jeopardy, there is the scary national debt. Xers do not believe that the self-indulgent Boomers will actually defer personal gratification and use the anticipated budget surpluses to reduce or eliminate the national debt. With this debt hanging over their heads, Xers see themselves paying huge taxes forever just to cover interest payments.

Most troubling of all is the economy. True, it behaves itself from time to time—witness the remarkable prosperity of the late '90s. But it also has a tendency to start and stop without warning, like a faulty car inadequately maintained, liable to break down at any time. Xers are constantly being told that they will not live as well as their parents, the first generation in American history to hear this dire prediction. Small wonder they are tormented by anxiety about the stability of the economy, the fear that it will some day go into free fall. The Nasdaq sell-off in 2000–2001 gave them a taste of what this would feel like.

Nor is this anxiety entirely without reason. Xer confidence in the Boomer elite's ability to guide the economy took a terrific beating in the brief but painful economic tailspin of 1990–91. This setback, which Xers denounced as the ruinous work of Boomer mismanagement, frightened the wits out of anxious Xers, who even now wonder if it could happen again—as it possibly could. Combined with other disappointments, the erratic economy indelibly imprinted on impressionable Xer minds a palpable distrust of the Boomer establishment. Xers doubt that the Boomer elite will provide them with the safety net earlier generations enjoyed. Will Social Security and Medicare be there for them when they need it? Probably not, they have concluded. A survey by *Third Millennium* found that 53 percent of Xers believe the TV soap opera *General Hospital* will outlast Medicare.[10] No wonder we are worried, Xers say. How can anyone feel secure when Boomers are in control?

Many Xers brim with resentment toward their Boomer bosses. According to Suneel Ratan, an investigative reporter, Xers refer to Boomers as "knotheads and control freaks." Ratan's interviews with 60 twenty-somethings and Boomer managers elicited a litany of complaints that sounds eerily like the echoes of a generational grudge match. Xers complained that the Boomers "claim to be seeking younger employees input when in reality they couldn't care less what Xers think. [B]oomers seem threatened by young, cheap-to-employ hotshots who come brimming with energy and superior technological savvy."[11]

Boomers respond by calling the Xers cocky, disloyal, self-pitying whiners and snivellers who disrespect authority—this from the Woodstock generation, the youthful rebels of the 1960s. About Xers, Michael Kinsley, Boomer columnist and editor, had this to say: "These kids today. They're soft. They don't know how good they have it. Not only did they never have to fight a war, like their grand-parents, they never even had to dodge one."[12] Perhaps Kinsley wrote tongue in cheek, but nonetheless his comment reflects the opinion of many of his generation.

A CONFLICT OF CULTURES

More difficult to pin down than the raw feelings caused by clashes of interest are the subtle irritations provoked by differences in gener-ational culture. Cultural differences across generations are nothing new, of course. Every generation tends to go its own way, marching to its own drum, humming its own tunes, dancing its own steps, worshipping its own celebrities. To illustrate, the GI generation pre-ferred the jitterbug to the Charleston of its elders, swing music to ragtime, Frank Sinatra and Jo Stafford to Rudy Vallee and Ruth Etting. Similarly, the Boomers thought the music and dance of their parents old hat and doted on rock and roll, the Beatles and Elvis Presley. And not surprisingly, Xers dismiss Boomer music and dance as uncool. They have fashioned a pop culture of their own, a mish-mash of rock and roll from the fifties and sixties, disco from the sev-enties, a few ballads beloved by the Boomers, flavored with a large dollop of heavy metal rock, hip hop, and rap. Their idols are rap and hip-hop artists, antiheroes such as Tupac Shakur, Dennis Rodman, and Kurt Cobain the first was killed by gangster gunfire, the last by suicide.

Differences in popular culture are perhaps the least important sources of intergenerational friction. Much more serious is the way the two generations look at work. As Boomers see it, Xers are lazy, infuriatingly casual about keeping appointments and meeting work quotas, seldom loyal to a company, likely to drift off to another job when they get bored, and all but impossible to motivate when the work becomes routine. What has happened to the work ethic, Boomers ask?

This question elicits hoots of laughter from most Xers, who call the Boomers workaholics and phony moralists. They reject outright the Boomers' portrayal of work as spiritually uplifting, valuable in itself. Work, the Xers say, should be fun, not a moral crusade. Fun is a mantra for Xers. They will rally around almost any endeavor that affords them fun. Without fun, work, even well-paying work, becomes dreary, a dehumanizing pursuit of lucre without any redeeming virtue. Stephan Paternot, age 25 and cofounder with Todd Krizelman, also 25, of Theglobe.com, an Internet company, put the Xer attitude toward the intrinsic value of fun very succinctly: "Todd and I have always had a philosophy since we started, that we're only doing this as long as we're having fun. The day that you're just doing it for money, that's the day we get out."[13] Linking work to an ideology of social uplift, as Xers say Boomers do, strikes the Xer as loopy rhetoric, empty and dishonest and self-serving.

Baffled and angered at the rejection of their work code, many Boomers have abandonded any hope of finding a way to win independent Xers to the Boomer way of thinking. Give control to these people? No way, say the Boomers, an attitude that infuriates Xers, already resentful and rebellious, and more than ready to throw off the yoke of Boomer control.

While the preferences of one generation often appear rather bizzare, even comical to another, they used to be seen as nothing to get terribly excited about. Why, then, this nasty disparagement of, and intolerance for, popular cultures other than one's own? What has changed? A lot has changed. Let us begin with the Boomers. This group is hostile to American subcultures, African-American culture aside, despite its rhetoric of inclusiveness and tolerance—though cultures located in distant lands, preferably inhabited by impoverished third-world natives, are more acceptable, in some cases even admirable. But at home the Boomers will not tolerate nonconformity in others.

After having set the standards for proper behavior for their times (actually, in their view, for all times), the Boomers see no value in ideas and behavior unlike their own. Karen Ritchie calls the Boomers "one of the most repressive and reactionary generations this country has ever produced."[14] Todd Gitlin accuses Boomers of forming neighborhood associations to push street people, nonconforming "alcoholics, drug dealers, and wing nuts," out of Berkeley parks and out of their lives.[15] Besotted with political correctness, bewitched by the splendor of their own moral superiority, the Boomers are prepared to come down hard on violators of their code of conduct—though, swallowing hard, they assented to Bill Clinton staying in office, his lying under oath to a grand jury notwithstanding.

Nonconformity in young people drives many Boomers up the wall. That is strange, because as youngsters themselves they made an issue out of challenging authority, raising angry fists in defense of nonconformity. Now, the same generation that celebrated free love, pot, LSD, and bra burning blanches at the sight of young, pierced, tattooed bodies whirling wildly to rap music ablaze with incendiary racist and sexist lyrics—hip-hop Xers doing their own thing, as the Boomers once proclaimed was the right of us all. The Boomers puritanically would put a stop to such disfigurement, such Dionysian abandonment, such nihilistic sloganeering—if they could.

MISSION IMPOSSIBLE

Exasperating as differences in pop culture, in appearance, and in public demeanor may be, they are trivial compared to the gap that separates Xers and Boomers over the issue of social equality. The Boomer elite sees as its primary social mission the creation of a just and egalitarian society—an urgent and entirely reasonable goal, they believe. A just society is, after all, what children daily pledge allegiance to in classrooms across the country: one nation, indivisible, with liberty and justice for all. Wasn't this what the founders had in mind when they declared that all men are created equal and endowed by their creator with certain inalienable rights, among them life, liberty, and the pursuit of happiness? The pursuit of justice and equality has been going on for more than two centuries, disenchanted Boomers point out. Why then is liberty far from secure, injustice rampant, and equality as distant as ever?

This blemish on the nation's escutcheon must be removed, the Boomers argue. Not only is it the right thing to do, it is entirely achievable, if only enough people get behind the Boomer leadership and do their share. By "people" the Boomers primarily mean the Xers. If only this large group of youngsters, energetic and outspoken, presumably idealistic and malleable, would do the right thing and join in, the Boomers could accomplish their mission in short order.

On first reflection, the Boomers' expectation of Xer cooperation seems wholly understandable. After all, Xers and Boomers have at least this much in common: they both think of themselves, and would like others to see them, as sincerely committed to fair treatment for all. Intolerance offends them; prejudice against harmless persons is anathema, and discrimination should go by the board, the sooner the better. They would not, for instance, legislate against homosexuality: sex in their opinion is nobody's business but the participants'. They would sanction the occasional use of marijuana and are toying with the idea of legalizing harder drugs. They favor a level playing field for everyone, particularly for the ambitious Boomer or Xer. They very definitely believe in a fair chance for everyone to enjoy life. They think of themselves as decent people, ready to live and let live—a mark of their superiority. Righteous indignation against injustice and discrimination makes them feel good.

But on the issue of equality of condition, Xers and Boomers part company. Many elite Boomers still favor this goal, though often their support turns out to be mere lip service. Xers, in contrast, will have none of it. Perhaps the most meritocratically oriented generation the country has ever known, elite Xers accept without question whopping inequality in wealth, provided it is based on merit. They may wince at the news of someone their age making it really big—the billionaire founders of dot-com companies, for example—they had hoped to be winners themselves by 23. But they would not penalize the winner. Winning means being rewarded, not punished with aggressive measures designed to level differences in income.

In contrast to their warm embracement of winners, elite Xers turn a cold and stony face toward losers. As Xers see it, the playing field is now level, and those who do not make it to the goalpost have only themselves to blame. Consequently, affirmative action, quotas, set-asides, and other measures developed to assist disadvantaged minorities to become winners have few adherents among Xers. They shun any ideology that makes the redress of minority grievances its major goal. To the Xer, "Issues like affirmative action and equality are a drag. Ideology is a cause for embarrassment, like your mother's soft spot for the Great Society."[16]

More than an embarrassment, egalitarianism seems to Xers nothing more than mere hypocrisy, another empty Boomer slogan, futile posturing. They note that during the period of Boomer ascendancy inequality has grown steadily: it is far greater today than at any time since World War II.[17] Whatever their original intention may have been, the elite Boomers long ago sold out. They have done well for themselves. Grossly materialistic, obsessed with self-fulfillment and the good life, the Boomers went from serving the underprivileged to serving themselves, Xers charge. Novelist Douglas Coupland has accused the Boomers of being "embarrassed by their own compromised "'60s values" and of "transferring their collective darkness onto the groups threatening to take their spotlight."[18] In the film *Reality Bites*, a quintessential Xer statement, the heroine, played by Winona Ryder, lashes out at the Boomer sell-out, exclaiming, "And they wonder why we aren't interested in the counter-culture they invented, as if we didn't see them disembowel their revolution for a pair of running shoes." Xers say they are not taken in by the Boomers' sham values, a welter of skimble-scamble stuff.

Made cynical by scandals and betrayal, from Watergate to Iran Contra to Whitewater, disillusioned by broken promises and frayed values, bored by political sloganeering, Xers tend to avoid organized social action. They are too young to have taken part in the radical–chic social movements that shaped Boomer sensibilities—anti–Vietnam War, civil rights, women's liberation—and hence missed out on the exhilarating highs those movements spawned. To most Xers organized social action means stifling coercion, dull speeches, and useless marching. Environmentalism, it is true, enjoys their support, but they tend to participate as individuals, not as part of a group.

They visit the ballot box infrequently. Why bother? Aren't all politicians venal, mealy-mouthed, and duplicitous? "In the old days at least politicians pretended to have principles," laments Beth Englander, 26, a former Vista volunteer. "Now they're not ashamed to switch values just to get elected."[19] Xer voting is the lowest of any age group. Only one-third of the 18–24 year olds voted in the 1996 presidential election. When they bother to vote they tend to support long shot candidates, such as Senator John McCain, or former professional wrestler Jesse Ventura, whose victory in the 1998 Minnesota election for governor stemmed in large part from the support of a disproportionate number of Xers. "We have a libertarian streak," says Richard J. Thau, a Boomer author. "We grew up in a period of one instance of government malfeasance and ineptitude after another. . . . We believe government can't be trusted to do anything right."[20] To sum up, whatever their reasons, Xers do not put creating an egalitarian society, certainly one imposed by governmental dictate, high on their list of personal objectives.

This cruelly offends Boomer sensibilities. Compassion, caring for the poor, attention to the needs of the underprivileged, particularly blacks, and devotion to social equality are cherished ideals, buzzwords to elite Boomers. Affirmative action was their brainchild, their redemption, their rebuff to allegations of Boomer selfishness and self-absorption, proof that their generation has indeed made a difference after all. To have the purity of their motives impugned and their ideals rejected—by Xers, of all people—is an unforgivable injury, more evidence that Xers are cold and heartless, selfish and indifferent to the feelings of others, a lost and abominable generation.

It is understandable that differences in ideals and goals would pit Xers and Boomers against each other. They prize different things, strive for different ends, worship different celebrities. How could they not rub each other the wrong way and seriously chafe each other's sensibilities? But, paradoxically, similarity can have the same effect, for both groups tend to possess two personality traits in common: perfectionism and chameleonism. This similarity, which neither the Xers nor the Boomers recognize, far from bringing them together, only increases their estrangement from each other.

Perfectionism, in particular, makes it difficult for either group to make allowances for the other's inconsistencies and erodes the confidence they must have in each other if they are to settle their differences. We have already looked at the effects of chameleonism. Let us now examine perfectionism, to see how it develops and what it does.

6

The Search for Perfection

Chameleonism never stands alone: it always comes sheathed in a bundle of values and attitudes, expectations and aspirations, stereotypes and perceptions. These will vary with the people with whom the chameleon associates, with whom he competes against, and what he fears. But the one invariant factor, the one trait that always accompanies chameleonism, is perfectionism: the demand that everyone and everything, oneself included, be without flaw—now and forever. Violation of this demand will arouse in the perfectionist gnawing fear and loathing, though these reactions to imperfection may be concealed for prudential reasons. Perfectionists, like chameleons, understand that it is wise to hide unwelcome appraisals and feelings. But the hatred of human flaw and social error is there in the perfectionist's mind all the same, caustically eating away at his or her confidence in the world.

Perfectionism has its roots in experiences that shake a child's self-confidence and damage self-esteem. For a variety of reasons, differing somewhat from generation to generation and from place to place, some children develop intense feelings of insecurity and low self-worth. They feel vulnerable to attack, and they fear that people will take advantage of them if ever they let their guards down. Anxious and perplexed, feeling rejected, they search for means to protect themselves, armor their enemies cannot pierce, a fool-proof way to fend off attack. Perfectionism is one such way.[1]

The development of perfectionism in children is an exceedingly complicated process, as yet rarely studied and not well understood. I can only speculate about its genesis. But though its origins may differ somewhat from person to person and from group to group, the following scenario seems reasonable as a first approximation. It provides, at the least, an approach to an understanding of the development of perfectionism in middle-class American Boomer and Xer children, male and female.

THE BOOMER SCENARIO

Among elite Boomers, perfectionism developed as a result of damage to self-esteem caused by excessive parental indulgence, by unrealistic parental expectations, by inconsistent parental behavior, and not least by peer rejection. Highly intelligent, skilled with words, precocious achievers, these young Boomers charmed their parents, who gave their offspring to understand how special they were. Being special merits attention and reward, and the young Boomers were usually showered with both. Their parents enthusiastically applauded their every achievement and made it clear that they expected great things. It would be remarkable indeed if such children did not come to think of themselves as extraordinary beings, almost godlike in talents and prospects.

All went well for a time; the child's self-esteem grew luxuriantly in the warmth of the parental approval. Then the demon of parental inconsistency entered the picture. At some point, usually between the ages of six and eight, parents tightened the reins. These are ages when parents in many societies around the world conclude that children have attained the level of physical maturation and cognitive ability to understand the reason why something is expected of them. To illustrate: in rural Taiwan, according to Margery Wolf, villagers think a child is incapable of understanding instructions until the age of six; the Nydeggers in the Philippines and the Maretskis in Okinawa found parents also zeroing in on age six as a time to begin seriously imposing parental standards of behavior on the child; David Landy thought Puerto Rican parents did so when the child reached age seven. I found this same age held true for parents in Brazil. Until the child reaches this magic age, it typically enjoys a great deal of leeway. But soon after age seven, parental indulgence tends to be replaced by firmer expectations and harsher treatment.[2]

So it was for some middle class, white Boomer children, future members of the nation's elite. Sometime between age six and eight their world changed in an unpleasant and inexplicable way. Children who were formerly pampered were now admonished to behave as other children did: to keep their rooms and themselves tidy, to do their homework and other chores, to stop behaving like spoiled babies and do as they were told. In addition, they were constantly reminded to be tops—in school, in sports, in comportment— onerous expectations that invited failure, as, to children's chagrin, occasionally happened. All this, initial indulgence followed by abrupt and inexplicable harshness, seemed unreasonable, not unlike rejection—and indeed they took it to mean rejection.

Unfortunately, their sense of rejection only grew deeper as they encountered peers outside the home. Often, their treatment at the hands of other kids was a problem and a pain. At school their peers, never indulgent or easily overawed, treated them just like other kids, brighter perhaps than most but withal merely human. This was a keen disappointment, hardly the treatment they expected, considering their parents' enthusiastic evaluations and remarkable lenience. Possibly the youngster became the target of attack from schoolmates who envied the achiever's high grades and popularity with teachers, a hard blow to endure in a peer-oriented culture.

The young Boomer was puzzled and hurt. Why are parents suddenly behaving so unreasonably? Why are schoolmates so unfriendly? And what can be done about any of this? Typically, a child's reaction to rebuff and an abrupt change in the rules is a surge of anger and an urge to strike back. Getting angry at parents and disobeying orders is usually counterproductive. As a rule, parents are not amused by a child's self-assertion and intransigence and only tighten the screws. Telling peers off usually turns out to be a loser as peers almost invariably return attacks with attacks of their own—not at all what the child wanted.

When counter attacks do not work, some children reexamine the problem and come to the conclusion that the fault must lie within themselves, in that they are underlings. They conclude that their parents and peers had rejected them for good reason: they had proved unworthy and hateful; they had done something wrong. What else could explain their parents' sudden strange behavior and their peers' nastiness? The effect of this self-destructive assessment is an avalanche of pernicious self-belittling that over time seriously damages the young Boomer's self-esteem. This self-doubt and anger that inexplicable attack and consequent self-denigration brought is in most cases eventually repressed, hidden within the child's mind, erased from conscious memory. But it is still there, nonetheless, doing its baleful work.

THE XER SCENARIO

The process by which self-esteem among young Xers is damaged takes a different form from that of the Boomers, because typically their early experiences markedly differ, a difference that begins in the family. Many Xers never knew the family stability and indulgence their Boomer predecessors enjoyed. As already noted, the divorce rate doubled from 1965 to 1975, just as the earliest Xers entered middle childhood. More than 40 percent of today's young adults have spent time in a single-parent home by age 16. Moreover, by that age the average Xer had already been moved from place to place, repeatedly dumped into the care of distracted baby-sitters, and loaded down with burdens an earlier generation assumed were really the responsibilities of adults.

Nor did most Xers receive the pampering and ego-boosting treatment so many Boomers experienced. Xers entered the scene just when the country was going through a severe antichild period. Neil Howe and William Strauss assert that "the pop culture conveyed to little kids . . . a recurring message from the adult world: that they weren't wanted, and weren't even liked, by the grown-ups around them."[3] This message was reinforced by the zero-population-growth movement, which maintained that each additional child was an unneeded claimant on already tight resources, a point of view that permeated the nation and led to parents' making freer use of contraception than ever before. Even when adults truly wanted children and had them, they couldn't help noticing how expensive children were to raise, how much they demanded of parental time and energy, and how difficult it was to pursue self-fulfillment when kids tied one down.

Life at school was no picnic. Like their Boomer counterparts, the future Xer elite frequently encountered humiliating treatment at the hands of their agemates. High school was an ordeal. Xer achievers tended to be outsiders, nerds, and geeks, misfits in a system that valued beauty and brawn, that adored football hunks and prom queens. Though brighter than most of their peers, good at math and skillful with computers or with the uses of language and literature, these young Xers became objects of ridicule. Dismissed as oddballs, clumsy and nonathletic intellectuals, risible clowns unfashionably dressed in funny clothes, many of them developed a lasting sense of insecurity and grievance.

Buffeted by unfriendly winds from an indifferent society, disoriented by broken family ties and shifting family boundaries, burdened by responsibilities they were not prepared to assume, and mocked by peers, some elite Xers came to feel rejected, to believe they were burdens to their parents and society, unwanted nuisances. Watching rerun images of happy family life on TV's *The Brady Bunch*, many Xers were puzzled: why are things different now, what had gone wrong? Too young really to understand what was going on around them, they concluded that they had done something wrong. Why else would their world and other people be so mean, so down on them? Of such an assessment is low self-esteem born.

An injury to self-esteem, is always a raw and ugly wound; it should not be treated lightly or ignored. Too much is invested in developing and maintaining a satisfying self-regard to let an injury fester under trivial treatment. A simple poultice to reduce the pain will not suffice. Something must be done, serious remedies must be applied. Consequently, when confronted with danger to their self-esteem, elite Boomers and Xers alike move heaven and earth to change things, to find a way to protect themselves.

PERFECTION AS A REMEDY

What can be done? Several things—to begin with, troubled youngsters can call upon pleasure for help. They may decide to bury their troubles and assuage the hurt of rejection by having lots of fun, on the principle that living well is the best revenge. Following pleasure's prescriptions, they pick on younger siblings, watch TV endlessly while letting homework slide, turn their bedrooms into rat warrens, gorge on Snickers bars and peanut butter sandwiches, play tricks on friends and strangers. All this is intrinsically very satisfying and may do the trick, at least for a while.

But in the long run, hedonism often fails to work, for a variety of reasons. There is, for one thing, the problem of satiation: how much candy can one eat before surfeit sets in? For another, bullying younger kids, defying parents, and offending schoolmates, though altogether satisfying in themselves, are dangerous shenanigans. They can easily backfire and cause more distress than they relieve, if parents and peers get nasty in return. Hedonism, it turns out, can't be depended upon.

What else, then, can young Boomers and Xers do to protect themselves from the hurt of malicious attack? They can become perfect
people. Perfection puts them beyond the reach of calumniating foes;
perfection armors them against backbiting criticism, the gibes and
jeers of envious peers; perfection stills self-doubt and smooths over
the jagged edges of failure; perfection gives life consistency and
meaning. Most important of all, perfection provides an illusion of
control. Perfect people know how things work. They understand the
forces arrayed against them and can master the world. This feeling of
being in control is perfectionism's most precious gift to troubled and
insecure children. It will influence their behavior throughout life.

So, unconsciously and without deliberate design, the hurt youngster develops an encompassing preoccupation with becoming perfect. This is no trivial goal, for perfection is not easy to achieve or put
to effective use in boosting self-esteem. But slowly, by repeatedly
glossing over their faults, blaming their failures on others and imagining that they possess highly desirable qualities, damaged youngsters acquire the feeling of being perfect. They are, of course,
oblivious to the fact that they have become perfectionists. They will
readily confess to being human, fallible like everyone else. But deep
down, once incorporated into the personality, perfectionism causes
them to believe they are always right—though, of course, they will
vehemently deny any such idea ever entered their minds.

In building their self-images, elite Boomers and Xers draw upon
materials at hand, varying somewhat with the circles they move in
but always containing elements infused with the imagery of excellence, since they work in a world saturated with the language of
achievement. The urge to create the flawless computer program, the
sales pitch no consumer can resist, the leveraged buyout to end all
buyouts, the initial public offering no other offering can match, the
tune, phrase, costume that catches the public's attention—this, they
maintain, is what lashes them on to ceaseless effort. When finally
constructed, the image of the perfect self, excellent in every way, is a
wonderful piece of work, one to which its author becomes narcissis-
tically bonded.

Unfortunately, the quest for perfection must inevitably fail: perfection is beyond the grasp of mere mortals. Consequently, the pursuit of perfection condemns perfectionists to constant disappointment, to quests that will never leave them in peace. Rational people
understand this about perfectionism and never attempt it; to put
oneself in the position of being repeatedly disappointed seems to

them perverse. But people in thrall to perfectionism are oblivious to good sense. Their pursuit of perfection is not rational; it is an unconscious defense mechanism, hidden in some dark recess of the mind, and its urgings cannot be ignored.

People who think of themselves as perfect are consumed with anger and bewilderment when others challenge or contradict them. Even the slightest disparagement or the most minute frustration upset them inordinately, though they ususally go to great lengths to conceal their anger. Other people seldom correctly gauge the depth of this fury, and they often offend the perfectionist without realizing it. Hence, the mistrust, the anger, the misery that perfectionism creates, the botched the relationships it produces with friends and strangers alike. Obsessive and doomed to failure, destructive of healthy relationships, perfectionism is the cause of much unhappiness.

Why then does it survive the challenge of reality, the stubborn and exasperating refusal of the world to accept the perfectionist's claim to superiority over all others? The answer, simply put, is that perfectionists do not recognize the futility of their passion for perfection. They screen out feedback that doesn't fit. Moreover, notwithstanding its long-term costs, perfectionism *works* for them, at least initially: it makes them feel superior and legitimates their searches for security and success. Also, they are unaware of perfectionism's terrible psychic price. They do not connect it with the disappointment and anger they feel about themselves and the world.

PERFECTIONISM AND SELF-FULFILLMENT

In addition to its function as a defense against rejection, perfectionism legitimates the search for self-fulfillment—which is itself a potent incentive to become perfect. Only the perfect person can achieve self-fulfillment, and only a self-fulfilled person can be truly happy. Happiness means realizing the potentials that are rooted in the organism, a genetic blueprint that must be followed. In their search for self-fulfillment Boomers and Xers obsessed with perfectionism become totally absorbed with their own needs and wishes, imperatives they pursue with the fierce determination that perfectionism always demands.

Psychologically sophisticated Boomers and Xers justify their determination to attain self-fulfillment (they are unaware of its relationship to perfectionism) by pointing to the theories of self-fulfillment psychologists, such as Abraham Maslow, Erich Fromm, and Carl Rogers.[4] These theorists reject the idea that life must be a continual struggle for instinctual satisfaction. Though they grant the importance of the instincts and cede to the unconscious a major role in shaping human behavior, they also believe the social environment plays a far greater part in the formation of personality than orthodox Freudians are willing to concede.

True, our efforts to adapt to an often unfriendly environment—the ego doing its job—can make us into the selfish creatures we all too often become. And true also, humanity's innate need for sexual pleasure and a tendency toward aggression can lead to socially undesirable consequences. Even so, there is more to human nature, fulfillment theorists believe, than lust and venom, more to life than fighting and fornicating. The search for self-fulfillment is also part of human nature. And if self-fulfillment enhances self-esteem, if it makes adjustment to life's vicissitudes easier to bear it seems worth any price. But what if that price is perfectionism? As we will see, this is a heavy price indeed.

Because it develops slowly out of our efforts to cope with the world, perfectionism once in place is difficult to change. Perfectionists interpret each new experience within the framework of their existing self-images, even though events may call into question the conclusions upon which those self-images are founded; this makes perfectionism relatively invulnerable to attack. Believing themselves guiltless victims of obtuse people, perfectionists bend unwelcome information to conform to their images of themselves as persons much put upon, rudely abused despite their faultless characters. Hence, only an exceptional experience, sharp enough to pierce the shield that protects perfectionism from disconfirming evidence, will cause it to change—not something that happens often.

PERFECTIONISM IN BOOMERS AND XERS

Critics discern clear evidence of perfectionism in Boomers. Neil Howe and Richard Strauss describe the Boomers as "distracted perfectionists" who, determined to resacralize America and make it perfect, cover themselves with ashes and sackcloth when they and the country fail to measure up to their ideals.[5] J. Walker Smith and Ann Clurman say Boomers see their mission as pushing the system and themselves "closer to perfection," an attainable goal, they believe, once the evil in society has been located and rooted out. Perennial optimists, Boomers believe themselves strong enough and smart enough to do that. Clearly perfectionism, as well as hubris, is at work here.[6]

Xers are different. Street-smart and cynical, clobbered by unruly times and unfair fate, elite Xers would seem to be immune to perfectionism. Xers say they are not under any illusions about themselves and are not misled by the Boomers' notion that the world can be made perfect. They are not perfect, they say, and do not expect things even to work out well for them, let alone become perfect. Unlike the young Boomers who, flush with the coin of youth, believed in a limitless future, bountiful and generous, always there for them when they needed it, Xers feel they can't count on the future. "Life is uncertain," they say. "Eat dessert first."[7] That terrible injustices exist, that social problems grow ever grimmer, and that the Boomers are responsible for this mess, is obvious to the Xers. But that they cannot remedy every wrong, that they need not and should not assume the burden of cleaning up other people's messes, is also obvious. Surely, you might say, this is not the screed of perfectionists.

And yet beneath this tough talk lies a solid foundation of perfectionism, mixed with naive idealism. For if Xers are not idealists, why would they care that the world is screwed up, as they claim it is? If they are not perfectionists, why would they complain about Boomer hypocrisy? There is, after all, nothing particularly new about the world being in a mess. When hasn't it been? Most people, not afflicted with perfectionism, simply shrug their shoulders, take the world as it is, and move on. But elite Xers tend to take the imperfect world as a personal affront. Though they can't bring themselves to do much about it, they find imperfection deeply offensive: it upsets them, it makes them feel cheated, it turns some of them surly and sour.

As to Boomer hypocrisy, why should it upset them? After all, hypocrisy is a fact of life, even among their peers, no cause for surprised resentment. Yet Xers boil with indignation when Boomers assume airs of moral superiority and blithely refuse to recognize their own imperfections and misdemeanors. In a better world, a perfect one in fact, the one for which Xers really yearn, the Boomers would candidly admit to their failures, promise to make amends, and humbly beg the Xers' forgiveness. No one but an unworldly perfectionist would harbor such unrealistic expectations.

PERFECTIONISM AND CHAMELEONISM

Perfectionism is not, of course, the only way Xers cope with the torment of damaged self-esteem. They have more than one string to their bow—they have chameleonism. Like perfectionism, chameleonism shelters the Xer from invidious comparisons and injurious attack, from the noxious tactics of envious colleagues and unscrupulous competitors that eat away at self-regard. As we know, chameleons seek to escape injury by pretending to be the allies, not the foes of their competitors. This tactic makes sense to some canny Xers, who have decided that a chameleon's life is their only choice in a hard world dominated by unsympathetic Boomers. Karen Ritchie writes, "The best educated and most affluent of Generation X chooses to fit in, to play it safe in order to achieve what they want and need out of life. They view it as a fundamental issue of survival."[8] Disguised as allies, Xer chameleons try to distract, befuddle, and charm their opponents, weaving webs of deceit that ensnare the unwary.

You might think that the Boomers, older and usually more economically secure, would have little need to conciliate their young opponents. But they too play the chameleon game when it suits their purposes. Wisdom advises them to be cautious, to assume the chameleon's role, the pretense of being the Xers' buddies rather than their enemies. Why not, say the Boomers to their younger colleagues, put aside petty differences and work together for our common good? Basically, we're just like you. Let's be one team and get rich together. They don't mean it, but they hope the pretense will work.

As mechanisms of defense, perfectionism and chameleonism are compatible and feed upon each other. Successful chameleons are exceptionally sensitive and very clever, as they must be to get away with the tricks they play on unsuspecting opponents. Therefore, it is easy to see how chameleons would come to believe themselves not only smarter than the people they gull but perfect at what they do. From perfection in chameleonism to overall perfection is a psychologically logical step that chameleons readily take.

As strategies of manipulation and dominance, the paths of perfectionism and chameleonism, though superficially attractive, are fatally thaumaturgic. What will happen when negotiations between Boomers and Xers reveal basic differences of interest? How will these be resolved? Not by calm discussion and compromise, if perfectionism and chameleonism call the tune, but by efforts to deceive and manipulate opponents, usually followed by bitter accusations of selfishness and bad faith when negotiations break down. Under the spell of perfectionism, neither group will moderate its rhetoric, lower its expectations, or settle for less. To do so would seem detestable, utterly forbidden to people of perfect stature.

The reasons for this are not hard to find. As perfectionists, Boomers and Xers alike, cannot admit to misjudgment or wrongdoing, cannot accept a compromise. To do so would be a sign of weakness and a betrayal of personal integrity. Any recognition of personal failing, which they see as the only legitimate basis for ceding advantage to an adversary, is inconceivable to perfectionists. It is also terribly dangerous. After so much time and psychic energy has been devoted to becoming perfect, any confession of weakness is a chink in their armor, which under pressure can widen until the entire structure collapses. In short, the possibility that they could be at fault is simply too absurd even to consider.

Even when they are in the wrong, and even when they recognize their error—highly unlikely though that is—to admit as much would be, as they see it, unwise, mere loony folly. Uncovering one's real intentions to the enemy and engaging in honest exchange could well be fatal. As chameleons (and perfectionists), elite Boomers and Xers fear being exploited if they let their guards down. Their goal is to gain security and personal advantage through subterfuge and artful deception, not through a rational discussion of the issues, open examination of areas of disagreement. A discussion of issues opens up the possibility of compromising standards and losing face—which is completely unacceptable to the perfectionist chameleon.

As a result, when chameleons exchange ideas with competitors and other adversaries, exchanges are more likely to be of claptrap and flapdoodle rather than useful information. Honest information, they believe, would in the end be used against them. They lack enough faith in fair play, enough trust in the good will of others, to take chances. This is how chameleons look at the world. This is why they became chameleons in the first place.

To sum up, perfectionism and chameleonism exacerbate the tensions that exist between Boomers and Xers, and will probably continue to do so, for they are rooted in complex socio-psychological forces that generate anxiety and resist change. These forces have created a miasma of frustration and suspicion in which chameleonism will continue to grow luxuriantly. Sadly, chameleonism, and its colleague, perfectionism, have made Xers and Boomers so touchy, so distrustful of each other, that good relations between them will be exceedingly difficult to achieve—if they can ever be achieved at all.

7

Gender and Chameleonism

Elite Xers dote on a meritocratic society: it gives them the freedom they treasure. In a meritocracy, few of life's important decisions—what work to do, where to live, whom to associate with or marry, for example—are dictated by custom or harsh reality, as they are in a traditional system, which uses ascribed status, particularly those associated with age and sex, to govern most social relationships. Instead, a meritocratic society makes these choices private matters, subjects of negotiation between consenting partners. Negotiation is possible because a meritocracy is fluid and in constant flux. Indeed, almost nothing seems fixed, nothing settled, nothing secure. To a large extent, therefore, Xers feel free to make their own rules, free to decide for themselves what work to do, with whom to associate, whom to conciliate or dominate, whom to flatter and deceive.

Xers yearn to be free, to be masters of their own fate. They would like to cast off the restrictions of a callous world and thumb their noses at people who have been indifferent to their needs. To the Xer freedom comes festooned with rights: the right to work or not to work at all; the right to marry or stay single, to have children or not; the right to be gay, lesbian, or straight; the right to change sex roles or ignore them altogether. In short, freedom means having choices.

Choices enchant Xers. Choices open the door to new experiences. Through that door rush ideas and images, transmitted by the media, that encourage people to break the chains of custom that tie them to the past, to explore the potentials of innovative suggestions, to seek out aggressively new experiences. They embolden people to dare to be different from their parents and to seize the opportunities the new age affords them. Until relatively recently such opportunities were scarcer for women than for men, but with the triumph of the Third Transformation, the range of choice has expanded enormously. One of the most important of these new opportunities is the chance for women to pursue success in the paid workplace with all the vigor long associated with ambitious men scrambling to get ahead.

This chapter will examine the story of women's changing place in the labor force, their successes and travails, and the part chameleonism and its associate, perfectionism, has played in all of this. I will argue that the women's increased role in the workplace inevitably heightened the competition between the sexes, changed gender roles, produced much confusion and anxiety, and inevitably promoted chameleonism in both men and women. I will show how women use chameleonism to good effect in the competitive marketplace and explain why they tend to be more expert chameleons than men.

THE TWO FACES OF CHOICE

Elite Xers in a meritocratic society face a difficult situation. They often have more choices than they can handle: not simply the choice between conformity or being expelled from the group, the dilemma people in traditional societies face, but the choice between different types of work, between competing ideologies, between multiple sources of satisfaction or pain. Life for elite Xers is one long exercise in decision making. Poised between right and wrong judgment, they must learn to discriminate between alternatives and to anticipate the consequences of their actions. This necessity to make choices among multiple options sharpens the mind and enhances critical judgment. The choice may not always be the right one, but the freedom to make it strengthens the spirit.

Stimulated to want more than an average existence, afforded numerous opportunities, trained to decide between options, elite Xers plunge daily into activities from which, if successful, they can gain a sense of competence. As part of a system, the meritocratic information society, which rewards competence, they acquire the belief that competence pays. And competence when rewarded generates self-confidence. Small wonder Xers tend to emphasize the benign face of freedom, a face that beckons them to enter the race for success.

But freedom is two-faced; it also has a malign countenance. The freedom to make decisions is also the freedom to make mistakes, and for elite Xers the mistakes can be whoppers. As they rise to positions of power, Xers acquire the authority to make choices whose consequences when wrong can be ruinous. To illustrate: a hot-shot Xer bond analyst who incorrectly estimates the direction of interest rates may cost an investment bank millions of dollars; a young designer who promotes an elegant but expensive line of apparel may produce the flop of the season; an entrepreneurial Xer who persuades venture capitalists to back his dot-com company with cold cash may see the company and the cash go down the drain when the idea proves impractical.

In brief, freedom is risky, and the price of failure can be ghastly. As a consequence, people have been known to flee from freedom like the plague. This is why, according to Eric Fromm, the German people in the 1930s abandoned the democratic Weimar Republic and embraced the totalitarian regime of Nazism, which abolished freedom and gave the freedom-wary German the sense of being protected by an all-wise savior, a *Führer*.[1]

Freedom also unleashes ferocious competitive forces. Elite youngsters today face competition from sectors of the population that in earlier times never dreamed of entering the big battles for power and money. One such sector was female; many women were prevented from competing with men—but no more. Now women challenge the notion that advancement is possible only for privileged males and no longer automatically accept sequestration in the low-status pink-collar ghetto. The result is an exciting fray in which men and women compete for advancement, a tumultuous free-for-all that can be frightening as well as exhilarating, for not everyone can cope with the anxiety that high-risk competition has created.

Ready or not, the competition for occupational success has become a wide-open sport in which almost anyone may take part. The playing field is not completely level, of course. Some people have a head start, put there by parents and friends. Others are handicapped by a despised color, a disliked religion, an unconventional accent or sexual preference. Still, on the whole, the meritocratic information society encourages competition and welcomes almost everyone to enter the race for success, a remarkable development. After all, what other society so actively recruits talent, so bemoans the waste of talent, and worries about the loss the nation sustains when gifted youths are neglected? What other society searches quite so earnestly for bright youngsters and plies them with fellowships and promises of golden rewards if only they will take part in the national game of success hunting? The result is a diversity of contestants without precedent in this or any other country.

Most elite Xers take for granted the sexual diversity of contestants in the competitive work arena. It is all they have ever known. Everywhere they looked—in the classroom, in the workplace, in the political arena—they saw a mixture of sexes. It seemed the natural state of things. But a little reflection and some knowledge of history would quickly disabuse them: they would see how extraordinary their current situation actually is. In truth, they are immersed in a competition whose tempo is uniquely intense, brought about in part by the movement of women into the workforce. Even its most privileged sectors—the corporate board of directors and the university inner sanctum—are now open to women, one of the most momentous changes to have occurred in the last fifty years. Its impact on the elite Xer deserves our attention.

WOMEN IN THE WORKPLACE

Until the last half of the nineteenth century, the American woman's position in the workplace reflected the country's predominantly agrarian nature. At that time, the country approximated Thomas Jefferson's dream. He had envisioned an America that would be forever rural, a democracy of farmers tilling their own lands. The farmer, in his view, was the salt of the earth: "While we have land to labor," he wrote, "let us never wish to see our citizens occupied at the work bench, or twirling a distaff, for those who labor in the earth are the chosen people of God."[2] When he died at age 83, in 1826, his dream still seemed reasonable, for in that year the country was overwhelmingly rural: only about 8 percent of the population lived in communities of 2,500 persons or more. At mid-nineteenth century, five times as many people lived on farms as in cities.

A century ago, rural Americans made a sharp distinction between the kinds of work they considered proper for men and for women. On the farm, men were expected to do most of the heavy work: clearing and plowing fields, sowing, reaping, then carting and selling crops. Of course, women helped out when needed, hoeing, weeding, and gathering in the crop, working beside their menfolk. But their principal assignment was domestic: spinning yarn and weaving cloth, cooking and preserving food, caring for small animals and children.

Moreover, not only did the sexes perform different kinds of tasks, they occupied different physical and psychological spaces. They kept out of each other's way and rarely competed in any kind of work. Also, they usually maintained considerable emotional distance from one another, engendering a degree of formality that modern Americans would find cold and unnatural. (It is, however, unfair to apply modern sensibilities to the relationships between men and women of an earlier century.) In any event, the traditional sexual division of labor prevented or reduced the tensions caused today by competition between the sexes for prestige, money, and power.

Unless necessity forced them to seek employment elsewhere, most women were content to work at home, as custom and the good opinion of their neighbors required. When they had to earn money outside the home, it was usually at work much like their normal household duties: sewing gloves and garments, caring for the infants of strangers, selling homegrown vegetables and poultry in the local market. Young unmarried girls might hire themselves out as domestics, doing woman's work in someone else's house, but this was a temporary expedient until marriage made it possible for them to stay at home.

The industrial engine changed all of this. It began to move, albeit slowly, in the early nineteenth century, dawdled up to the Civil War, built up a head of steam after the war, and finally took off during the last quarter of the century. One of the effects of this change was the separation of the homeplace from the workplace, which forever changed the role of women in the paid labor force. Women began working outside the home in significant numbers, drawn by the prospect of steady wages. At first many worked as servants or as quasi domestics in hotels, hospitals, restaurants, and bars. But slowly the industrial system began to attract women into its factories, mills, and workshops. In time the garment lofts of New York and the shoe factories and textile mills of New England drew large numbers of women into their employ, until factory girls became a common sight on the streets of all manufacturing cities.[3]

At first most of the women in the industrial work force were unmarried girls from poor rural or lower-class city families. Middle-class women turned up their noses at the idea of working in dirty, noisy factories; it was not the kind of thing ladies did. These privileged wives and daughters of industrialists, merchants, and professionals shuddered at the thought of working for pay, and yet before the nineteenth century was out, they had entered the labor force in large numbers. A movement that began as a trickle in the nineteenth century became a torrent in the twentieth.

Consider the record. In 1870, the first year in which reliable national data on working women were collected, women made up 14.1 percent of the labor force. Each decennial census thereafter reported a steady, if modest, increase in the female component of the workforce. Thus from 1880 to 1900, women's share of the workforce increased from 14.5 percent to 17.7 percent, a 1 or 2 percent increase per decade. As a result, by 1920 the percentage of women in the labor force had grown to 20.2 percent; by 1940, women made up a quarter of the paid working population. After the Second World War, however, the pace of growth quickened dramatically. From 1940 to 1990, each decennial census revealed an increase of 4 to 6 percent in the female component of the labor force. By 1980, women's share of the labor force had grown to 42.4 percent, and by 1990 it had risen to 46 percent, approximately where it is now.

But the sheer number of women in the labor force does not tell the whole story. Equally interesting is the presence of women who for family reasons had been reluctant to work outside the home—married women and mothers of small children. At the turn of the twentieth century, the typical working woman was young and single: 46 percent of single women worked outside the home, as compared with only 6 percent of all married women. By 1962 this number had increased to a third of all married women, and by 1982 it had risen to 51 percent.

That is not all. Many of these women had children of pre-school age, a marked contrast with the past. Thus in 1948 only 10.8 percent of women with children under six years of age worked outside the home, whereas by 1984 three out of five women with children under three, and 52 percent with children under six, were in the labor force, approximately the present number. Since 1980 most of the increase in female employment has been among women with preschool-age children. For the first time in American history, young children at home no longer keep the majority of women out of the labor force.[4]

WOMEN AND THE TECHNO-SERVICE ECONOMY

These changes were the work of the rising techno-service economy. The service economy did something the factory system never dreamed was possible or even desirable: it brought middle-class women into the labor force. The industrialization of production had meant little to these women, except to make cheaper certain products, such as cloth, thread, and needles. If middle-class women concerned themselves at all with the factory, it was to view with alarm the presumed evil effects of factory life on the morals of young working girls or to complain that factories were luring away girls from domestic work, making the problem of finding and keeping servants exasperatingly difficult. So, unlike many lower-class women to whom industrialization opened a new world of opportunity, most middle-class women resisted the lure of paid employment and stayed at home.

But the needs of the service economy would not be denied. Its technology eventually entered the home and changed the lives of privileged middle-class women. Labor-saving appliances made managing a house less time consuming, and with servants to do the dirty work, middle-class women found themselves with more free time than they had ever known. Some women gave themselves over to having fun, giving parties and attending social events. Some devoted their energies to charity, helping out in hospitals and schools, and setting up private agencies devoted to ameliorating the condition of the poor; in the process, they created an entirely new profession, social work. Some turned to jobs in the burgeoning service sector, in part just to get out of the house, in part for the intellectual challenge, in part for money with which to buy their freedom from irksome patriarchal control.

Competition between the sexes in the workforce was carefully controlled and muted. In factories and mills, most women avoided the skilled crafts that tradition had assigned to men, a decision enforced by labor unions and accepted as right and proper by most employers. As long as women stayed by themselves in the ranks of unskilled or quasi-skilled labor, the tension between the sexes over competition for jobs, salary, and promotion remained low.

Surprisingly, most women accepted this situation quietly, with a minimum of grumbling or open complaint. For in truth, many women did not relish the idea of competing with men. They had entered the work force reluctantly and looked forward to leaving it. Indeed, it has never been easy to get women into male-dominated occupations, especially in factories and mills, not even in time of war—not even during the Second World War, when the pressure on women to work in war-related factories was terrific. According to

Walter Karp, "there was nothing spontaneous about the unprecedented influx of women into the wartime shipyards and factories.
Far from picking up rivet guns with joy, American women had to be
exhorted, cajoled and browbeaten to take traditionally male jobs."[5]
Rosie the Riveter, the sweetheart of the homefront, always enthusiastic and smiling, loving every minute at her job, was a figment of
wartime propaganda.

Almost as radically as it had changed the production of goods,
technology changed the delivery of services. Before the growth of
modern technology, work in the service sector, mostly performed by
women, had been associated mainly with dirt and slop, with brooms
and mops, with bedpans and soiled sheets, with demeaning toil
requiring little intelligence or skill. Technology gave the service worker
new tools and interesting skills. Working in offices, hospitals, stores,
schools, a woman could operate equipment of wondrous complexity.
Soon the typewriter and telephone, the thermometer and the stetho-
scope, became the familiar tools of middle-class women at work.

Service work appealed to middle-class women in ways that factory work never had. For one thing, service work seldom made demands on physical strength that women could not meet. A hand
strong enough to hold a skillet can easily hold a sales pad, punch a
typewriter keyboard, or carry a briefcase. For another thing, service
work connoted helping others, an idea congenial to women who
think of themselves as helpers of their families, of their friends, of
their communities. Before the turn of the twentieth century, many
women had gained valuable experience dealing with people in their
roles as volunteer workers in charities that helped the sick and poor.
In this way they acquired a proficiency in supervision that was later
translated into jobs as visiting nurses, truant officers, child-labor in-
vestigators—work to which few men were then attracted.

Service work also attracted women because it often permitted
part-time employment and usually allowed easy exit when domestic responsibilities required a woman's presence at home, as well as
reentry when the situation at home eased. Moreover, the pay in service work was at least comparable to that earned in factory work, often better, and service work was less subject to layoffs than a job in a
mill or factory. But perhaps most important of all, service work was
generally safe, clean, and respectable, something a middle-class
woman could do without jeopardizing her status as a lady.

It was not altruism that prompted employers to recruit women
into the service economy; women were welcomed because they

were needed. Had employers limited themselves to hiring males, the cost of labor in the rapidly expanding service economy would have skyrocketed. Skilled service workers were scarce, and competition for intelligent staff was ferocious. Eventually, even tradition-bound companies were forced to toss aside old prejudices. Like it or not, they had to open their doors to women, even in management, even in businesses as stuffy and hidebound as banking. Said Barry M. Allen, first vice president of the Bank of Boston, explaining a recent change in hiring practices: "We can't afford to keep out any talented person."[6] Being a woman no longer means automatic exclusion from the manager's desk.

Government statistics show that women who join the workforce today gravitate overwhelmingly toward jobs in the service economy. About two-thirds of all working women are in the service sector; only one in six holds down a job in a goods-producing industry. How different it was a century ago. Then, six out of the 10 leading occupations of working women were in the goods-producing sector; now only one of them, sewers and stitchers, can be called goods producing. Most of the rest are service positions, principally in the personal care and health, educational, recreational, insurance, merchandising, and finance industries.

Equally significant, most of the jobs created in the next decade will be in the service sector—and these will be women's jobs. Apart from the 20 occupations traditionally held by women—all in the service sector, and all expected to grow—the new positions being created in data processing, legal services, health and education, and government are even now being filled mostly by women. The Bureau of Labor estimates that of the 10 occupations most likely to add workers in the early twenty-first century, eight are considered women's jobs. Women will account for 65 percent of all new workers. As far as new jobs are concerned, the future belongs to women.[7]

Women now work in all sectors of the economy and compete with men, often successfully, for advancement in fields long dominated by men. Women hold positions of managerial responsibility in companies across the country, including many in the Fortune 500 category. According to Department of Labor data, 43 percent of all business managers are women. In some fields, such as insurance and nonprofit social services, more than half of the managers are women. They are also doing well in high-growth businesses like Internet services, biotechnology, and health care.[8]

Perhaps most significant, women have broken through the glass ceiling that kept them out of top managerial positions. A study released by the Census Bureau in April 2000 revealed that more than 7.1 million women worked in full-time executive, administrative, or other managerial positions in 1998, a 29 percent jump from 1993. Some of these women are filling top-flight positions. For example, in 1995 Ann M. Fudge, a 44-year-old black woman, became the president of Maxwell House Coffee Company. Brenda Barnes manages a six-billion-dollar business as chief operating officer of Pepsi-Cola North America. In 1999, Carly Fiorina took over at Hewlett-Packard, a quintessential computer maker, the first woman CEO of a Dow 30 firm. These are only a few of the stars that dot a constellation crowded with achieving women.

Looking at salaried work alone misses a big part of what is happening to women; they have become a dynamic part of the business world. According to the Census Bureau, the number of businesses owned by women increased 40 percent between 1987 and 1992, to 6.4 million, one-third of the total. A recent study by the National Foundation for Women Business Owners estimates that almost eight million businesses are now owned by women, employing one out of four workers. More female achievers are in the making, for the enrollment of women in law, medical, engineering, and business schools has more than doubled in the last decade. Women make up about a third of students at business schools, 40 percent at medical schools, and half at law schools. Clearly, still more female luminaries loom on the horizon.

To sum up: many women, no longer content to stay at home, impatient with ties that kept them in the kitchen and the nursery, are exchanging the apron and the baby carriage for the business suit and the computer, and now seek new experiences and rewards in paid employment outside the home. But women have done more than join the labor force; they have changed it. Elite Xer women have achieved important jobs in government, in the skilled professions, and in science and business, irreversibly changing the composition of the work force—a revolutionary break with the past, one that is changing women and society. They have become part of the new meritocratic elite.

CHAMELEONISM AND THE FEMALE ELITE XER

More than a need for workers motivates employers to hire women for positions in the service economy: commonly held notions about the character of females are also important. To many male bosses, women appear ideally suited to service work. Women are thought to be exceptionally sensitive to other people's moods, inclined to be sympathetic to their needs, and quite skillful at putting others at ease—thus making it relatively easy for a woman to deal with clients in face-to-face encounters. Women seem more flexible than men, more skillful at mixing with different kinds of people, more able to blend into any group. When it comes to soothing jangled nerves and handling irate customers, the sensitive female can generally be counted on to succeed where the more obtuse male would fail.

This notion that their temperaments (as men see it, that is—women tend not to share the male perception of the female temperament) are more pliable and accommodating gives women an advantage over men in certain areas of the job market. For instance, the rapid movement of women into personnel work, a growing job category for women, has been attributed to the belief that women possess a natural talent for dealing with people, adjusting grievances, and maintaining proper working standards.

In effect, what male employers are saying is that women are chameleons and that this makes service work easier for them than for men. But have men have got it right? Are women, in fact, inclined to be chameleons? There is reason to believe so. The behavior of women, the comments they make about their own sex, and a spate of recent research on the socialization of girls all point to widespread chameleonism among women.

As we have seen, peers play a big role in the development of chameleonism. This is true for both sexes, of course, but in some circumstances peers are more salient for girls than for boys—particularly in connection with dating and mating. This intriguing fact showed up in a study I conducted in three American cities and later replicated in seven English cities and two Italian ones. Although research revealed that industrial societies have been successful in reducing centuries-old attitudinal and behavioral differences between the sexes, when it comes to competition with members of the opposite sex, a sharp difference still exists: girls appear more worried about competing with boys than boys are with girls.

Why is this? Perhaps it is because many girls believe that maintaining good relationships with boys becomes difficult when the boys lose out in competitions with them. Most girls learn this early. My survey of adolescent girls found that 64 percent believe that boys would like them less if they did better than the boys in a test. Some girls hide or deprecate their accomplishments, fearful that others will think them vain: 40 percent of the girls said they worried that other people would think them "stuck-up." Many girls use chameleon-like tactics to fend off antagonism from boys, such as "acting dumber than I really am" and " doing what other people want me to do, even when I don't really want to." These girls use chameleonism as a tool to protect themselves from the belligerence and rejection of peers.[9]

Why this sensitivity of females to the possibility of rejection by males? It appears to be tied to their anxieties about dating and eventually finding a marriage mate. This is not a trivial concern. Eventually, most Americans marry and in time become addicted to the marital state (four out of five remarry after divorce), an attraction that stems in large part from the emotional gratification marriage provides. But there are also intense pressures from family, married friends, and society on the unwed adult to get hitched, a weight that falls more heavily upon females than upon males. Bachelorhood is socially acceptable, but spinsterhood alarms almost everyone. Popular and professional opinion have combined to make many an unmarried woman feel incomplete, an unfinished identity awaiting a man to give it form and meaning.

But first a man must be found. Trying to be helpful, the woman's parents, friends, and the mass media shower her with advice and admonitions. She is told to nurture the frail male ego and to avoid anything that might frighten her quarry or make him skittish. Aggression must be avoided, or muted and disguised. An attitude of passivity must be assumed, because the traditional female is expected to play the passive role in courtship—or appear to be doing so; a posture of compliance should be feigned, within reason. Ellen Fein and Sherri Schneider, in their 1996 book *The Rules: Time Tested Secrets for Capturing the Heart of Mr. Right*, gave this advice to hopeful brides: "The man must take charge; while the woman must be coy and demure, forbidden to talk to a man first, to smile at him or make eye contact."[10] Underlying this advice is the assumption that a woman seeking a husband operates in a buyer's market, in which the man is the buyer.

In the mating game, many men, including elite Xers, seek to play the traditional male role, no matter how modern they profess to be. Despite what women may want, and the unfairness of it all, this greatly influences the attitudes men have about women. Traditional men in particular tend to hold an ambivalent, stereotypic, schizoid views of women. On the one hand, they cannot deny that women possess highly desirable resources and skills, and for this reason they may decide that if it takes marriage to get access to these resources, so be it. On the other hand, listening to tradition, they believe that women are inherently devious, capricious, powerful creatures, who will castrate the male, psychologically and perhaps literally, in order to get their way.

As boys they came upon this image of women when listening to adults talk about the wiles and wickedness of women, or perhaps from hearing other boys speculate about girls. As any boy knows, sharing gossip and information about girls is one of the greatest joys of belonging to a peer group. Whatever its source, the stereotypic image of the female is frightening, at least to traditional males.

Their vision clouded by fear and hostility, by wonder and puzzlement about a woman's intentions, traditional males search for any evidence that confirms their prejudices. Even the smallest sign of female competitiveness and aggression is enough to inflame male paranoia. When women behave assertively, when they threaten to win in any contest with men, the anger and fear of traditional males are aroused, because losing to a woman is intolerable to them. Faced with the prospect of not doing as well as a woman, some men withdraw and sulk, or flare up in anger. But whatever the response, traditional men feel deeply threatened by female superiority.

To defuse any potentially explosive element in their relationships with men, women with marriage on their minds become very circumspect. They strive to anticipate the expectations of men, conceal anger, leave offensive opinions unexpressed, say what is expected, "making nice" and fitting in as best they can. They avoid doing anything that would frighten off men, in the belief that the most important relationship of their lives is with a man in marriage. In effect, where men are concerned many women tend to behave like chameleons.

THE FEMALE ADVANTAGE

In the game of chameleonism, women have several advantages over men. For one thing, they tend to be better than men at establishing relationships with others. To cement these relationships, they talk about their troubles, share confidences, and seek comfort and reassurance. They spend precious time and energy cultivating personal ties and developing skills that strengthen relationships—skills that come in handy when they employ chameleonism to protect themselves against the pugnacity of others, especially men. For another thing, according to Helen Fisher, women are more flexible than men, less bound by rigid rules, more willing to embrace alternatives better suited to their needs. Skilled at dealing with people, alert to the importance of connections, women dissemble when the situation requires, even at some personal cost. "Women suppress their personal views, their interests, even their careers, to accommodate others and maintain harmony in their social worlds."[11]

In pursuit of consensus and harmony, the accommodative woman carefully obeys the first rule of chameleonism: avoid confrontation, don't appear dominant, don't seem like a threat. According to Deborah Tannen, women use self-mockery and self-disclosure to ward off envy and hostility. They are also more likely than men to ingratiate themselves with potential critics, by using "ritual apologies" to smooth out imbalances in relationships. Above all, say Elinor Lenz and Barbara Myerhoff, the career woman, likely to be an elite Xer, "is a skilled compromiser and negotiator, she fits in, straddling her two worlds with a commendable degree of poise and equilibrium."[12] This kind of behavior is less acceptable for many men, who think it would make them appear weak and vulnerable.

In order to avoid confrontation and win acceptance, women always keep their social antennas tuned. "They pick up the tiny signals that people send, detect their motives and desires—[they] have a knack for decoding your emotions by looking at your face. They swiftly decipher your mood from your body posture and gestures—and deftly navigate their way into [your] heart."[13] Determined to maintain social relationships and skillful with words, a talent demonstrated in IQ and SAT test scores, women can "fathom what you want to hear . . . and then proceed to manipulate you with words."[14] This "uncanny ability to read [people's] minds and then tell them what [they] want to hear" is the hallmark of the chameleon.[15]

No doubt some Xer women find the idea of faking congenial agreement with men both silly and demeaning. They think chameleonism is an archaic relict of the past, rubbish to be ignored, certainly not applicable to themselves. They will have none of it. Men are put off by competitive, assertive women? So what? In a competitive world, sometimes men win, sometimes women do; winning and losing are all part of the game. Isn't this the rhetoric of the meritocratic workplace, as likely to fall off the lips of a woman as a man—nothing to take offense at, nothing to worry about, right?

Not really: Actually the female meritocrat is in a quandary. She works under immense pressure in a winner-takes-all scramble for high stakes, often competing with male superiors or colleagues. She is expected to excel and to get ahead in her career. She has been taught to evaluate herself in terms of occupational success, the same standard by which men have long been gauged. But what matters winning if it drives away friends, male and female, who have been made envious by her success? How can she feel content if she believes that competition with males will be thought unfeminine and that victory over men will earn her kudos from society but cost her love and marriage? Even if she is already married or not interested in marriage, or if she works primarily with other women (as many women do in the welfare, health, and educational industries), she cannot fail but notice the chill that her success introduces in her circle of friends.

Yet if she withdraws from the occupational contest, not only will she pay dearly in money and prestige, but she will also suffer a blow to her self-respect. For in withdrawing she confirms the negative stereotype of women: that women are dependent, moody, and flighty, uninterested in work that requires long-term personal commitment, unable to take seriously the demands that success in a career entails. If her actions confirm this stereotype, is she not in danger of thinking it true of herself? The result may be that she comes to hold a poor opinion of herself, to accept as true of herself all the hostile things misogynists have been saying about women. In that case, she runs the risk of becoming depressed, listless, self-denigrating and anxious—exactly as the image of women embedded in the traditional gender role portrays them to be.

THE WAR OVER GENDER ROLES

Since traditional gender roles may make women feel weak while encouraging men to behave aggressively, adding unnecessary tension to the already stressful relations between the sexes, why not change the roles? Better yet, why not get rid of them altogether? After all, gender roles are artifacts of the remote past, products of conditions long since abolished. Since abolishing the old to make way for the new is an Xer goal, a rallying cry for a disaffected generation seeking a place for itself in an unfriendly world, getting rid of traditional gender roles would seem to be in order. Moreover, dismantling gender roles should be no problem for elite Xers, who openly disdain all arbitrarily imposed rules and seek to evade them whenever possible.

But changing a gender role is no easy task, as Xers are finding out. Why is that? In part it is because few men consider their gender role a problem and hence see no reason to change it, in part because women cannot agree on what should be done. Men's indifference to the consequences of their own gender role—the outcome, no doubt, of their self-satisfaction and inability to imagine themselves at fault in the gender-role brouhaha—could probably be overcome if only women would make up their minds to do something about it. However, strange though it may seem, women will not marshal their considerable resources to make the old roles go away.

This is true even of dedicated feminists. Though currently in some disarray, the women's movement is still one of the most articulate and organized groups in the country. But far from getting together on a common agenda, feminists are in fact engaged in a nasty internecine war. Currently, factions of the feminist movement (or what is left of it) are quarreling over what their objectives should be, including what is to be done about gender roles.

That women are at war with one another will probably come as news to most men. Absorbed with themselves, with sports and work, they simply have not been paying any attention. Women are less surprised; they tend not to be sanguine about the possibility of amity among women. Still, needless to say, surprise or not, this war dismays feminists. Its ferocity also startled them: they were not expecting the amount of infighting, its implacable viciousness, that presently plagues them. In the beginning they were remarkably united. As a small, embattled group, they could not afford the luxury of fighting among themselves. But time and success has brought inherent divisions within the women's movement out into the open.

One source of division is disagreement among feminist leaders over the parts nature and nurture play in the formation of gender roles. Divided into angry factions on this issue, many feminists—a mostly white, middle-class, well-educated group—have begun to direct at each other the fury they once hurled solely at men, charging one group or another with either ignoring the dictates of biology or overestimating its importance.

One faction gives to nature the dominant part in the fashioning of gender roles. Theorists in this group, variously called "essentialists," "biological determinists," or "evolutionary psychologists," see biology and evolution as the source of gender differences. They argue

that hormonal and other biochemical factors, abetted by natural selection, have made the sexes into two distinct groups, unalterably
different and directed by nature toward mutually antagonistic
goals. Following the dictates of natural selection, males have developed into aggressive and unemotional creatures, an independent,
cold, linear-thinking breed obsessed with rank. Females, also under
the direction of evolution, have become compassionate, sensitive,
nurturing, warm, unassertive, passive, malleable, and pliant, eager
to please and be helpful.

As the evolutionist sees it, the differences between males and females came about as a product of the reproductive strategies that
primordial men and women employed to ensure their own survival
and that of their offspring. The male sought to increase the number
of his progeny by having many mates. He wandered where lust
listed and strove for dominance as a way of gaining access to females. In seeking females, he preferred youth and beauty, signs of
fertility, but would take his pleasure where he could find it. Since
success in mating tends to favor this sort of promiscuous behavior,
natural selection favored the production of aggressive, risk-taking,
adventurous, competitive males, so much so that they have become
dominant in the population.

The female, on the other hand, wanted to be protected: she needed
a mate who would take care of her and help protect her young. She
was looking for a male with status and resources, or with the potential for obtaining them, for she thought, not without reason, that
they were indications of his ability to provide for her family. Over
time, so the evolutionist's argument goes, these attitudes, male and
female, became embedded in the architecture of the brain, so that as
John Stossel, a politically incorrect gadfly, put it, we have become
"hard-wired to be different."[16]

On the opposite side of the nature-nurture debate are the "social
constructionists." These theorists, sometimes called "liberal" or
"radical cultural" feminists, rule out any part for nature in the fabri-
cation of gender roles. They maintain that gender roles are hand-
made, mere cultural artifacts socially constructed to fit the uses of a
society dominated by men. Writes feminist Susie Orbach, in a typical
presentation of this point of view, "Gender roles are culturally prescribed—they've nothing to do with genetics."[17] Social constructionists see traditional gender roles as nothing more than pieces of a
shabby tale concocted by patriarchal males to justify their domination of women. The patriarchal male was abetted in this endeavor by

traditional women, who reared their daughters to be accommodating to the needs of men. For in the biologically based explanation that legitimates traditional gender roles (an explanation as acceptable to traditional women as it is to men), women are weak and helpless, in constant need of male help. Consequently, accommodation rather than confrontation seemed the wisest stance a woman could take in her relationships with men.

Radical feminists and other social constructionists claim that traditional gender roles make women easily exploitable. Weakened by the commandment that they be submissive to men, these women are predisposed to be losers in any contest with men. The men, on the other hand, born aggressive and trained to dominate others, are encouraged to believe they can have their way with women—or at least to give it a try. It is expected in traditional circles that men will seek to dominate women, though this submission, unless care is taken, could well lead to the woman's ruin.

Social constructionists object to this, of course. They believe that what some people have built up, other people can tear down. This emphatically includes gender roles—a logical conclusion, as they see it, because if anatomy is not destiny, gender roles can be changed at will or even abandoned entirely.

ANDROGYNY AND GENDER ROLES

The division between different sorts of feminists comes into sharp focus in their contrasting attitudes toward androgyny: the blending of masculine and feminine characteristics within a person. Androgyny has two faces, one benignly humanistic, the other malignly political. As a humanistic ideology, androgyny urges men and women to incorporate into themselves the positive characteristics of both sexes—that is, to adopt the assertive, agentic qualities of the male, while softening them with the nurturant, compassionate qualities of the female. The androgynous female could then pursue success and self-fulfillment as forcefully as males have long done, unhampered by ambivalence or fear of societal reproof. There would be benefits for the male as well. The androgynous male would be spared the damaging effects of unrestrained male competitiveness: the hard work, the fatigue, the emotional tension, the medical problems that tax the health of men who frantically pursue success.

As a political ideology, androgyny favors leveling the barriers that keep the sexes apart, physically and emotionally, and that stig-

matize women as inferior. So effectively have these barriers separated the sexes that at times men and women appear to have become
separate species, inhabiting different worlds, unable to bridge the
chasm that divides them except for occasional orgiastic coupling.
Like ships that pass in the night, the two sexes send out signals to
one another—sometimes of distress, at other times of support—but
the messages are often muffled, misunderstood, and all too seldom
acted upon.

On the surface the message of androgyny seems conciliatory:
eliminate the gender roles that keep us apart, put an end to the
causes of friction between the sexes, let amity flow. Let us, the message reads, build a new model of humankind, a multifaceted person
who embodies the best of both sexes, honoring the potential for
wholeness in each of us. This potential is stronger in women than in
men, it is true. But even so, androgynists maintain, a world free of
gender roles, the liberation of both sexes from the constraints of tradition, is attainable, a wholly humanistic goal.[18]

But in fact, on balance, the mission of androgynists is more political than humanistic. Granted, they seek to demolish the barriers that
separate men and women, eliminate the subordination of women to
men, and put the sexes on equal footings. But the unspoken goal of
radical androgyny is not parity; it is female superiority and dominance over the male. To achieve this ambitious goal, androgynists
have taken to denigrating systematically things masculine and cele-
brating attributes considered feminine. In this way, androgynists
hope to change the outlook and aspirations of girls and women.

As a start, androgynists are promoting a radically new regimen of
child rearing aimed at feminizing boys and masculinizing girls.
Androgynists want to change the toys children play with, the games
they engage in, the ways they dress. They favor, for example, giving
dolls to little boys and trucks to girls, and dressing little boys in bits
of girls' attire, and vice versa. Fernanda Moore, a graduate student
in comparative literature at Stanford University, was charmed when
her three-year-old son asked to wear a tutu (he had become smitten
with a tutu-wearing little girl his own age). She readily agreed and
threw in some barrettes for good measure. Delighted that her boy
would be a role model for little boys, she saw him as a crusader for
the empowerment of little girls; she was soon crushed when the boy
decided to abandon the tutu for a dinosaur, with horns and a tail.

Ms. Moore would no doubt fall in that category of females Christina Hoff Sommers accuses of seeking to "unman" boys. In her book

The War Against Boys, Sommers blames women for producing men who are insecure about their masculinity, out of touch with their identities, and wracked by feelings and fears they cannot express. Sommers maintains that most of the women in boy's lives—mothers, teachers, counselors—do not understand masculinity, feel threatened by it, and treat boys as protosexists and potential sexual harassers. The traditional masculine virtues—the aggressive pursuit of victory in sports, the manly display of courage in competition, the stoic acceptance of pain—get little approval from these women, who urge boys to curb their appetite for competition, get in touch with their feelings, and open up to others, particularly to girls, the all-too-frequent victims of male aggression.[19]

Androgynists have succeeded in changing the books children read, to include stories and pictures of girls and boys doing similar work for similar objectives. For example, girls are shown as fire fighters, soldiers, police, doctors; boys are shown as care providers, nurturers of children, nurses for the sick, cooks preparing the family meal. At school, girls are counseled to take courses once considered unfeminine—science and math—and encouraged to challenge boys at games and sports, or at very least play games once thought unfeminine. Presumably, as a result of this new orientation, girls will grow up to be self-confident women, ambitious and assertive, and hence more able to take on men in any competition and win.

As part of their plan to bring men down a peg or two, androgynists seek to create a general revulsion against man-the-aggressor. Androgynists picture men as offensively pursuing money and power, being obsessed with rank, and lacking in empathy, thus incapable of connecting with others. All this will end, androgynists claim, when males are freed from the chains of their traditional roles and can become new men. Unfortunately, they argue, this task will be the mothers' burden, because the fathers are too emotionally inhibited to handle the work of creating the new man.

The new man, feminized and sensitized, refurbished with womanly qualities, will be empathic, warm, and compassionate, an altogether different human being—one, to use the words of Olga Silverstein and Beth Rashbaum, who is "responsible to self, to family and friends, and to society, and capable of understanding how those responsibilities are, ultimately, inseparable."[20] He will also be much easier for women to handle in any competition for jobs, promotion, and power. Androgynists deny, of course, that this is what they have in mind, though they admit that the blurring of distinctions between the sexes could have the effect of reducing the competition between men and women. But this, androgynists say, would be in the best interests of both sexes.

So far it hasn't worked out that way. Most men resent being told that they must become more like women, seeing this as just another female trick to weaken and unman them, and they resist becoming anything faintly resembling the feminine ideal. For their parts, young women today are turned off by the idea of becoming more like men, the unisex ideal explicit in the androgynist model of humanity. Witness the current popularity among young female Xers of face makeup, of attractive hair styling, of high-heel shoes, and of close-fitting clothes—all of which sharply accentuates their femininity.

By seeking to change the balance of power between the sexes, androgyny has disturbed the relationship between men and women, with serious consequences for both sexes. Two things are reasonably clear. First, androgyny has heightened anxiety among both men and women. Urged on by androgynists, men and women increasingly find themselves competing in the same arena, and embroiled as seldom before in a rancorous contest for influence and power. As a result, both sexes have become edgy about the intentions of the other. Second, androgyny has increased confusion in the minds of both men and women, for by trashing traditional customs, androgynists have left both sexes bereft of time-tested solutions to many of their everyday problems. People must now work out for themselves new sets of rules to govern their relationships. This is hard and uncertain work, permeated with anxiety, a task whose end is nowhere in sight.

The close connection between androgyny and anxiety-producing confusion and competition may become clearer when we understand that androgynists believe men and women are engaged in an endless battle for dominance. That this battle creates a nagging sense of frustration in the souls of androgynists and many of their opponents, a boiling cauldron of resentment that frequently spills over into vituperative rhetoric, should surprise no one. But more than rhetoric is at work here; simmering hatred also contributes its embittering bit. Christina Hoff Sommers maintains that radical androgynists hate men, or at the very least view them with a degree of suspicion that borders on paranoia.[21] She argues that to such women as Catherine MacKinnon, Paula Rothenberg, Elizabeth Minnich, Eleanor Smeal, and Diana Scully, the doyenne of feminism, as well as their younger colleagues Elizabeth Wurtzel, Katha Pollit, and Susie Orbach, all men are oppressors and natural brutes. Men don't just have sex with women, they rape them. Even voluntary sex is nothing less than rape, for what is sexual penetration but a violation of a woman's bodily integrity? That some women obstinately insist on having sexual relations with men baffles and angers radical androgynists almost to tears.

FROM IDEOLOGY TO ACTION

Androgynists, diligently at work carrying out their program, have enjoyed remarkable success. By skillfully piggy-backing their ideology onto the civil rights movement and justifying their programs to remake society as simple extensions of the fight against prejudice and discrimination, they have penetrated the culture. Working carefully and with great persistence, often unnoticed, they have managed to sell themselves as agents of benign change, supporters of cultural diversity and multiculturalism, and champions of tolerance and inclusiveness. Highly organized and well funded by foundations, universities, and departments of education, they have insinuated themselves into positions of power in schools, colleges, and government agencies.

Their influence is especially strong in elite colleges and universities, in departments where critical theory, literary deconstructionism, and multiculturalism have taken hold. They dominate women's studies programs and strongly influence English and history departments, law schools, and divinity schools. They are disproportionately represented in the ranks of deans of students, in dormitory administration, in offices devoted to discovering and punishing sexual harassment, and in counseling centers. Skilled at administration and committed to gaining control of the curricula, they insert themselves into the academic power structure and use their clout to denounce "phallocentric oppression." They organize demonstrations to demand more money for women's studies, and they set up seminars to examine the ways in which male-dominated establishments work to exclude women from jobs and positions of power.

For a time androgynists met little opposition. Early on, they found that resistance to their pursuit of power was fragile and rickety. In many cases the door to change stood ajar, and the guards blocking their way were often shamefaced, disarmed by ambivalence and doubt. Males in the faculties and college administrations generally kept quiet, frightened of being called sexists if they objected to feminist excesses. The few who spoke up were harassed in the classroom and surrounded on the campus by enraged female students who shouted curses and threats. This generally frightened the enemy into silence. Academics are not trained to be warriors; on leaving home when they were young, they preferred college and graduate school to boot camp. In most cases, then, they opted for withdrawal; silence seemed to them the better part of valor. As for most women academics not of the androgynist persuasion, they played along, not wanting to appear disloyal to the women's movement. Many of their students, attracted to the ideology of feminism, enrolled in women's studies courses and became disciples.

But in time a reaction set in. Some women, mostly outside the academy—such prominent writers and critics as Camille Paglia, Katie Roiphe, and Cathy Young, to name only a few—began to decry the excesses of androgyny. They accused certain feminists of subordinating scholarship to ideology, of recruiting students to the extreme wing of the women's movement, and of stirring up hatred between the sexes. In articles and books, and in lectures before large audiences, they attacked the androgynists' viewpoint as mere manipulative sophistry intended to advance personal campaigns for attention and influence. They have made it clear that androgynists do not speak for all women and certainly not for them personally. They have caught the attention and to some extent the support of many Xer females, who say they want nothing to do with androgyny and even reject the label of feminist.

Notwithstanding their adamant refusal to call themselves androgynists, elite Xer women accept the principle of gender equality. They jeer at the idea that they are incapable of competing on equal terms with men. They reject the notion that women are timid and irresolute as embedded in the traditional image of women, and they demand that this old chestnut be thrown in the scrap heap. Why, Xers ask, shouldn't women be encouraged to act assertively, compete against the standards applied to men, and pursue achievement as aggressively as men have always done? They ask for no favors. They reject the idea that the state should mandate equal numbers by sex in every occupation—a goal of androgynists. What they want is fair treatment on a level playing field. Given a fair chance, women will show that far from being unfit to work in the hurly-burly of the marketplace, they can more than hold their own in competition with men. Refusing to be stymied or sidetracked, Xer women plow ahead in pursuit of their goals: equality and occupational success.

AMBIVALENCE AND AMBIGUITY

But the pursuit of occupational success has created problems few women anticipated. Women today face a challenge their ancestors seldom encountered: how to reconcile the conflicting claims of family and career. Work outside the home, which was supposed to liberate women, has left some of them feeling exhausted and overwhelmed. In trying to juggle the demands of career and family, some women discover that they have taken on more than they can handle. They are finding that they simply are not up to it, that there are not enough hours in the day, that there is not enough flexibility in the mind, not enough resiliency in the body, to do both jobs properly.

Perhaps there are superwomen who can effortlessly juggle the demands of family and career: satisfying employers who require complete commitment to the job, appeasing husbands who insist on services only a full-time housewife could provide, mollifying children who want total attention to their needs—and do all this without wrenching physical and emotional costs. But ordinary women, torn by conflicting demands and desires, may end up feeling exhausted and strung out. To some women the price of success at work appears excessive, not worth the time lost with husband and children, marital bickering and alienation, nerves strained to the breaking point. Still, to many other women the rewards of being in the labor force are irresistible. Notwithstanding the costs, they pursue occupational attainment with zest and, it should be noted, with considerable success.

The success of women in the labor force has not, of course, gone unnoticed by men. Some men applaud female achievements, others simply welcome a second income in their marriage; very few voice strenuous objections. But it would be naive to believe that female competition does not threaten many males, even the quite young ones. When the Ms. Foundation for Women sponsored a "Take Our Daughters to Work Day," a newspaper reporter found boys as young as 14 expressing alarm; they feared the experience would put the girls one-up in the job search years hence. "They may take over my job. . . . They will take over every job that is in the world in the future," was a typical teenage reaction.[22] Adult men are generally chary of expressing such chauvinistic sentiments, but anxiety must surely churn their stomachs when they witness the swift ascent of women into the high positions that were once set aside for the men.

Perhaps all of this was foreseen. After all, competition often has worrisome side-effects. What was not foreseen was the confusion and anxiety, experienced by men and women alike, that are created when social demarcations between the sexes become blurred and familiar moorings to tradition are dissolved, leaving many people adrift. Xers in particular now find themselves in unfamiliar waters, without the guidelines for workable gender relations that earlier generations took for granted.

This is not simply a matter of abandoning the little civilities that once eased the relationships between the sexes, that reassured women of their femininity and boosted male self-esteem. Such simple courtesies as opening the door for a woman, rising when she entered the room, and helping her to be seated have been thrown overboard, discarded as useless junk from times gone by. But most Xers seem not to have noticed, or if they have, they appear not to mind.

Far more difficult to handle are the problems caused by the demise of many of the rules that once governed intimate relationships between the sexes. The blurring of gender roles created much confusion, leaving young people without the guidance a generally accepted code of conduct once provided. For example, what is to be done when no rules exist to tell the Xer when it is proper to take the initiative in developing a relationship with a member of the opposite sex, or when to stop, or when not to start at all? Who is to set the boundaries in dating or other sexual matters? Should the man, the woman, either one? Does it depend entirely on conditions and the participants' temperaments? No one is authorized to say. Xers must figure this out for themselves. What custom once made clear is now a matter of private arrangement.

Make no mistake, these are not trivial matters. In the dating game, a misstep, an unwelcome sexual advance that once might have evoked a chilly look or a slap in the face, may now land a miscreant in court on charges of sexual harassment. In marriage, confusion as to how money and authority should be allocated, how household tasks should be divided, or how child rearing chores should be distributed can destroy an otherwise satisfactory relationship. Even a truly happy marriage can founder if no agreement can be reached on these matters, and agreement has become more difficult in the absence of culturally prescribed answers to basic questions about proper marital deportment.

On their own in an environment awash with ambiguity, embroiled in relationships without a firm architecture and where mistakes can be fatal, many Xers flounder, anxiously searching for a way out. Some assume a posture of cheeky bravado, adopt a what-the-hell, let's-do-it attitude, hoping to bluff their way through the crises caused by baffling social change. Others become cantankerous and withdraw, professing an indifference they really do not feel. More inventive Xers have taken to faking it. They dissimulate and prevaricate intrepidly, throw up smoke screens to mask their confusion and intentions, and weave stories to suit situations. They test the winds and go with the flow—the usual responses to danger of the true chameleon.

Even if Xers can surmount these difficulties, other challenges await them. Not the least of them is how to deal with the new immigrants, a source of competition and anxiety their immediate predecessors seldom encountered. As we have repeatedly remarked, competition and anxiety are progenitors of chameleonism, and for this reason I have made immigration the topic of the next chapter.

8

Immigration and Diversity

Elite Xers tend to be of two minds about immigration. On the one hand, as descendants themselves in many cases of people who came to this country only a few generations ago, they feel attracted, however tenuously, to the Old World cultures of their ancestors. They proudly assert that the United States is a nation of immigration and that immigrants have always been a major source of its vitality. Feeling virtuous about America's liberal immigration policy, these Xers shudder at the suggestion that the borders be closed to outsiders.

On the other hand, they find the immigrants' presence somewhat threatening. Who are these strange newcomers anyway, jabbering away in incomprehensible languages, dressing in strange clothes, eating bizarre food, expressing crazy ideas? Will they not change the very nature of the country, its culture and institutions, and in time take over the nation? Are they not taking jobs that belong by right to native-born Americans? Any one of these forebodings is enough to create more than a modicum of anxiety, but collectively they add up to a substantial bundle of trouble the Xers could just as well do without.

In this chapter we will examine how Xers view several of the problems that have been linked to immigration, and whom they hold responsible. This is a touchy matter, because immigration is an emotion-laden subject, making rational discussion about it almost taboo. Some people who talk about immigration become apocalyptic, conjuring up images of racial miscegenation, cultural decadence, and national decline; others, conversely, become enthusiastic, seeing

the immigrants as promoters of the nation's destiny and contributors to its cultural splendor. Such rhetoric aside, however, the ambivalent attitudes of Xers toward immigrants can be understood as
responses to problems that boil down to three.

First, as some Xers see it, immigration is a mess, the work of the
Boomers, who opened the door to a vast new wave of immigration
and then walked away, leaving the Xers to cope with its consequences—just like the Boomers, Xers say. Second, the new immigration is hugely expensive to the nation. Indigent immigrants must be
helped, their sick cared for, and their children educated. Xers believe
the bill for all this will be their burden for many years to come. Third,
and by no means least, many of the immigrants are highly skilled
technicians and professionals, keen competitors for jobs that nor-
mally would be filled by elite Xers. This last problem is particularly
painful to success-hungry Xers, who are finding it hard to compete
with crackerjack talent imported from abroad. The world is already
hectically competitive, Xers say, somewhat plaintively. Who needs
more competitors?

WE'VE BEEN THERE BEFORE

It would be tempting at this point to jump right into an analysis of
the perceived effects of contemporary immigration on the Xers,
treating it as sui generis, unique to our time and place. Probably
most Xers would be comfortable with this: they tend not to search
the past for explanations of the present. But they would be mistaken,
for whatever Xers may think of present-day immigrants, good or ill,
their attitudes are unavoidably touched by the experiences of earlier
generations of Americans with immigrants.

Modern attitudes toward immigration are colored by memories
of the past, those ethereal footpads who waylay us on our way to the
future and fracture our complacency. These memories are part of the
heritage our parents, grandparents, and great-grandparents left us,
handed down from generation to generation: stories told around the
kitchen table, offhand remarks about one group or another, recounts
of hurtful incidents and cutting remarks. American culture is larded
with these stories, the residue of the prejudices and ill feelings that
Americans in earlier times bore toward the immigrant. The suspicion of outsiders, fear of competition, and discriminatory practices
to keep the immigrant down and away that we see today—all have

their counterparts in previous times, and all color the attitudes of native-born Americans toward today's immigrants.

It is not surprising that the hopes and prejudices and fears of earlier generations of immigrants and of native-born Americans resemble those found today. After all, immigration has been part of the American experience for a long time. It behooves us, therefore, to examine the vicissitudes of earlier immigrants and of their often reluctant hosts. Only then can we truly understand what immigration means to contemporary Americans.

WAVES OF IMMIGRATION

Leaving aside the Asians who crossed the Bering Strait in prehistoric times—little is known about when they arrived exactly or in what numbers—immigration may be said to have begun in colonial times. Fortunately, the records for this period are fairly good, and we know much about who came, how many, and when. Most of the early immigrants came from northern and western Europe. The English and Scots-Irish settled in the North and South; concentrations of Dutch and Germans and scattered elements of Welsh, Swiss, and Swedes took up residence in the middle-Atlantic areas; the Spanish and French founded communities in the far South. Together, they gave the nation its language and much of its culture, dominated its economy, and established its government. At first their influence was sovereign, but they were not to have the country to themselves for long.

Soon after the white man arrived, another kind of newcomer arrived on American shores: African blacks, forcibly transported and enslaved to fill the need for cheap labor. By the time the legal importation of slaves stopped, about half a million black Africans had been brought. Even though new slaves could not legally be imported after 1808, natural increase kept the slave-holding states fairly well supplied with workers. But in the rest of the country, labor was scarce and expensive. As a consequence, immigration was encouraged, and periodically for a century and a half newcomers seeking work and new lives flocked into the country.

Demographers distinguish between different streams of immigrants, depending on their countries of origin and the times of their arrival.[1] Three times in the past 150 years the United States received huge waves of immigrants, each markedly different from the others in the origins of its people, in their languages and customs, in their skills and aptitudes. Yet all were in some respects remarkably similar: almost all had difficulty adjusting to their new home, and all had long-term impacts on the nation.

The first wave arrived mostly between 1830 and 1860, mainly from western Europe—Britain, Ireland, Germany, and the three Scandinavian countries, places much like those the early settlers had left. They came in unprecedented numbers. In just twenty years, 1830–50, the proportion of foreign-born in the United States rose from one in a hundred to one in ten. Many came during the two decades before the Civil War: in the 1840s about 1.7 million, and in the 1850s about two and a half million. For a decade after the Civil War an average of 300,000 to 400,000 immigrants were attracted to the United States each year. But the number of Western European immigrants began to dwindle sharply in the 1870s and then slowed to a trickle at the end of the century.

The second wave of immigration began about 1880, this time mainly from eastern and southern Europe—Slavs from Poland, Russia, and the Austro-Hungarian Empire; Jews from Poland, the Ukraine, and Russia; Italians mainly from southern Italy and Sicily; and Greeks, Bulgarians, Armenians, Turks, and others seeking relief from poverty and persecution. This wave peaked in 1907, when more than one and a quarter million newcomers arrived, an extraordinary influx that put great strain on the cities in which they settled. Between 1890 and 1920, a total of 18.2 million immigrants came to the United States, probably the largest voluntary movement of people in history.

The reaction to this influx was the Quota Act of 1921 and the Immigration Act of 1924. Quotas were set to reflect the racial and ethnic composition of the existing American population, then predominantly of northern and western European extraction; the effect was to reduce immigration sharply. These bills, in combination with the Great Depression and the Second World War, produced a lull in immigration that was to last forty-five years.

NO WELCOME WAGON

The reception many immigrants received was not cordial: it was, in fact, downright unfriendly. The immigrant was viewed with suspicion and contempt, and was blamed for soaring crime rates and welfare costs. There was some basis for this hostility; immigrants were disproportionally afflicted by social pathologies. To illustrate:

in Cincinnati the crime rate tripled between 1846 and 1853, including its murder rate, with the influx of German immigrants. Boston's expenditures for poor relief rose threefold during the same period, and its arrest rate climbed sharply. Many of those arrested were from the city's Irish immigrant population.

Many of the immigrants were Roman Catholics, and much of the native-born American's attitude toward immigrants was shaped by endemic anti-Catholic sentiment. Roman Catholics were seen as intruders in a Protestant world, agents of the pope, who was craftily using the immigrant as an entering wedge of Catholic imperialism. In 1850, a newspaper published by an anti-immigrant and anti-Catholic party whose members were known as "Know Nothings" declared that Catholic immigrants "march and countermarch with the precision of regular soldiers at the tap of the Popish drum."[2] A nativistic reaction set in, especially against the Irish, taking the form of discrimination in employment, access to housing, and entry into social clubs.

Protestant immigrants fared somewhat better, but they too encountered hostility. German immigrants (some were Catholics) evoked memories of Hessian mercenaries and national peril; their industriousness frightened lazy natives who had lost the appetite for work. The German inclination to beer gardens and leisurely Sundays, devoted less to prayer than to the casual enjoyment of a day off from work, struck native Americans of a Calvinistic bent as irreligious and self-indulgent. The Scandinavians, almost all Protestant, escaped calumny by migrating to the upper-Midwest, where they established prosperous farming communities and blended into the landscape.

Immigrants were made the butt of ridicule: their manners and accents aroused much mirth, not altogether kindly. Ethnic slurs were commonplace a century ago, and little effort was made to hide bigotry and prejudice. Jokes at the immigrant's expense were the daily fare of popular entertainment well into the twentieth century. Vaudeville and burlesque shows routinely contained a skit or two in which comics lampooned stereotypic Irishmen, Jews, Germans, or Swedes. Not many people would find this funny any more—at least admit it.

Native-born Americans from all social strata tended to view immigrants with strong misgivings and alarm. To the worker, the immigrant was an unfair competitor, who would work for less pay and more hours and would tamely accept abominable working conditions. To the patrician, relatively safe from economic competition but appalled by foreign ideas and customs, the immigrant was a threat to the integrity of the nation's Anglo-Saxon heritage. One alarmed matron later remembered in horror, "These hordes of new-comers maintained strange customs, spoke peculiar languages, dressed oddly, and practiced alien Catholic and Jewish religions; they had not the proper reverence for American values, symbols and heroes. . . . One's home, family, or community could hardly remain safe with such barely civilized people around."[3]

Truth to tell, these aliens, working at menial jobs in dirty sur-roundings, crowded into noisome slums in the disreputable sections of town, unafraid openly to frequent saloons and bawdy houses, noisily arguing among themselves, not embarrassed by public dis-plays of anger or love, presented a strange and unprepossessing sight. To the nativist, they threatened, as Mrs. Matthew T. Scott, the president-general of the National Society of the Daughters of the American Revolution, put it in 1910, "to trample American tradi-tions and ideals into the mud."[4] Her audience roundly applauded these sentiments. Even so enlightened a figure as the economist Henry George referred to the new immigrants as "garbage" and wor-ried what effect their getting the vote would have on the country.

These sentiments were soon translated into action: restrictive measures were introduced, more drastic than ever before. Religious groups endorsed prohibition and compulsory Sunday observance as ways of countering the European notion of Sunday as a day of en-joyment and relaxation. The legislatures of Wisconsin and Illinois in 1889 forbade teaching in foreign languages in the public schools. Organized labor favored laws to restrict the employment of nonnaturalized foreigners as factory workers; the immigrant's movement into white-collar jobs met with hostility from business. Anti-Catholic and antiforeign organizations sprang to new life in the 1890s. The American Protective Association, an organization de-voted to controlling, even expelling, the immigrant incubus, grew to 500,000 members.

Ideologists added a new wrinkle to anti-immigrant feelings: a rac-ist philosophy, this time directed at white immigrants rather than solely at blacks and Asians. A wealthy New York sportsman, geneal-ogist, and author, Madison Grant, argued against the belief that the environment could overcome the pull of heredity and warned that the new immigrants would permanently dilute and soil the purity of the northern European stock.[5] Grant and others like him found appreciative audiences. Many organizations and clubs closed their doors to Jews and Catholics, even those whose education and financial success would ordinarily have made them acceptable.

Other groups, more sanguine about the possibility of fashioning Americans out of unlikely immigrant material, pressured the immigrant to assimilate as rapidly as possible, exhorting the newcomer to be a loyal citizen, urging him to abandon his old ways and adopt without reservation the customs of his new country. But many doubted that this could be done. The immigrant, it was said, would stick in America's throat and eventually choke it.

IMMIGRANTS IN THE AMERICAN MAELSTROM

But who would choke first, the native-born American or the immigrant? Many immigrants thought it would be themselves. The immigrant had come to America with high hopes and grand illusions. In most cases he had been an illiterate peasant, laborer, artisan, or marginal retailer in the old country. Poverty, insecurity, and quasi-feudal servitude had been his normal condition. He had left the squalor and misery of his village with little regret. When America beckoned, he was glad to enter through the golden door, expecting to find a rich and open world in which life would be easier and freer. What he found was not a country of easy living whose streets were paved with gold—surely only the naively credulous had believed this fantastic description of America—but a bustling industrial society, the likes of which he had never before encountered and for which he was ill prepared. To his dismay, he discovered that he had entered a fiercely competitive, impersonal world in which survival, to say nothing of prosperity, could not be taken for granted.

Many immigrants felt lost. Life in America was a trial and a puzzle. That Americans spoke a different language and followed different customs was to be expected. But that their customs would be so bizarre and their bigotry and hostility so open the immigrants had not forseen. Nor had they expected that life in America would be so competitive and harsh, that poverty and congestion, the very things they were seeking to escape, would be so intense.

Working in mills and factories, operating noisy and dangerous machines, enduring long periods of closely supervised work, six days a week and for ten to twelve hours a day, all for wages barely sufficient to keep body and soul together, many immigrants felt harried, exhausted, and dazed, as though "caught up in a storm that would soon tear them limb from limb."[6] Life in the village had been harsh, it is true, but in many ways it had been more humane. Time had been governed by the movement of the sun, not the clock. Work had been fixed by the season, not the production schedule. The boss had been a fellow villager or a familiar landlord, not a stranger determined to sweat every last ounce of labor out of his workers.

Immigration took a terrible toll on the lives of immigrants: in health destroyed by days in dark workshops and nights in dank tenements; in families ground to pieces under the pressures of urban living; in precious Old World cultures obliterated by industrial civilization; in minds confused by inexplicable American rules and regulations; and in spirits reduced to melancholy by the insults and jabs of a hostile world.

THE NEW JERUSALEM

Consider, for instance, the experiences of immigrant Jews in New York City. Their history in this country provides a useful and cautionary tale—in part because their experiences were typical of the life endured by many immigrants in the late nineteenth and early twentieth centuries; and in part because some elite Xers are of Jewish descent, and many non-Jewish Xers stem from immigrants who landed in New York at about the same time as did the Jews. The stories these immigrants told their children and grandchildren still reverberate several generations later in the minds of Xers, whose attitudes toward immigrants are colored by the tales of their ancestors' travails in adjusting to American life.

As a major port of entry, New York was a magnet that attracted immigration. At the beginning of the twentieth century, fully half of the population of the city was foreign born. The bulk of the Jews arrived between 1880 and 1910, part of the second wave of immigrants from eastern Europe. There had been trickles of Jewish immigrants to America in the years before 1820, a tiny rivulet of 7,500 between 1820 and 1870, a modest stream of about 40,000 in the 1870s. Then came the pogroms of the Russian government in 1881, and the stream of emigration from the czarist empire to America turned into a river and then a torrent. Perhaps a third of Europe's Jews came to the United States. Many landed in New York and stayed there. In 1880 there were approximately 80,000 Jews in New York; by 1910 that number had risen to about 1,100,000, more Jews than lived in any other city in the world.[7]

On arriving in New York, they usually made their way to the Lower East Side, where most of their coreligionists lived. To their dismay, they found conditions there worse than those they had left behind in the old country. Crowded into unsanitary tenements, scrambling for jobs, working for barely subsistence wages, overworked and undernourished, many immigrants lived lives degraded by hunger and disease. Irving Howe recounts the reaction of a young immigrant to his first encounter with the New World: "Orchard Street. The crush and stench was enough to suffocate one: dirty children were playing in the street, and perspiring Jews were pushing carts and uttering wild shrieks. . . . Was this the America we had sought? Or was it only, after all, a circle that we had traveled, with a ghetto at its beginning and its end?"[8] Not every immigrant, of course, found conditions in his new home unexpected; misery was not an entirely new experience for Europe's Jews.

Housing was scarce and expensive. The congestion was horrific. Single men slept four or more to a room; two families might share a tiny apartment. One modest-sized building of sixteen apartments, two rooms each, quartered about 200 people, and that was common. The Lower East Side became the most densely populated area in the city: in 1890 it had 522 inhabitants per acre; by 1900 that number had grown to more than 700, a population density that rivaled the city slums of East Asia. According to the University Settlement Society, the population density of the 10th Ward at the turn of the century was worse than that of the worst sections of Bombay.[9] In this pressure-cooker of dirt, disease, and violence, many immigrants became desperately sick, only precariously alive.

Jobs were hard to find, and many Old World skills proved of little value in modern industrial America. Jewish poets, writers, and scholars, for example, though greatly admired in the old country, seldom found work in their callings. About half of the Jewish newcomers worked in the garment industries, at needle trades infamous for their exploitation of workers. Unscrupulous factory owners used child labor when they could get away with it, contracted work out to women and children at home at cutthroat piece-rate wages, and set up factories in unheated or overly hot, dark, packed, unsafe rooms and lofts that became death traps when fires broke out.

Working hours in the sweatshops were 60 a week; at home, 84 hours a week was common. Wages were just enough to live on, provided everyone worked, including the women and their children. In 1885 the average wage of a semiskilled worker in the garment trades was seven dollars a week. The New York State Bureau of Labor Statistics reported in 1885 that the best workers received 10 dollars a week, while many were earning three to six dollars a week. The report went on to say: "Some even with the aid of their families and working fourteen hours a day could only earn 12 to 15 dollars a week. Others could make only four dollars by working ten hours a day." Still others tried their hand at peddling, the second most popular occupation among immigrant Jews; some did well, though many failed at entrepreneurship and fell back into the ranks of wage earners. Not all, of course: Marshall Field, R. H. Macy, and Jacob Gimbel were celebrated exceptions.

It would be a mistake, however, to think that Jewish immigrants' disappointment with America was entirely the result of disillusioned expectations and harsh conditions. In fact, their problems were at least as much cultural and psychological as material. Many felt like lost souls, alone in a strange and cold world, starved for spiritual sustenance in a mechanistic civilization, cut off from the cultural roots that had once fed them. Cried one poet, "There is too much materialism here, too much hurry and too much prose—and yes, too much machinery."[10] Immigrants who had abandoned their traditions and blocked their memories often had difficulty finding something to replace them.

They could find little meaning and solace in the culture of their new homeland. There was too little time for reflection, too few chances to pause in the frantic search for a livelihood, to wonder at the purpose of the life around them. The tempo of life in America, its intensity and hurry, stretched their nerves to the breaking point. "Curse you, emigration," wrote Abraham Cahan, editor of the *Jewish Daily Forward*. "How many have you broken, how many brave and mighty have you rubbed out like dust!"[11] Demoralized and exhausted, a few went home, many more stayed, some broke down under the strain and went under.

ANGEL OF MERCY

Just as conditions threatened to become overwhelming, aid came to the needy, sick, demoralized immigrants in the shape of nurses and social workers who devoted their lives to succoring the poor and afflicted. One of them was Lillian Wald.[12] To the immigrant Jews of the Lower East Side she was a godsend. Born in 1867 in Rochester, New York, the daughter of middle-class Jewish parents, a self-described "spoiled child" unaware of the suffering around her, educated at Miss Cruttenden's English-French Boarding and Day School for Young Ladies, Lillian Wald seemed destined for the conventional life of solid bourgeois womanhood. Perhaps this would have been the case had Vassar accepted her application for admission. But someone at the college decreed that age 16 was too young to begin college. If Vassar did not want her, she decided, she would do something else instead; she entered the New York Hospital's School of Nursing.

Several years after graduation, she began running a class in home nursing for women in New York's East Side. One day, a visit at the insistence of a little girl to the dismal home of a sick family changed the course of her life. Face to face with the squalor, misery, and despair of that afflicted family, she almost immediately decided to move to the East Side, there to set up a settlement house, and from that time on to devote her life to caring for the poor and distressed. "There are two kinds of fastidious people," Irving Howe wrote: "those who recoil from the messes and those who stay to clean them up. Lillian Wald stayed, not out of exalted sentiment or angelic temperament, but because there was work to be done and no one else seemed likely to do it."[13] She founded and ran along the "principles of anarchic matriarchy" a place to help the needy, a place eventually to become famed for its humane and beneficent works—the Henry Street Settlement.

She gave her heart and soul to the immigrants who came to the Henry Street Settlement for help, afflicted people without work or money, sick and lonely, wretched people adrift in a heartless city that cared nothing for their misery. With her small staff of nurses she visited the squalid, overcrowded tenements of the poor to nurse families with typhoid, pneumonia, consumption, and other contagious diseases. She fed, washed and dressed their children, and she helped clean up the squalor of the tiny rooms in which several families lived, without privacy or privies, without the bare rudiments of civilized living. She worked hard to start a program of public nursing and persuaded the Board of Education to put nurses in the schools. She charmed millionaires for money, badgered City Hall to enforce the sanitary regulations, and was called in mock terror "She-Who-Must-Be-Obeyed" by awed journalists. Of her Jacob Riis said, "The poor trust her absolutely, trust her head, her judgment, and her friendship."[14] Never married and yet a mothering figure to countless children, a superb woman who touched the lives of thousands, she had become by the time of her death in 1940 a model to which social workers could point with pride.

NATIVISM UNLEASHED

Most second-wave immigrants—Italians, Greeks, Armenians, Poles, Czechs, Romanians, Hungarians, Jews, and others—survived their initial privation and confusion, adjusted to their new surroundings, and eventually gained general acceptance. But acceptance did not come easily. It was the immigrants' bad luck to come to America just as an earthquake of massive economic change shook the country, leaving angry, anxious, and frightened people in the rubble. The economy had decisively moved away from agriculture to manufacturing.

Ambitious politicians were stirring up controversy over the currency; the business cycle and bad planning had pushed the country into a terrible depression, culminating in the Panic of 1893. Unemployment was widespread. Many native-born Americans accused the foreigners of taking their jobs, of soaking up the nation's charity at a time when the country seemed to be growing poorer, undermining the nation's health with indigestible lumps of foreign matter. As the native-born had done during previous periods of heavy immigration, they now showed their resentment in a spectacular rise of openly expressed prejudice and discrimination.

For a time it was open season on immigrants. From the late 1880s to the beginning of the Second World War, demagogues in the pulpit and on the political platform felt free to take potshots at various immigrant groups. Hostility toward Catholics rose to levels not seen since the heyday of the Know-Nothings of the 1850s. Anti-Semitism, negligible when the Jews were a tiny minority living in a few coastal and inland cities, enjoyed a new lease on life. Italians were routinely linked to the Mafia and regarded with distrust. Slavs were viewed with contempt and treated as inferiors.

Despite bigotry and discrimination, despite hard times and disappointments, most immigrants, from every ethnic, religious, and racial group, stayed in their new country, married, and raise families. Most found jobs or opened businesses; many prospered or saw their children do so. Some of their children or grandchildren have become members of America's most recent ruling elites: Boomers and Xers.

LEGALS, WETBACKS AND BOAT PEOPLE

By the mid-1960s the long war between native-born Americans and immigrants appeared over. Assimilation had done its work, and the earlier tensions between ethnic groups had appreciably subsided. It seemed that Americans of different national origins had finally learned to live more or less at peace with one another. But no sooner had the nation adjusted to the earlier influx of immigrants than this lull was broken. In 1965 the Immigration and Nationality Act Amendments eliminated national origins as a criterion for admission. New regulations that emphasized family reunification replaced the old quota system based on national origin, setting in motion a huge new wave of immigrants.[15] This wave came principally from non-European countries, mostly in Asia and Latin America, thus adding to the usual problems of assimilation the daunting challenge of threading into the nation's fabric peoples of different races as well as of vastly different cultures.

The push to change the immigration laws had ostensibly come from politicians seeking to satisfy the demands of their ethnic constituents. But the strongest force behind the change was the indignation of liberal intellectuals, many of them Boomers, who considered the existing policy discriminatory and racist, a clear case of social injustice, unworthy of the just society the Boomers wanted to fashion. As they saw it, the old immigration policy was an affront to Asians, Latin Americans, and Africans, an explicit statement of the white man's belief in his superiority, and a violation of America's vision of itself as a nation dedicated to equality, open-mindedness, decency, generosity, and concern for the poor and oppressed.

In order to make their proposal acceptable to the white majority, the pro-immigration group argued that opening the door to non-Europeans would erase the blot of racism on the good name of America, while changing the mix and number of immigrants only slightly. This argument, at a time when the country was engaged in a titanic struggle to eradicate racism at home, carried much weight, and a historic change in immigration policy swept through Congress with minimal debate. The old quota system was abandoned and replaced with a policy designed to make it easier for people from non-Western countries to enter the country.

In the period from 1968 to 1993, some 16.7 million immigrants came to the United States; a record 1.8 million were admitted in 1991 alone. But this is not the whole story. During the 1970s illegal immi-

gration began rising and continues strong to this day; it is now estimated at 300,000 to 500,000 each year. The size of the new wave is not
the only issue: race and ethnicity also worry many Americans. Today, for the first time in American history, nonwhites outnumber
whites among the new immigrants.

This is no accident. The Immigration Acts of 1921 and 1924 se-
verely restricted immigration and at the same time gave most of the
slots to northern and western Europeans, restrictions reflecting the
national bias against immigrants from eastern and southern Europe.
As for Asians, they were considered beyond the pale and were for
the most part excluded. It is true that under the 1921 and 1924 Immigration Acts, immigration from Asia was once again permitted (the
Chinese had been excluded in 1882 and the Japanese in 1907), but the
quotas were so constructed as to keep the number of immigrants
tiny. In the 1950s, the annual immigration quotas for Asian countries
were 105 for Japan, 105 for China, and 100 each for Korea and the
Philippines. Immigration from Latin American countries, though
somewhat larger, was also small.

But when the 1965 Immigration Act replaced quotas based on national origins with a system that emphasized kinship, the racial and
ethnic composition of immigration changed dramatically. Under the
new rules adult children could bring in their parents; brothers and
sisters could vouch for one another; aunts and uncles could sponsor
their nieces and nephews; and so on. Since many of the new immigrants belonged to large extended families, immigration from Asia,
Africa, and Latin America exploded. Where previously immigration
from these areas had numbered at most in the hundreds, it now bal-
looned into the tens of thousands. In the late 1990s the United States
accepted annually about 1,000,000 immigrants, almost four times
the number legally admitted in 1960. Some 85 percent of the legal
immigrants arriving in the United States between 1968 and the late
1990s came from less developed countries: 47 percent from Latin
America and the Caribbean, 20 percent from Mexico alone, and 34
percent from Asia, mainly Korea, Vietnam, China, and the Philippines.
With less than 5 percent of the world's population, the United States
accepts nearly half of all legal immigrants to the developed world.

In addition, and though good numbers are hard to come by (illegal entrants are by their nature difficult to count), it is estimated that
about four million illegal immigrants currently live in the country.
The true number may in fact be much higher. Perhaps as many as
half a million illegal immigrants flood into the country annually,

many wading across the Rio Grande, others slipping across the Canadian border, still others arriving by raft or by boat from nearby Caribbean countries or distant China.

An undetermined number, those who can come up with the fare, arrive by plane on visitors' visas, deliberately overstay their allotted time, and blend into the anonymous population. Some are found and ejected; most escape detection. The Immigration and Naturalization Service, admitting that it has no idea how large this group is, has in effect thrown up its hands. In short, whatever the reason, whether because of ignorance, bureaucratic bungling and indifference, or sheer helplessness in the face of a seemingly impossible task, the country has been unable (or unwilling) to manage the flow of newcomers into its midst.

Annual immigration—including illegals, asylum seekers, and visa-overstayers—is at one of its historic peaks, currently well over two million. Furthermore, far fewer of them leave than did in the past. In earlier times, many immigrants came to make their fortunes, intending to return home as soon as possible, and many did, particularly when luck proved elusive and hard times became impossible to endure. Now a variety of welfare programs ease the immigrant's adjustment to American life, and staying has become a reasonable alternative to leaving. As a result, at more than 28 million, a March 2000 Census Bureau estimate, the foreign-born population today is bigger than was the entire United States population 150 years ago.

IMMIGRATION ANXIETY

A growing number of Americans, including many Xers, are upset about current levels of immigration. Popular pressure is building to amend the immigration laws and to restrict immigration or even cut it off entirely, at least for a while. Why is that? After all, though the absolute number is large, the proportion of foreign-born in the overall population today—about 10 percent, an increase from 4.7 percent—is still less than it was in 1925, when Calvin Coolidge was president (about 15 percent). That there is concern cannot be denied; opinion polls report that 60 percent of respondents feel the current level of immigration is bad for the country. They are echoing President Coolidge, who put his concern about immigration bluntly: "America must be kept for Americans."[16] What's going on here? Can it be, as advocates of easy immigration aver, that the hostility to immigration is mere xenophobia, prejudice, and racism?

To some extent, perhaps—but surely this charge hardly holds for elite Xers. They pride themselves on being open to diversity; they frequently express willingness to welcome outsiders into their midst, provided, of course, that they possess the requisite merit; they proclaim a readiness to judge others as individuals, not just as members of a group. All this is true enough. Nevertheless, behind their friendly exterior lie worries and fears, impalpable as smoke, about the long-term consequences of immigration.

Xer worries and fears fall roughly into three groups. There is, first, the fear among whites generally, and plausibly among elite Xers as well, that they will become a powerless minority, outnumbered and outvoted by the darker-hued immigrants pouring into the country. Second, like many Americans, Xers believe that immigrants have become an economic liability, draining the nation's resources and contributing less than they consume. And third, elite Xers fear that immigrants will take the bread out of their mouths, competing unfairly for jobs in a fiercely competitive economy—and getting them.

THE THREAT OF IMMIGRANT NUMBERS

How valid is the fear among whites that they will become a beleaguered minority? It is hard to know exactly. For one thing, deciding who is white is a complex business: the Census Bureau and the courts are continually being forced to confront this problem and have never been able to resolve it to everyone's satisfaction. Moreover, the demographic trends and projections undergirding the popular sense of where the country is moving are based on data and assumptions of varying solidity. Past demographic predictions, founded on presumably solid population trends, have sometimes proven to be hilariously mistaken. For instance, before the Second World War demographers were predicting that the population of the United States would peak at 150 million; now some experts foresee a population of at least 300 million or 325 million by the middle of the twenty-first century.

Nevertheless, one demographic fact is firm: the racial and ethnic composition of the country has definitely changed. In 1900, nine in 10 residents of the United States were whites, mostly of western European ancestry. At the close of the twentieth century, this proportion had shrunk to less than three in four.[17]

All things considered, if present trends continue the majority status of whites will slowly melt away. As things stand now, the birth rates among nonwhite Hispanics and some other nonwhite groups exceeds that of native-born whites. Indeed, the white birthrate is presently below the replacement level. Extrapolating from census data, Sam Roberts estimates that early in the twenty-first century the proportion of whites among the country's children will shrink to less than two-thirds; it is already less than half in three states—Texas, New Mexico, and California, the home of many elite Xers.[18]

By the middle of the twenty-first century, whites in America seem destined to become a minority. Then again, perhaps whites will hold on to a slim majority. But as Ben Wattenberg, author and political columnist, points out, "There's a big difference between being a 90 percent majority, a 70 percent majority or a 55 percent majority."[19] Whatever the future may hold, many whites already feel they are becoming an endangered species, a declining part of the labor force, increasingly irrelevant to the economy. The World Bank shares this impression. It estimates that early in the twenty-first century whites will make up only 45 percent of the workforce.

What about the issue of immigration's financial costs? Opponents of immigration are saying to harassed taxpayers that easy immigration doesn't make economic sense, that it puts an unnecessary burden upon the citizen's pocketbook, that it costs too much, we can't afford it anymore, that if it continues unchecked we are going down the drain. To elite Xers, worried about taxes and the national debt, this warning makes sense. Liberal though they may be on social issues, though less so than their Boomer predecessors, on money matters they are true fiscal conservatives. Xers who feel sheepish about expressing hostility toward immigrants can get worked up about the fiscal burden immigration is imposing on the nation.

To illustrate: Xers complain that immigrants are abusing the welfare system, eating up scarce resources, costing the country a bundle, and forcing the taxpayer to foot the bill. In 1998 almost a quarter of immigrant households were receiving some type of public assistance, as compared with 15 percent of native households.[20] Opponents of immigration maintain that the cost of providing services to immigrants is bankrupting the nation's biggest cities. New York City, whose population is 28 percent foreign born, has 1.14 million residents, many of them immigrants, on welfare. The nation's second-largest city, Los Angeles, has a population that is 38 percent foreign born. Los Angeles County must find money to fund welfare for 967,692 of its residents, quite a few of whom are immigrants. In 1994, this burden sparked a taxpayer's revolt—California's Proposition

187—which would cut off welfare for illegal immigrants. Despite loud protests from immigrant advocates, it passed easily with overwhelming white support.

Educating the children of immigrants is also costly. They are numerous; they make up a majority of students in a growing number of school districts; and more classrooms must be built and more teachers hired to take care of them. Often they do not speak English. An earlier and less tolerant America forced immigrant children to sink or swim in a school system that employed only English-speaking teachers. It was a brutal way to teach English and other subjects, and there were casualties. Some children couldn't make it, but for the vast majority the system worked. Painfully but with remarkable speed, the children of immigrants learned English, many becoming proficient enough to move on to college and become teachers themselves.

Now, in a kinder-hearted America, many schools employ bilingual teachers, who teach immigrant children in their native languages. This is more humane, and it may for some children facilitate learning (though it retards the learning of English), but it is most certainly more expensive. Bilingual teachers tend to be costly and sometimes extremely rare; for instance, trained people who can teach Hmong children in their native tongue as well as in English are not plentiful. Though bilingual education has been modified in some states or even abandoned (such as in California), its proponents are still active.

IMMIGRANT COMPETITION FOR JOBS

It is the cruel fate of many third-wave immigrants to be caught in a time warp. They come from countries with essentially nineteenth-century economies that depend mostly on low-cost, manual labor. Unfortunately, they now find themselves in a twenty-first-century economy that requires workers with educated, trained brains. On average, third-wave immigrants have had less schooling than earlier waves and substantially less than native-born Americans. In fact, a significant number of immigrants are unable to read or write at all, in any language: 10 percent of Mexican illegals, for instance, are illiterate. With manufacturing in decline, good-paying factory jobs have become scarcer; while service jobs are increasing, many of them paying quite well, they often require education, technical training, and skill in using English. Sadly, many of the immigrants from Latin America, Africa, and some parts of Asia are poorly equipped with these skills.

This mismatch between the needs of the economy and the skills of some immigrants has produced several unpleasant consequences. For one, it has in many cases made the immigrant's adjustment exceptionally difficult, with all the attendant social ills—welfare dependence, crime and juvenile delinquency, addiction to drugs—that such painful adjustment entails. For another, it has forced many immigrants to seek employment in overcrowded, poorly paid, unskilled manual and low-level service work. This is nothing new, of course. As already noted, earlier waves followed precisely the same course.

Some immigrants are, however, well educated and highly skilled. Immigrants from Europe, though fewer in number than in the past, often bring with them college educations and well-honed entrepreneurial skills. Asian immigrants, especially Koreans, Indians, and Chinese, on average have more years of schooling than native Americans: 15 years for immigrants, as compared with 13 years for natives. Seventy-five percent of Indians working in the United States are college graduates. In 1998, almost 13 percent of all immigrant men had at least master's degrees.[21] A significant number of them have become highly successful in well-paying occupations.

It is these educated immigrants whom elite Xers have in mind when they think of immigrants competing with them for good-paying jobs. Most people can understand intuitively that unskilled immigrants would drag down the wages of working-class natives. Unskilled immigrants are often willing to work for less pay and fewer benefits; they also tend to be nonunionized. But that skilled immigrants would have a similar effect on the elite Xer is generally hard to imagine. Do not elite Xers command fine wages, and is there not a shortage of them, particularly in the computer-related industries? The owners of software-writing companies, for instance, say so. They deride the idea of immigrants taking Xer jobs and successfully petitioned the U.S. Congress to issue more visas in 2001 to highly skilled immigrants. On the other hand, Norman Matloff, a computer scientist at the University of California at Davis who also studies immigration, denies that a shortage of homegrown software labor exists. There is only a shortage of *cheap* software labor, he says.[22]

Most elite Xers are silent on this issue. They flinch at giving the impression of being prejudiced against immigrants. Liberals on most social policies, they see advocating immigration restriction as politically incorrect, and they tiptoe around the subject. Nevertheless, the competition for jobs in the software industry is especially keen in California, which in the late 1990s was the home of 28 percent of all immigrants with college degrees. Many of these immigrants can be found working in California's Silicon Valley, the quintessential home of information-based industry and the origin of many computer-related innovations.

Particularly notable has been the influence of immigrants on the development of the Internet. In his book *The New New Thing*, on how a new Internet service took shape, Michael Lewis describes the ambiance of the workplace. He was struck by the number of immigrants, especially from India, employed in the enterprise—so many, in fact, that it seemed to him the air reeked with odor of curry. Relatively small in number (about 725,000), Indians, native and immigrant, have had a disproportionately large impact upon the information-age sector of the economy.

But it would be a mistake to think of all Indians as mere scribblers of cyberscript. Immigrant Indians do more than produce innovative computer programs; their entrepreneurial skill and financial muscle are also impressive. Some of them are running Fortune 500 companies. Vinod Khosla cofounded Sun Microsystems, and Sabeer Bhatia, founder of Hot Mail, became seriously rich when he sold the company to Microsoft for $400 million. In fact, Indian-American millionaires number in the thousands, headed by Gururaj Deshpande, cofounder of a number of network-technology companies, who is said to be worth between $4 billion and $6 billion.[23]

Not all these immigrant entrepreneurs are Indians, of course. Many are from Chinese-speaking parts of Asia. According to economist Paul Krugman, almost a quarter of Silicon Valley start-ups are owned by Asians, immigrant or native born. AnnLee Saxenian, a Berkeley associate professor of regional planning, estimates that 7 percent of Silicon valley high-tech firms are led by Indian CEOs. Together with Chinese entrepreneurs, Asian Indians were responsible for 29 percent of Silicon Valley's new start-ups, creating 60,000 jobs.

An example of Indian success at the non-CEO level is Ramesh Radhakrishnan. A native of Bangalore, the son of an upper-middle-class Indian family, he is a marketing-intelligence supervisor at Cisco (computer software) and is living the tech immigrant's dream: a high-paying job and a home in the hills. "I wouldn't trade this for any other place," says Ramesh. Add his story to the fact that one-third of the engineers in Silicon Valley are of Indian descent, and it does not seem at all surprising that Elite Xers worry about the competition from this sector of the immigrant population.[24]

Much in demand, riding high on the swiftly moving surf of technology, what have elite Xers to fear from clever young Indians or Chinese? A lot, they think. In fact, in today's ferociously competitive society, bright young people are dangers to one another. A coveted job in a sprightly new dot-com company could be lost to someone else, perhaps a foreigner, and with that loss would go the prospect of getting the stock options or shares in an initial public offering that would make one rich. For all their bravado, Xers become frightened at the thought of losing out in the competition for advancement or of even losing their jobs. Losing one's job is bad enough; losing to an immigrant is too much. And yet this is what many Xers think is happening, or could happen.

To sum up: elite Xers, overwhelmingly white and native born, cannot help but be affected by the large number of the immigrants in the country and their ethnic-racial character. For immigration has always been accompanied by social, economic, and political perturbation, a maelstrom of aggravating problems that have invariably distressed the native population and made it anxious. Moreover, large-scale immigration has always been associated with major social change, with sometimes disagreeable attendant psycho-social consequences, among them a rise in chameleonism. The present wave of immigration is no exception.

Sophisticated Xers worry about what change has in store for them. That the world is changing is obvious enough; where that change will take them is far from clear. They want answers to questions: what is going on, and why, and with what consequences? Xers feel the need for guidance, and they are turning to theories of social change, some of them regrettably decrepit and discredited. This is the topic of the next chapter.

9

Paradigms Sought

Xers take change for granted. They see change everywhere, constant and intrusive, touching their lives at almost every point, sometimes creating vexatious problems and headaches, at other times bringing new sights and sounds to excite the imagination and new opportunities to fill the pocketbook. Every year, Silicon Valley and Seattle invent new electronic contraptions: faster computers, ingenious programs, and tempting applications. Every year, Paris and Milan dictate new fashions in wearing apparel, perhaps a new skirt length or a novel frou-frou fabric. Every year, Hollywood and New York churn out new songs and dances, performed by an ever-changing galaxy of stars whose meteoric rises to popular fame are matched only by their equally rapid falls into obscurity.

Small wonder, then, that it has become common for enthusiasms in dress and speech, in eating and entertainment, in self-care and emotional repair, in political sympathies and spiritual uplift, to have short shelf-lives, coming and going with dizzying speed, destined almost every one for oblivion. Surely, Heraclitus had it right some 2,500 years ago when he wrote that change can only be understood as the effluence of continuous motion.

But skeptics demur: is motion really social change? It is not always so, and certainly not necessarily. Fashions and fads, quintessential examples of motion and commotion, flit in and out of the popular consciousness in kaleidoscopic bursts. Yet they rarely represent significant social change, except perhaps when a change in fashion signals that something important is in the works. For example, following the Second World War, when women's clothes became more casual and comfortable, when walking shoes replaced high heels, and tight skirts gave way to loose-fitting pants, the change in fashion pointed to major changes in a woman's role in society, especially her place in the workforce. But usually fashions and fads and other flashy alterations in consumption have no lasting effects on society. Like iridescent bubbles on the surface of the sea, fads and fashions, though eye catching, rarely give useful indications of the currents of change hidden from view deep beneath the surface.

Locating the true currents of change, learning to ignore the claims of charlatans who proclaim change when there is no change, being able to avoid being distracted by irrelevancies and identifying the true core of change is not easy. Sometimes obscure people and events, though hidden from view and ignored by analysts, leave imprints on their times. At other times, it may appear that change is under way when no change is taking place at all. To the exasperated question "What is going on here?" the accurate answer may be, "Nothing much." As a result, careless observers, Xers included, often misjudge what is happening and never manage to get handles on the furious changes that are affecting their lives.

But apart from the die-hard skeptics who feel they are being conned by an establishment that professes support of change but in fact resists it, most Xers sense that important changes are indeed taking place all around them. To them, change is real enough—if anything all too real, too fast, too disorienting. They want to understand what is happening to them and are having trouble doing so. This is one reason why many of them feel cranky, anxious, and angry.

In all fairness, it should be pointed out that Xers are searching for answers. For despite their indifference to politics, their preference for pragmatics and contempt for theorizing, their what-does-it-matter attitude, it is characteristic of the Xer generation to want predictability and stability in life. But predictability requires understanding. Without a guide to social change, Xers intent merely on pursuing the good life will become confused and lost.

Eager to understand the perplexing changes buffeting them, desperate for an inkling of what the future has in store, and determined to find something that works, Xers have adopted a stance of pragmatic eclecticism. They selectively borrow from a mixed bag of facts and theories, some of which have been in the air for centuries, seeking in this way to construct a practical paradigm of social change. It is true that facts appeal to Xers far more than mere theories; as they see it, an obsession with theories is what got the Boomers in trouble. Facts, however, are never enough. They are fine as far as they go; no one should be without some; they help give us a handle on what is going on. Nevertheless, facts do not speak for themselves.

Facts need theories to give them tongue, to articulate confused feelings, to pull together chaotic experiences, to give shape and meaning to change. And so Xers have begun to rummage through some old theories, the intriguing work of poets and philosophers, scholars and scientists, mountebanks and mystics. In their search they have encountered two time-worn theories of social change: cyclical theory of change, ancient but still serviceable; and the more modern evolutionary theory, which, cleverly garbed in Darwinian costume, is currently enjoying considerable vogue.

From the cyclical theory of change, some Xers have borrowed the idea that similar events may have similar effects, and the notion that change proceeds along a more or less predictable path, good and bad following each other in an inexorable circle. Other Xers, however, are not convinced by cyclical theory. They have turned instead to evolutionary theory and taken from it the idea that social change develops out of the competition for scarce resources and that successful adaptations to change will survive, to become in the long run generally accepted modes of thinking and behaving.[1]

Let us look at these theories of change to see what can be learned from them, and to understand why many Xers have found them attractive. We begin by examining the oldest theory, the still-popular paradigm of cyclical change.

THE WHEEL AND THE PENDULUM

When men first took up the challenge of explaining change, it seemed to them to be without direction and purpose, an endless coming and going, a ceaseless pushing forward and retracing of steps, a random movement through time. This view of a change as mere commotion governed by chance did not satisfy tidy souls, who found a chaotic world hard to live with. They needed order and predictability in their lives, so they converted change from a chaotic shuffle through time into a predictable trundle, a wheel-like movement that has direction and purpose.[2]

The ancient Greeks were the first to hit upon the idea of change as a circular movement through time. They were struck by the patterned alternations of history, by the regular ebb and flow of human experience. Perhaps the Greeks appear so often as innovators in the history of ideas because, as Winston Churchill said, they were the first to enter the fields of science and literature—an advantage, coupled with a language well suited to epigrams, that gave their reflections on life a priority upon which their fame is based.[3] Be that as it may, as early as the eighth century BC the Greeks had begun thinking of change as a wheel-like movement through times punctuated with strife.

This is hardly surprising. The Greeks were a warlike people who gloried in military conquest and the martial virtues, quite as Homer had portrayed them in his great epic poems. True to the Greek spirit, the poet Hesiod, in the eighth century BC, described change as a circular movement through conflict-laden stages of ever-increasing dreariness, from a golden age of harmony and splendor to progressively more fractious times, ending in an iron age of great brutality and strife. In time the cycle would repeat itself, and a new golden age would appear—though Hesiod never explained why this would happen. Aristotle also believed change to be circular. Reflecting on political change in his time and place (fourth century BC Athens), Aristotle concluded that the political structure of the city-state went through predictable stages of change, moving in a circular fashion from monarchy to aristocracy to oligarchy, to democracy, to tyranny, and then back to monarchy again. What it was that moved the polity through this series of fixed stages in an endless circle, Aristotle did not say.[4]

The ancient Chinese modified the cyclical theory of change somewhat: they saw change as a process of perpetual oscillation, a pendulum-like movement from a period of order to one of disorder and then back again. Good government could prolong order and prosperity, delaying disorder and poverty for a while, but come they would eventually. A wise government would make preparations for hard times. Chinese authorities always acted (they still do) as though they were in thrall to this ancient philosophy and treated every challenge to their power as an invitation to social breakdown and chaos. Feeling themselves strapped to the pendulum of change, they struggled to slow its movement. But knowing that change (nearly always for the worse, in their opinion) is inevitable, they awaited the future with resigned apprehension.

THE ARAB CYCLE

The most innovative exponent of the cyclical theory of social change was the great Arab historian Ibn Khaldun.[5] A native of Tunis, the descendant of an aristocratic family that included many prominent officials and scholars, and an important official himself, Ibn Khaldun was in a position to observe the interplay between social character and social change. Out of these observations came an opus that became a tool for an understanding of social change.

Khaldun lived during the declining years of a great empire: the Arab caliphate. Beginning in 632, united by the new religion of Islam, Arab armies swept out of the deserts of Arabia and in an incredibly short time established Muslim hegemony over the Middle East, the whole of North Africa, and parts of Europe, including Sicily and Spain, stopping only when they were defeated by the Franks in fighting near Potiers in 732. This halted the Arabs' advance on Tours, a lose of momentum from which they never fully recovered. Before that setback they had enjoyed a string of remarkable victories, intimidating the Byzantines and Persians, and creating in the process an empire of their own.

But fortune is notoriously feckless, and fate is fickle. By the mid-fourteenth century, the political deterioration of the Arab world was far advanced, its unity shattered by wars between Islamic sects and rival claimants to the caliphate. The martial spirit and vigor of Arab armies had become a thing of the past. Looking about him (he lived from 1332 to 1406), Khaldun saw Muslim armies in retreat in the Middle East and Spain. Muslim borders were everywhere becoming increasingly insecure and violated, even in the Maghreb (northern Africa), his native region. Great Muslim cities, famed for their culture, commerce, and industry, were under attack from barbarian invaders.

Much of the Middle East had already fallen into the hands of nomads from the steppes of central Asia. In 1258, the Mongol chieftain Hulegu, having conquered Persia, defeated the armies of the Abbasid caliphate (roughly the Iraq of today), captured Baghdad, put the caliph, Al-Muzt, to death by strangulation, and massacred many of the city's citizens, though Hulegu had promised to spare their lives. In Spain, the Christian knights of the *Reconquista*, fighting with a ferocity and ruthlessness that would have won the respect of Genghis Khan, Tamerlane, and other Mongol chieftains, drove the Muslims out of Grenada in 1492, finally ending centuries of Islamic rule in the

Iberian Peninsula. Khaldun did not live to see the final defeat of Muslim forces in Spain, the jewel in the Islamic crown, but the pattern of defeat and withdrawal had been well established in his lifetime.

In the final years of his life, after a career filled with enough adventure to fill several picaresque novels—high civil appointments under various sultans in North Africa, Syria, and Spain; participation in several rebellions, a couple of incarcerations, refuge in a monastery; command of a large force of desert Arabs under the sultan of Tlemcen; capture by Tamerlane after a hair-raising escape over the walls of Damascus—Khaldun set for himself the task of discovering the causes of Arab decline. In 1377, in a village in Oran, he sat down, "with ideas pouring into my head like cream in a churn," to write a history of the Arab people.[6] Superbly equipped by experience, intelligence, and erudition, Khaldun produced a masterpiece of which, the introduction, the *Muqaddimah*, presents a theory of social change whose originality and depth of scholarship has given it an influence that persists to the present.

Khaldun's great contribution was to elucidate the link between social character and social change. He believed that each society creates a dominant character type, which originates in the organized activities of the people, particularly the way they earn their livings. Two contrasting character types dominate Khaldun's analysis of social change: Nomadic Man and Sedentary Man. As Khaldun saw it, the transformation of the Arabs from Nomadic Men into Sedentary Men (city dwellers) was the principal cause of their misfortune. In the city the Arabs produced a character type fatally unable to cope when attacked, lacking in the ability and the grit to defend itself.

The Arabs had once been herders, moving from place to place in search of food and water for their flocks. Life in the desert had been hard and only the hardy had survived. Food, water, shelter were scarce, the sun and wind were merciless, and fighting between rival tribes was common. The soft and weak did not last long. But hardiness was not enough. To survive in this harsh and unyielding environment, the nomad had to be more than tough; he had to be courageous, cunning, and ruthless, ferocious toward his enemies yet generous toward relatives and friends, with whom he developed intense bonds of solidarity and without whose help life would have been unbearably precarious. Toughened in a constant struggle for survival, the desert nomad became, in Khaldun's words, "the most savage human being that exists."[7]

Nomadic Man was not squeamish about spilling blood. The desert was no place for the weak stomached. Constantly culling herds, routinely killing the weak and deformed, slaughtering animals for food—a job he did himself without flinching, not something he relegated to professional butchers working far from the public's queasy eye—he became accustomed to bloodletting. It was all in a day's work, something anyone with a knife could do. Of necessity, the nomad became a hardened killer. Untroubled by bloodletting, physically tough, able to travel long distances over difficult terrain, and energized by a religion that mandated war against the infidel, the desert nomad was a formidable warrior. It was inevitable that he would bring his skills and temperament to the work of war.

Trading with his neighbors at border crossings, exchanging horses and slaves for weapons and food, the Arab nomad became aware of how vulnerable and rich the settled peoples of the Tigris-Euphrates Valley were and decided to help himself to their property. Sweeping out of the desert and brushing aside local resistance, the Arabs pounced upon their hapless victims, sacking towns and cities, butchering or enslaving many of the inhabitants. Wherever he went, the Arab nomad planted the banner of Islam, creating a vast empire whose political and cultural achievements still reverberate throughout the world.

But the nomad did not make war merely because an ideology encouraged him to do so; he made war because it paid and because he enjoyed it, brutal and bloody though it was. Not that he was more brutal or bloodthirsty than other nomadic warriors—in fact, he was relatively restrained in the way he conducted war, being under the influence of Islam, which required the Muslim warrior to treat his prisoners mercifully. But people get hurt in war, and some warriors enjoy hurting people. A hint of the pleasure the fighting nomad derived from victorious conflict can be seen in this comment by Ghengis Khan, perhaps the greatest of the nomad conquerors, on the pleasures of life: "Man's greatest good fortune is to chase and defeat the enemy, seize his total possessions, leave his married women weeping and wailing, ride his gelding and use the bodies of his women as a nightshirt and support."[8] This frame of mind explains why the onslaught of the nomads evoked such terror in the hearts of their victims.

But in time success spoiled the Arab nomad. Inexorably, the conquerors became like the conquered. Drawn to city life, covetous of city wealth and luxury, they became Sedentary Men: artisans, clerks, shopkeepers, merchants, doctors, courtiers. They fell prey to the same corrupting influences that had made the earlier residents of the city weak, self-indulgent, and easy to conquer. And therein lay the explanation of Arab decline—city life had ruined them.

In the city the Arab indulged his craving for luxury and vice. Made soft by easy living and believing himself safe behind walls manned by professional soldiers, he became a cautious creature, without martial skill or physical endurance, acquisitive, submissive to authority, fastidious in dress and consumption, and refined in de-meanor and behavior. His soul, as Khaldun saw it, was suffused with evil. City life had made him "devoted to lying, gambling, cheat-ing, fraud, theft, perjury, and usury." Self-indulgence had made him soft, vice had made him weak, security had made him cowardly. In consequence, when hard, cruel, and energetic invaders—the fero-cious Mongol nomads from the East and the Christian horsemen from the north—appeared before his walls, the sedentary Arab fell easy victim to their arrows and swords. But history would not end when the Arabs are conquered, Khaldun predicted. Eventually a new horde of barbarians would appear at the gates, and once again the city's conquerors, now a soft and weak people, would become victims.

History, as Khaldun saw it, is the record of empires built by one character type, hardy Nomadic Men, who in time develop into soft and corrupt Sedentary Men. This breed will always be impotent to resist the fury of predatory invaders who, invincibly armed with martial vigor and courage, overwhelm the city dwellers and become their masters.

This conception of change as a cycle, though ancient in origin, still maintains its hold on popular imagination, because it appears to conform to the realities of experience. Also, old social theories, like old soldiers, never die. They do not even fade away. When out of fa-vor they live a twilight life, nurtured by a few devoted believers, un-til fresh minds breathe new life into old ideas, thus giving the old soldier new vigor and appeal.

CYCLICAL THEORY REDUX

In the twentieth century, three such fresh minds—those of Oswald Spengler, Arnold Toynbee, and Pitirim Sorokin, Europeans by birth and training—gave cyclical theory new popularity, modifying and elaborating it in long, multivolumed works, unfortunately marred by neologisms (Sorokin), Germanic philosophical obscurantism (Spengler), or religious dogmatism (Toynbee).[9] Unhappy with the strife endemic in their times, trying to understand why things had come to so sorry a pass, they imagined a time when life seemed more satisfying, and, seeking to solace the unhappy, they held out the hope of better times to come as the wheel of change turned.

Though they aroused renewed interest in cyclical theory, to examine their ideas here seems not worthwhile, for nothing much came of their work. Their books languish, mostly unread except by specialists and graduate students rummaging through the detritus of ideas long out of fashion, looking for material for monographs and dissertations. This is not to say that cyclical theory no longer engages the minds of people. True, no contemporary European theorist of stature explicitly promotes cyclic theory; even so, its hold on the popular mind continues. The latent fear that fighting between major nations will once again break out, despite NATO, SEATO, and Pax Americana, is an expression of the notion that war must follow peace, inexorably, as the night the day.

Cyclical theory's impact was not, of course, restricted to Europe. In America, numerous pundits and intellectuals also found the cyclical approach to change irresistible and still do. For example, Ralph Waldo Emerson thought history alternated between periods of conservatism and innovation, though he left unanswered the question of how long each period lasted. Henry Adams was more precise; he believed that American politics swung pendulum- like from a period of centralization to one of diffusion, each period lasting twelve years. Arthur M. Schlesinger and son, Arthur, Jr., each in separate books published years apart, advanced the notion that American politics oscillate from conservatism to liberalism. Schlesinger the elder thought each period of the cycle would last about sixteen and a half years. His son, though living in faster- moving times, tied the cycle to generational change: he thought that each period would endure for about thirty years.

To their credit, both Schlesingers took their theories seriously, and they bravely sought to forecast the future. In 1924, during a long period of Coolidge-style conservatism, the elder Schlesinger predicted that a new era of liberalism would commence in 1932, a prediction that proved right on the mark when Franklin Delano Roosevelt ushered in two decades of liberalism with his New Deal. The younger Schlesinger has been less successful. In a book published in 1986, *The*

Cycles of American History , he predicted that the 1990s would be a period of liberalism, a time when absorption with private interest (conservatism) would be replaced by a greater willingness to use government to further the public interest (liberalism). Thirty years having elapsed since the liberalism of the 1960s, Schlesinger thought the cycle was ready to turn in the direction of liberalism. Sadly for his theory, events proved otherwise: national social policy in the 1990s turned out to be generally conservative, even though nominally under the charge of a liberal president.[10]

Perhaps the cyclical theorists most visible to the public are the investment managers and technical analysts, some of them elite Xers, who scan the historical records for portents of the stock market's future. They look for auguries of the market's health and direction in the statistical entrails of the beast—patterned changes in put-call ratios, trend lines, measures of price volatility, price-earnings ratios, price highs and lows—and then sell their opinions to credulous investors who dream of making killings in the market.[11] The public rarely seems to wonder why these market gurus make their expertise available to the public rather than put it to work solely for their own private advantage. Why does the public not ask, whence comes this altruism? No one knows. On the other hand, not everyone is so kind. John Pierpont Morgan, regrettably less helpful than the run-of-the-mill investment counselor, took a more intuitive and selfish stance: no complex tables or charts, no advice or handouts for him. When asked what the stock market would do, he would respond curtly that it would fluctuate, for reasons no one knew or could do much about.

Curiously, people who think in circles—that is, who believe change occurs in cycles—seldom have much to say about the causes of cyclical change. Cyclical theorists are never very good at predicting the direction and duration of change, and they are even weaker when trying to explain it. Sadly, what little speculation there has been about the causes of change has not added much to our understanding of what keeps the wheel turning or the pendulum swinging.

The Ancients, who started all of this, said little about the forces that propel society through the various stages their ingenious minds conjured up. It is as though having described the stages of change, they thought their job was done. In the main, they tended to be fatalistic, to see people or societies as cogs in a vast clockwork world, doomed to turn endlessly in circles; or as donkeys imprisoned in a treadmill, fated to move throughout eternity from one stage to another, staying nowhere permanently, eventually ending up where they began.

When pushed to explain why anyone stays on the treadmill or submits to being nailed to the pendulum, cyclical theorists usually fall back on generalities about how the innate nature of the prisoner keeps him locked in place. The elder Schlesinger, for example, felt that the root cause of political change lies in human nature, in the tendency of the electorate to become bored and discontented with one philosophy or party and out of vexation to turn to its opposite, whether that be liberal or conservative. The younger Schlesinger also believes human nature is at the core of social change. He argued that personal factors—a weariness with the endless clashes of interests in the body politic, a revulsion against ideas that never bear fruit, a mounting frustration with the slowness and disappointing results of change—eventually cause people to turn in fatigue and exasperation to the opposite pole of the pendulum.[12]

The problem with cyclical theory, as Xers drawn to this perspective will discover, is that a human society is not a wheel or a pendulum. Societies do not bounce from one stage to another along predetermined paths. Though this idea appeals to Xers who believe every action must evoke a counteraction, providing them with the predictability they so desperately want, and however analytically convenient dividing history into stages is, nothing in cyclical theory enables us to explain with anything approaching precision why or when a society will move from one stage to another. The idea that change resembles the circular movement of a wheel or the swinging to and fro of a pendulum along a predictable arc ignores the many times no movement takes place. Even when movement does occur, the theory fails to account for the highly variable periods of time that pass before the pendulum completes its arc or the wheel its turn.

The nub of the matter is the observable fact that metaphors, though attractive as literary devices, are lamentably faulty scientific tools. Predicting future events on assumptions based on the swing of a pendulum or the turn of a wheel is a highly risky business, not unlike predicting the results of a horse race with the help of a racing form—which also makes assumptions about future events based on past performance. But as we know, people who make bets based on past racetrack performance often lose their shirts.

Nevertheless, despite its failings, the cyclical paradigm is attractive to some Xers who have become frazzled by rapid social change, though they are attracted for reasons that are disheartening. For the

cyclical paradigm taps into deep veins of cynicism in their characters, into their skepticism, into their sense that change is illusory, that
what appears to be change is simply chimera, the work of Boomers
playing their usual tricks. Xers believe they are being manipulated
to think things have improved when in fact nothing important or enduring has happened. But they are not fooled, they say. There is no
wizard behind the curtain: only a charlatan operating a machine that
generates smoke and illusion, a technique chameleon Xers know all
too well.

There is, however, more to this than cynicism and skepticism:
there is also pessimism, a trait common to many Xers. The description of change as simply another turn of the wheel or swing of the
pendulum fits in well with the Xers' feeling that the future is likely to
be painful, that the next turn of the wheel could well bring disaster,
confirming their worst fears. Many Xers cannot shake the feeling
that just around the corner gimlet-eyed trouble lurks—the inevitable consequence of Boomer incompetence and malice. To the skeptical and pessimistic Xer, cyclical theory is simply a sugar-coating of
the truth: that life is unpredictable and often unpleasant—and that
they are helpless to do much about it. At best, cyclical theory can
promise only temporary relief, the belief that bad times will be followed by good. But then again, they point out, good times are invariably followed by bad.

Pragmatic elite Xers prefer to take their medicine straight—a
long, bitter drink of pessimism and regression undiluted by the
sweetness of false hopes. This is the reason many of them are attracted to Darwinian social evolution as a paradigm of social change.
It is strong medicine, but it fits in well with the world as they know it,
and as they fear it will continue to be. First, however, we must examine the notion of change as progress, for like regression it bears upon
the Darwinian social evolutionary theory of social change.

CHANGE AS PROGRESS

The skepticism of many Xers about the inevitability of beneficial
change seems un-American, as indeed it is. Xers are, in fact, the first
generation in the country's history not to have been smitten by the
idea of progress. In the past, as numerous foreign and domestic observers have noted, most Americans at some time in their lives lost
their hearts to the notion that things were bound, in the long run, to
get better and better.[13] This point of view gave them the confidence

to settle in cold, rocky New England or to establish towns on the fever-infested lowlands of the Atlantic tidewater, then to push into the frontier against the objections of hostile Indians, to build cities in the mountains, deserts, and desolate prairies. Their experience justified that confidence, so in time few dared challenge it. Indeed, it came to be seen as downright unpatriotic to question the inevitability of progress.

The idea of progress has a long and honorable genealogy in America. It arrived on the *Mayflower* with the Pilgrim fathers, for it was implicit in their dream of improving their lives in the New World and of building a city on a hill, a light to the nations. It can be found in the notion of America's manifest destiny to expand across the continent, to settle new lands, and to bring the blessings of Western civilization to savage peoples. It is there in Frederick Jackson Turner's theory of the moving western frontier as outlet for American energy and ambition, and it was a source of pioneer optimism, the expectation that Americans would prosper as they overcome the challenges of surviving in a rugged unsettled continent. It is loud and clear in the ebullient rhetoric of Theodore Roosevelt, who saw no end to American expansion, influence, and prosperity. Even today it can be found among Americans who wish to export their vision of the future by getting other peoples to adopt the American Way of Life.

Of course, the idea of progress did not originate with Americans. Much before they latched on to the idea of progress, it had made deep inroads in the minds of Europeans, beginning in the seventeenth and eighteenth centuries. Why the seventeenth and eighteenth centuries? In part because it was during this period that the effects of technological change, slowly building over centuries, and then spreading rapidly across the West, pushed into every aspect of life and burst into a new crescendo of innovation. The changes had been building for some time. Even in the Middle Ages, creative minds, optimistic about the possibility of bettering mankind's condition, had slowly been adding to the store of human knowledge and capital, inventing new machines or improving upon old ones.

New or improved farming equipment, such as the harrow and the heavy plow, opened new lands to cultivation and increased the production and variety of grains, vegetables, and fruits. New mechanical devices—the overshot watermill, the cam, crank, gear, cog, flywheel, and triphammer—greatly aided manufacturing and laid the groundwork for the industrial revolution of the eighteenth and nineteenth centuries. New construction devices—the brace and bit, the truss, the flying buttress, to name just a few—made building houses, castles, and cathedrals easier and safer. New machines and techniques made weaving and spinning faster, and metal founding more efficient.[14]

These innovations were possible because Europe had been blessed with an interval of relative peace. In the eleventh century the depredations of foreign invaders diminished. The Muslim wave was halted and gradually pushed back. The Norsemen settled down to enjoy the fruits of their conquests in Normandy, England, and Sicily. The nomadic horsemen, unable to consolidate their penetrations of the West, returned to their eastern grasslands. And perhaps most important, central governments finally curbed the power of the barons and brought their incessant quarreling and fighting under control. Concurrently, peaceful commerce, especially international trade, which had all but stopped when the roads and waterways became too dangerous to use, returned to life; markets and fairs appeared in the Champagne, in Lucca and Bruges, in Frankfort and London, and elsewhere. Merchants with capital, courage, and an outsize hunger for profits outfited ships, loaded them with local products—for example, textiles, wool, grain, and kegs of salted herring—and sent them to distant ports and, when successful, became fabulously rich.[15]

Other changes, also important, helped make the idea of progress appear both logical and inevitable, especially to people of a rational turn of mind. Travel and exploration, which flourished in the seventeenth century to a degree unparalleled in history, even in the halcyon days of ancient Greece and imperial Rome, opened the eyes and minds of Europeans to the richness and variety of cultures and peoples beyond their own small world. The stumbling of Europeans upon the Americas in 1492 (the Viking landfall on Greenland in 982 and Newfoundland in 1000 having long been forgotten) excited the imagination of philosophers and poets, who projected upon those unknown lands their own utopian fantasies of unspoiled societies inhabited by noble savages living together in peace and collectively enjoying nature's bounty.

Adventurers, merchants, and governments, enriched with the gold and silver taken from Mexico and Peru, provided capital for investment and stimulated economies—and not incidentally brought on a roaring inflation that contributed to the decline of the Spanish empire. (Xers take note: an abundance of unexpected riches can have a downside.) Historian Paul Johnson writes: "In Spain commodity prices rose 500 percent during the sixteenth century, about twice as much as in England and France over a longer period (1475–1663); and in Spain the inflation continued for a half century after it had exhausted itself elsewhere."[16] More money in private hands and government coffers meant greater support for schools and universities, which grew rapidly in this period. More plentiful and better food, and improvements in medicine and public sanitation led to better health and lower mortality rates, particularly among the very young, touching off a population explosion that energized economic growth and generated a general sense of excitement and well-being.

Excited by the exuberant growth of science and industry, drunk with rationalism and optimism, men like Voltaire, Diderot, Condorcet, and other *philosophes* of the French Enlightenment announced to the world that mankind had begun a march of progress that was both certain and without end. Their optimism was founded on the belief that progress moves in step with the growth of knowledge: every generation adds to the store. It is in the nature of knowledge to accumulate, like money growing at compound interest in a safe bank, and man's innate need to enlarge his understanding of the world causes him continually to make new deposits to his account. So it seemed incontrovertible that progress was inevitable.

Believers in progress argued that we cannot help knowing more than our ancestors, no matter how bright they may have been, because we have the benefit of their achievements. Thus a student today who is competent in the calculus, the contributions of Newton and Leibnitz, knows more mathematics than did Euclid or Pythagoras. Progress, not superior intelligence, makes this curious fact possible.[17]

But times have changed. The old complacency about the inevitability of progress has evaporated, and questions are being asked, enough questions to suggest that many Americans have no faith in progress—prominent among them, the elite Xers. To skeptical Xers the idea of progress seems a loony fantasy. The conviction that mankind will go on developing and improving into the illimitable future requires a suspension of disbelief, a willingness to ignore cruel reality, that seems to the Xer more appropriate to the theater of the absurd than to the theater of everyday life.

CHANGE AS REGRESSION

It needs also to be remembered that an idea older than the notion of progress also has a respectable genealogy: the idea of regress, the pessimistic philosophy that things are in inevitable decline, that the golden age is past and will never return. Many elite Xers are drawn to this old fellow, and they are not unique. There has never been a scarcity of pessimists in the world. Westerners have long mined a deep vein of pessimism in their culture, a mother lode of gloom that runs through their history.

The ancient Greeks, for example, were generally glum about the possibility of things getting better for most people. As they saw it, the future was in the hands of Moira, the personification of fate, whose intentions and actions no effort on their part could change. In their view, Moira was not especially inclined to make things easy for the Greeks—and that was that. Fatalism became especially strong during the late Hellenistic period, after the death of Alexander the Great and the disintegration of his empire, when his generals and their descendants took to fighting one another. Not surprisingly, continuous war, the devastation of cities, the looting and plundering and killing that rapacious soldiers visited upon innocent civilians caused the harried populace to retreat into fatalism as a defense against feelings of helplessness and despair.[18]

In different times and places other peoples have been similarly pessimistic. The early Christians, no strangers to violence and social turmoil themselves, felt deeply gloomy about the human condition and saw few prospects for its improvement. Writing to his friend Demetrianus, the Roman proconsul of Africa, Cyprian, bishop of Carthage in the third century, enlarged on a popular theme of general decline. The crops, he wrote, were doing poorly, silver and gold veins were dwindling, less and less marble was being quarried each year. "The husbandman is failing in the field, the sailor at sea, the soldier in the camp. . . . [T]he whole world is failing, and is about to die."[19] Cyprian was less disturbed by all of this than he sounded. Man's earthly fate, he believed, was in the hands of providence, and his reward would be an afterlife in a better world—the existence of which he never doubted.

In predicting the end of his world, Bishop Cyprian—now St. Cyprian—was right on the mark. The Roman Empire in the west fell as he expected. But the manner of its dying and the length of time it took, he did not predict. The sweep of Germanic tribes into Gaul, Spain, and North Africa in the last part of the fifth century; the sack of Rome by the Visigoth chieftain Alaric in 410; the gruesome march of Attila the Hun across northern Italy in 452, leaving in its wake a string of burned and pillaged cities; and the forced retirement of the last Roman emperor, Romulus Augustulus, in 476—these were events he could not have foreseen. But that they were messy, bloody affairs would not have surprised him one bit. After all, the New Testament had predicted a catastrophic end to the world, and the catastrophe that befell the Roman Empire in the west was entirely in keeping with this prediction.

For the next 1,200 years, life for most people was dull and dreary. Hunger was an ever-present companion and famine only one failed harvest away. Lawlessness and violence were ways of life for some people and the daily experience of many others. Kings, barons, and bandits warred upon each other almost continuously, and the common people, caught in the middle and helpless to defend themselves, suffered cruelly. Invaders from foreign lands added to their misery. From the south came Muslim pirates who raided coastal cities and inland towns. From the north came the Norsemen, Danes, and Norwegians, who laid waste to large stretches of the Atlantic coastline, and the Swedes, who pushed into the Baltics and Russia, burning and destroying whatever they could not carry away. From the east came nomadic horsemen who "spread nothing but ruin wherever they went, and nothing remained of their invasions but the memory of a savage and stupid work of destruction."[20]

Real economic growth virtually stopped. Not until commerce and manufacturing picked up in the eighteenth century did living standards rise appreciably, and then only in advanced countries like England and Holland. John Maynard Keynes, perhaps the most influential economist of the twentieth century, put it this way: "Down to the beginning of the eighteenth century, there was no very great change in the standard of living of the average man living in the civilized centers of the earth. Ups and downs certainly. Visitations of plague, famine and war. Golden intervals. But no progressive change."[21] Eventually, the growth of commerce and the industrial revolution gradually raised the standard of living, but they also created much misery in the process of change.

And so, to sum up, when lives were ruined by violence and poverty, when the poor had to endure the raw cruelty of their masters, and when industrialization caused much dislocation and upheaval, it is not surprising that pessimism also flourished. The residue of this pessimism, reinvigorated by periodic social calamity, still persists in Western culture and provides ready at hand a draught of disenchantment that is strangely attractive to many elite Xers.

SOCIAL EVOLUTION AND DARWINISM

Why so? In this noxious mixture of pessimism and estrangement many elite Xers have found a paradigm of social change that suits their characters, their situations, and their views of society. They have found Social Darwinism—an offspring of evolutionary theory that nicely bolsters the elite Xers' self-esteem, even though it promises disaster for many of the nonelite. For, seen from the Darwinian perspective, elite Xers have demonstrated their superiority, by proving themselves fit and morally exceptional in the most exacting of arenas: the laissez-faire market place of the information society.

This is strange, really, because Charles Darwin never considered evolutionary fitness a matter of moral excellence. To Darwin, evolution was purely a biological matter, an impersonal process of natural selection during which some creatures, having been made fiercely competitive by a constant struggle to gain access to limited resources, manage to adapt and reproduce. These creatures transmit their winning characteristics to progeny, while those who are poorly adapted fall by the wayside, losers in the game of life. Darwin carefully avoided making moral judgments about the ability of a species to survive. The shape of a bird's bill or the color of its plumage might help in the search for food or the evasion of predators, but these were matters of unplanned variation, not results of a creature's moral stature or of careful planning and intentional change. To Darwin, survival is survival and nothing more.

Herbert Spencer saw things differently. He discerned in the evolutionary process purpose and direction that Darwin had denied was there, and he announced his discovery to enthusiastic audiences in numerous highly popular books, articles, and lectures. In Spencer's hands Darwin's theory underwent transformation. Evolution ceased being solely a biological explanation of how species change; it became a social explanation of how societies change—it became, in short, Social Darwinism, perhaps the most ambitious and systematic theory of social change ever imagined.

The Social Darwinist conceived of social change as the movement of a society toward ever greater complexity, differentiation, specialization, and individuation. This movement gains energy from the conflict between individuals and groups as they struggle to win access to the limited resources upon which their survival depends. Individuals who survive have proven themselves to be fit. It was Spencer who introduced the phrase "survival of the fittest" into the

popular lexicon. And it was Spencer who turned a value-free idea—
the survival of the best adapted—into a moral indictment of failure.
Failure became the mark of the unfit and unworthy—a highly popular idea today, as it was then.

Philosopher, journalist, biologist, engineer, psychologist, and not
least sociologist, Spencer was above all a rationalist, a devout be-
liever in science, and an individualist. His distrust of government
was monumental. He never tired of castigating governmental inter-
ference in private affairs; he opposed state-financed education; he
objected to governmental protection of the gullible from the machi-
nations of the crooked. At one time he even argued for the private
management of war. The government's clumsiness in conducting
public affairs appalled him. Will Durant writes, "He carried his
manuscripts to the printer himself, having too little confidence in a
government institution to entrust them to the Post Office. . . . He was
a man of intense individuality, irritably insistent on being left alone;
and every new act of legislation seemed to him an invasion of his
personal liberty."[22]

In Spencer's opinion the evolutionary process, if left to its own devices, unfettered by governmental restrictions and unmitigated by
private benevolence, would be unsentimental about whom it selected for survival. Only the most deserving individuals would get
to pass on their physical characteristics, cultural values, and psychological traits to their progeny. The dross of social selection would be
eliminated.

In the late nineteenth century, Social Darwinism arrived on American shores, where it found eager and appreciative buyers. The tim-
ing could not have been more opportune. It was a time of rapid
economic change, growing wealth, rampant materialism, and reckless display. Americans in the Gilded Age thirsted for ideas that
would explain to the world the nation they were building. They
needed a philosophy that would sanction their mastery over nature
and would justify their sometimes brutal domination of weaker
neighbors. Social Darwinism was for them the right idea, in the right
place, at the right time.[23]

In the United States no one epitomized the Darwinian Man better
than William Graham Sumner. The son of humble parents, a graduate of Yale in 1863, a clergyman for several years, and the holder of a
chair of sociology at Yale University for thirty-odd years, Sumner
passed every test of fitness and became in the late nineteenth century (he died in 1910) a national figure, America's foremost spokes-

man for Social Darwinism. His path to success had not been easy. It had been marked by struggle (as befitted the life of an exponent of social evolution), by hard work, and by prodigious scholarly productivity. In a slew of lectures, papers, and books (his most important scholarly work, *Folkways*, became a classic) he spread the gospel of Social Darwinism. His work, unlike most publications by today's scholars, won a popular audience, whose members were eager to hear a message that sanctified their success. As Sumner saw it, the fit are the benefactors of humanity. It is their hard work, their willingness to plan and defer gratification, their dogged determination to get ahead that provide the human capital on which society depends.[24]

Elite Xers take to evolutionary theory like ducks to water. Like the Social Darwinians of the nineteenth century, they see life as a cutthroat struggle in which only the fit survive. And they are determined to be counted among the fit, among those who come out on top. This won't be easy, Darwinians Xers believe, since the future is out of their hands: it is the marketplace that will decide the shape of the future and their fates in it. Of course, they will do what they can to protect themselves, but there is no certainty that things will turn out well. A laissez-faire economy that rigorously culls the fit from the unfit and measures success by the accumulation of money and power is bound to produce losers as well as winners. Some elite Xers fear—indeed may expect, given their tendency to be pessimistic about the future—that when the competition is dangerous, they may turn out to be losers after all.

That the Darwinian market place celebrates winners and scorns losers does not bother elite Xers. They consider themselves more fit than the common run of humanity and hence likely to be winners. But there is more to this then youthful hubris. Perhaps, as their detractors claim, they are not particularly lovable; still, they are admirably suited to the information system and at home in it. Fit and energetic, busy working toward material success, they can spare little time for the losers, whom they consider their moral, as well as intellectual, inferiors. More than that, as Social Darwinists who see in their success visible proof of their superiority, Elite Xers hardly bother to hide their contempt for the unfit, the inferior people who clog the system and burden the successful with high taxes, useless philanthropies, and unwanted children.

Nor can they entirely hide their satisfaction in their triumphs over rivals, other elite Xers. To the contrary, contemplating the failure of rivals is pleasurable, and crowing about their own successes would be delicious if they were not worried about the retribution of envious losers. They are, therefore, somewhat circumspect about lording it over their fallen competitors; still, the pleasure they feel in victory is palpable and hard to conceal.

How pleasing it must be to the ears of elite Xers, weary of being made to feel guilty of avarice when they energetically pursue profits and wealth, to be told, as Social Darwinism does, that material success is nothing to be ashamed of—rather, that it is a mark of moral superiority. How soothing it is to the sensibilities of ambitious Xer youths, wounded by the accusations of less ambitious peers who see in the Xers' yearnings for success the root cause of unseemly aggressiveness, to be told (to paraphrase Joseph Epstein) that ambition is the fuel of achievement and achievement the motor of progress.[25]

This may be all very well as long as elite Xers feel assured of winning, but where does Social Darwinism leave them when defeat looms? Whatever its favorable view of the winner, the Darwinian paradigm has its downside: it affords the elite Xer a singularly bleak view of life. Its emphasis on the unremitting struggle to survive in a grimly competitive world, its refusal to comfort the weary and the laggardly loser, its promise to punish anyone who falls behind in the race for success—all this can be brutally exhausting. Elite Xers, riding high on the Internet, their skills much valued and in demand, may wonder what will happen if the cyberworld collapses and the safety net dissolves. What could the high-flying Xer then expect from others? Very little, for in the Social Darwinian system the loser has only himself to blame for failure. As a result, Social Darwinism in a ferociously competitive world is a huge generator of anxiety— which is almost the last thing the anxiety-ridden elite Xer needs.

Nevertheless, in most cases anxiety cannot be avoided. Yet it must be dealt with. Chameleonism, as we know, is the elite Xer's preferred defense against the buffets of unendurable competition. There is another way, however, a defense mentioned in an earlier chapter: withdrawing from the competitive fray, either by becoming free agents or by assuaging anxiety through unfettered hedonism. In a few cases, anxious Xers may withdraw entirely into private worlds of their own.

Though not as common as chameleonism, withdrawal has long been used by some Xers, as Douglas Coupland pointed out in his seminal novel *Generation X*, as a way of coping with anxiety when things do not go one's way, when boredom threatens to overwhelm the spirit, and life appears meaningless. It was Coupland who first noted the tendency for some young Xers to opt out of the rat race for success and to withdraw into their own private worlds. Since withdrawal may grow in popularity as some elite Xers exhaust themselves in frenetic competition for money and prestige, let us round out this analysis of chameleonism and the Xer elite by examining the efficacy of withdrawal as a defense against intrusions from an unruly and threatening world. Xers who are thinking of taking this route need to know what they can expect. This is the task of the next chapter.

10

Staying the Course

To many a frazzled elite Xer, tired and hag-ridden with worry, things sometimes seem to be falling apart. The glue that keeps society together looks weak, as if it may not hold. The social system feels wobbly and about to lose its equilibrium, its parts moving in opposing directions or rubbing angrily against each other, heating up and seemingly in danger of breaking down. This is not a far-fetched possibility. Indeed, at times eventual breakdown seems certain. For when people perform their social roles negligently, when they airily dismiss society's rules and customs as mere nuisances, and act on the urgings of their own characters in ways that disrupt society, stress and strain are inescapable and breakdown a genuine possibility.

We have looked at the sources of strain in the elite Xer's life, and there is no need to cover this ground again in any detail. Still, in this final chapter it may be useful to note again a few of these tension points and add several others, so that we may understand why some Xers are thinking of withdrawing from society or, as they put it, escaping from the box society has put them in. To begin with, there are the terrible pressures a fiercely competitive society puts upon anyone competing for success—pressures exerted by competitors, by members of the opposite sex, by talented immigrants, by an ethos that measures individual worth in dollars accumulated and merit badges garnered and treats failure with cold disdain.

There are other sources of tension worthy of mention. One is the rapid increase in population, caused mainly by the nation's newcomers. Immigrants are pouring into the country, and since they tend to have higher birth rates than the native born, substantial numbers are being added daily to the overall population. Rapid population growth produces overcrowding in schools and an excess of claimants for available resources. Battles then ensue between individuals and groups that seek to retain or to increase their shares, noticeably adding to the national level of frustration and tension.

Faulty training is another source of tension. Elite Xers complain that often the people they have to work with are not adequately trained or motivated to do their jobs. In the jaundiced opinion of anxious Xers, the world teems with incompetent people. Consequently, important work is performed poorly or not at all, causing all kinds of trouble and making the elite Xers' jobs more difficult. The problem begins with poor training in the schools and continues later in life as people fail to keep abreast of the most recent innovations in technology, a particularly dangerous condition in a time of exceedingly rapid technological change.

Another serious problem is the sabotage of society by people who, dissatisfied with the status quo, tamper with the system or reject it altogether, in the process setting off chains of events that are difficult to control. Some of the tamperers are idealistic rebels who want to replace the existing system with a perfect one; a few are anarchists who object to any system at all; others are well-meaning people whose innovations unsettle the conventional mind. Perhaps they advocate ideologies that challenge the old order; they scoff at old ideas and show how useless they have become; or they may introduce inventions that create new jobs but finish off many old ones. Whatever the innovation may be, it is likely to reorder time-honored relationships and unsettle people who are accustomed to things as they were and are unwilling to change.

Exceptionally sensitive to changes in human relationships in a society that is boiling with change, elite Xers quickly pick up signs that the times are out of joint. How could they not? Everyone knows about disaffected people who are openly resentful and worried, who march and countermarch, demonstrate and shout, and sometimes threaten to bring the system down unless they get their ways. Among the disaffected are certain Boomers, who complain bitterly that their dream of a perfect society has been wrecked and who fault Xers for not sharing their dreams and coming to their rescue. And then there are those women and men, quintessential termagants and macho spirits, who carry on at ever more strident levels the ancient

war of the sexes. Add to this witches' brew the bickering of some immigrants and native-born Americans who get in each other's way as
they push for personal advantage in a harshly competitive society—
witness the fighting between certain natives and immigrants over
jobs and promotions.

Truth to tell, and try as they may to protect themselves from its
baleful effects, Xers cannot escape the consequences, of unchecked
change. The emanations of change seep into their lives. Although
elite Xers are less vociferous than most other groups about their discontents and have not taken to the streets, many are covertly show-
ing their dissatisfaction with rampant change by gestures of
resentment, in sullen indifference to conventional norms of dress
and sex, in derogation of the old work ethic, and in some cases by
threats to pull out of the system and go their own ways. Aptly
enough, in a nation devoted to abolishing scarcity, there is no scarcity of complaint, of strain and stress.[1]

As some elite Xers see it, socially induced stress and strain is
blocking their paths to a world of blissful harmony, which they
imagine is only a hop, skip, and jump away if only the malefactors of
power and privilege would get out of the way. What these Xers
would like is a place where they can live at peace with themselves
and others, where people work together in mutually supportive
units, without dissension and conflict. In this community government is enlightened, coercion is unnecessary, and disputes are resolved by gentle reminders to everyone of their responsibility for
promoting the general good. Change is unnecessary, because such a
community is perfect and timeless. This is a dream, of course. Inevitably every system contains flaws, which left unrepaired tears it and
its members apart.

Paradoxically, the dissatisfactions many elite Xers feel grow out of
the very changes they have done so much to create. The information society they helped create is, as we know, agog with social change, whose
speed and complexity have made many of them uneasy and resentful.
Even though they see themselves as the bearers of change and as major
beneficiaries, they also recognize that change threatens their well- being, that it has created a degree of competition and economic instability
inimical to their peace of mind. It is these unanticipated consequences
of change that appear especially frightful to some elite Xers— in no
small part because they feel powerless to resist them.

Resistance seems futile because they confront a foe they do not
fully understand. A powerful personal enemy may be difficult to re-

sist, true, but at least it is recognizable and presents a choice that is easy to grasp. When, figuratively speaking, the enemy stands at the gates brandishing arms, shouting insults and threats, the choices are simple: fly or fight, submit or seek safety under the cover of dissimulation and deceit. But when the enemy is the impersonal force of change, whose effects are often intangible, the challenge is immensely more complicated.

Resistance to impersonal social change inevitably creates confusion. What is one to do, whom is one to fight, and with what weapons? When the answer is not clear, as it often is not, bewilderment reigns. This is nothing new, of course; it is a common problem whenever a new social system replaces an old one, whenever new values and practices and technologies take over, causing some people to feel out of place and no longer safe, tragically lost in an unfriendly world. Feeling unwanted and under excessive pressure, they may suffer a crisis of identity: they do not know who they are or what to do.

Some elite Xers feel this way—at loose ends, drifting aimlessly, like flotsam bobbing about in troubled waters. What can they do? They can do any of a number of things. They can tread water, jumping from one dead-end job to another, hoping that something will turn up, that someone will come along and rescue them. Other Xers take an assertive stance toward change. They believe they have a right to control it, at least as it affects them, and this thought marvelously concentrates their minds. They decide to take charge of their lives, to control change's discombobulating effects. Among these Xers, as we have seen, are those who use chameleonism to fend off the depredations of unfriendly competitors, seeking in this way to cushion the consequences of change.

But there are other responses to rapid social change. One of these is to strike out on one's own, to become a free agent not tied to any organization, the sources of so many unpleasant changes. Another is to withdraw, to isolate oneself from change by withdrawing from the system. In this chapter I will round out my discussion of the Xer elite and chameleonism by examining the efficacy of free agentry and withdrawal as mechanisms of defense against insecurity in a rapidly changing, highly competitive society. Let us begin by looking at free agentry.

FREE AGENTRY: ITS PLUSES AND MINUSES

Becoming a free agent appeals to some harassed elite Xers—the very term "free" titillates their imagination. Free agents are not shackled by conventional job demands and changes. To some extent they are outside the system, independent contractors working on projects for periods ranging from a few days or weeks to several months. They do their job and then move on. Tethered only by lap-top and cell phone, they may telecommute, work at home, coming to the office irregularly or hardly at all. Ideally, as free agents they can choose only congenial assignments and set their own pace, free from the irritations of company politics and the disconcerting changes mandated by management. And, an added plus, as free agents they can tend to their kids and spend more meaningful time with family and friends, living the perfect lifestyle.

No one knows exactly how many Xers have chosen to go the free-agentry route. The Bureau of Labor Statistics reports that 12 million people work under "alternative arrangements"—a category into which free agents fit—but most of these people are relatively unskilled temporary workers; such as cashiers, waiters, and sales clerks.[2] Just how many of them are highly skilled Xers is not clear, but that number seems to be growing, due in part to corporate downsizing and the normal dislocations of a rapidly changing market economy, which make free agents of people whether they like it or not. Not all free agents have willingly cut their ties to the corporation; some had no choice. Their jobs disappeared or they were let go.

The Internet boom has greatly promoted free agentry by providing Xers with information about job opportunities and encouragement to break away from companies and strike out on their own. Web sites extol the advantages of being a free agent. "Be your own boss!" exhorts an advertisement for Guru.com, a Web site for free agents. "Work where you want, when you want. No supervisors. No commuting hassles. Freedom to balance your priorities and work in your pajamas."[3] Another Web site, oddly named Monster.com, allows free agents to post their resumes and offer their services to the highest bidders. For Xers with highly valued skills—such as Java programmers, computer program debuggers, Internet consultants, marketing experts—the bidding can be brisk and liberating.

HEDONISM AND FREE AGENTRY

Not the least of the attractions free agentry has for elite Xers is the opportunity it affords them to satisfy the fun-loving side of their characters. Free agentry permits elite Xers to take time off without suffering the harassment an organization is likely to inflict on workers who want release from the nine-to-five, five-day-a-week routine, and who desire to devote their free time to the pursuit of fun. When this pursuit becomes excessive—that is, when it is obsessively hedonistic—it can become a way of justifying one's existence. Hedonism seems entirely acceptable to many Xers: they see nothing wrong with treating themselves to a good time. Also, some Xers see hedonism as a way of striking back at a cruel society.

Moreover, for the well-heeled elite Xer the pursuit of pleasure in a consumer society is easy, indeed difficult to avoid, almost obligatory. On every side messages pour in, from friends, colleagues, and especially the media, telling the Xer that life was meant to be enjoyed. The media constantly hammer away at the idea that self-indulgence makes sense. Advertisements promise beauty and everlasting sex appeal through the faithful application of skin creams and hair lotions, and a regimen of exercise and diet to keep bodies young and exquisitely trim. Tantalizing commercials hold out the prospect of moving up in the world by being seen in expensive cars and taking costly vacations, flying now and paying later. Xers are exhorted to believe that new experiences in exotic lands will change their lives. What is wrong, thinks the hedonistic Xer, with changing one's life and enjoying oneself?

Hedonistic Xers dismiss self-denial and frugality as silly holdovers from an earlier period of scarcity. As believers in the contemporary fun culture, they scoff at the blue-nose, puritanical abstinence of earlier times. Appealing to Keynesian economic theory, hedonists claim that self-denial and thrift are not even in the country's best interest. Where would the economy be if we all pinched pennies? In big trouble, that's where—buying would decline, shops would cut purchases, and factories would shut down. To be sure, with more savings more money would be available for investment, but to what end if buying becomes unpopular and the economy goes into a tailspin? Therefore sensible people take their pleasure wherever and whenever possible.

Sad to relate, hedonism has an Achilles' heel. Apart from the problem of satiation, hedonism may appear to others as mere self-indulgence, a sign of immaturity—and hence anathema to Xers eager to be accepted as adults. Hedonism may also become a religion, in which material enjoyment is worshipped as the surest road to salvation. As religious practice the pursuit of pleasure may give focus to life, and for some people pleasure is an important component of self-esteem. Still, Xers who pride themselves on living well—convinced that joy is strength, that the road to fun leads to self-fulfillment, and that having a ball is an essential part of what life is all about—may face social opprobrium. They risk being regarded as shallow materialists. This is not a label Xers covet.

THE COST OF FREE AGENTRY

Free agentry has other problems: job insecurity and isolation, dead-end assignments and intermittent income. According to the Economic Policy Institute, a Washington research group, free agentry, despite its vaunted freedom, comes with a large amount of insecurity. Free agents are especially vulnerable to the economic cycle: a business downturn can mean lengthy unemployment, often with inadequate insurance to fall back on. There is no group life insurance or pension plan—401(k) plans are outside the free agent's purview. So are sick leave, group medical insurance, and dental plans, a potential catastrophe for free agents with young children.[4]

Income may be a problem; it comes unpredictably and goes all too quickly. There are always bills to pay: office supplies, long-distance telephone calls, photocopying, postage, Internet services. Medicare and Social Security taxes are double what company employees pay. Permission to take an income tax deduction for a home office must be wrenched from a suspicious Internal Revenue Service, which tends to cast a skeptical eye on this kind of claim. The pay may be less than royal. Except in Hollywood or Silicon Valley, where remuneration can be fabulous, the free agent may find the going difficult. Paulette M. Glassman, who posted her profile on FreeAgent.com, said to journalist Nina Munk, "I keep hearing how good the job situation is, but for me. . . . it's tough to find work. I'm struggling to stay solvent."[5] To add to their discomfiture, free agents receive no annual bonuses, no stock options, no paid vacations.

Then there is the loneliness of the unaffiliated agent and the indifference of employers who feed off the talents of temporary workers. Said Randy Nelson, who made the decision to never again be tied to one company, being a free agent outside the conventional job circuit, working for one's self can be exciting but also painful: "It's a hard, grueling lifestyle. . . . You can't do it if you're not a self-driven person who's happy being lonely. You'll always be an outsider; you'll never be accepted as a full member of the team."[6] Probably few employers give much thought to the loneliness of temporary workers. What many employers care about is that free agents don't complain about their salaries, don't ask for insurance, vacations, stock options, and annual benefits, and can be easily fired if they prove to be lazy or incompetent.

A NICHE OF ONE'S OWN

If free agentry is flawed and unalloyed hedonism doesn't work or perhaps is not available, what are distracted, anxious, alienated elite Xers to do? They may turn to a drastic way of coping with anxiety: withdrawal into their own worlds. The Xer tries to shut out the forces of change that cause unease by deliberately avoiding the people and situations that hurt their self-respect and peace of mind. For these Xers, confronting hostile competitors outright, if they had tried that at all, proved too unnerving. Pain and failure usually followed in the wake of self-assertiveness. Hostility only evoked counter-hostility and attack only produced counter-attack. And so, fearing rebuff they choose withdrawal.

These Xers have given up trying to fashion a livable life in a hostile world. They have concluded that since change cannot be avoided or even slowed down, they will go elsewhere, psychologically and perhaps even physically. I am not alluding to recluses who, perhaps for clinical reasons, shut themselves off from the outside world. There is no evidence that the Xers who opt for withdrawal are necessarily clinically disturbed, at least not more so than most of their peers. They simply want to put aside the demands and irritations of combative life and carve out quiet places for themselves, small and exclusive niches—individual or collective—that are friendly and humane.

As yet, disaffected Xers have made no movement toward collective withdrawal. Perhaps its creation is not on the minds of many of them, not a part of their dream of escaping from the irritations of competitive existences. But, if a society entirely to one's liking cannot be built, there is always the hope of finding solace alone or as a member of a small group. Such hopes are human enough, though pathetically naive. For whether collective or individual, withdrawal has serious drawbacks. To believe otherwise is to misunderstand the human psyche and social change.

It also demonstrates a deep ignorance of history. A keener sense of the past would caution Xers against imagining that change can be halted or at least kept at bay; history provides numerous cautionary examples of the futility of trying to shut out change. To students of millenarian movements and utopian communes this may seem obvious, but to some harried Xers the very thought of a quiet place free from conflict-ridden change has such appeal, fantasy though it is, that sensible reservations are put aside. Nevertheless a few examples of what happens when people try to shut out the mauling of social change through withdrawal into separate communities may be instructive.

The history of efforts to isolate oneself from the imperious demands and contaminating influences of the outside world in communes of like-minded folk is dismal. Most attempts to set up communes in America failed in short order. New Harmony and Brook Farm in the nineteenth century and most of the myriad communes set up in the euphoric 1960s and 1970s fell apart quickly. Even the Oneida Community, among the longest lasting of American communes, could not outlast the lifetime of its founder. Internal dissension, financial chicanery, administrative incompetence, and the hostility of neighbors eventually brought all but a few communes down.[7]

The successful ones tend to be farming communities, marked by religious fervor and social consensus, and by a serious attachment to traditions rooted in preindustrial civilization. In these respects, the Old Order Amish (and to a somewhat lesser extent, the Mennonites and Hutterites) come to mind. They are characterized by religious commitment, a remarkably effective form of group self-governance based largely on patriarchal control, and a form of agricultural cooperation that promotes economic success. (But elite Xers tend to be secularists, and there is no evidence that they aspire to become farmers.)

The Amish, for example, isolated from the outside world, devoted to ascetic Protestantism, turned their backs on the gear of industrial life: cars, tractors, electricity, fancy clothes, movies, television. They also eschewed fighting and individual ambition; self-aggrandizement is refused entry into their lives. Dressed in eighteenth-century garb and traveling in horse-drawn buggies, they excite the curiosity of city folk, who travel long distances just to view these exotic denizens of a mostly forgotten world. Peaceful, prosperous and self-sufficient, seen as presenting no threat to outsiders, they are left alone.

NO WAY OUT

On the surface, there appears to be little similarity between the situation communes face, on the one hand, and the one confronting individual Xers. No neighbors plague the Xers with hostility, threatening to crush them into submission; no government restricts their freedom to live as they please. And yet a similarity exists. Like many communal groups, many elite Xers see rampant competition as a threat to their security. They believe the system they helped develop denies them the safety and the freedom from enervating anxiety they believe is their right. Many of them are angry, and some of them want out. There is no sign, however, that they are moving into communes as havens from a cold and unfriendly world, and it may well be that elite Xers are too individualistic ever to take this route.

Even so, the urge to withdraw from the messy fray for success may eat away at the resolve of some of them to stay the course. Nothing much may happen as long as the economy stays ebullient, providing elite Xers with ways to comfort themselves and still stay in the system. But if the economy should falter if it sinks into sharp and prolonged decline, turns sour and tensions grow ugly, a significant number of Xers may well decide to leave the field of competition to others and seek safety in stress-free arenas. Perhaps some of them will search out soul mates and found sympathetic communities; if they cannot find others with whom to share their withdrawal, they may decide to do it on their own.

These Xers will have made up their mind that success is a prize not worth the trouble of winning—too much hassle, too much work, too much anxiety. As they see it, success is not their only option; they can do other things beside pursue the bitch goddess. They can become, if they want, *luftmenchen* living on handouts from parents and friends. They can devote themselves to self-improvement, to working out in gyms at all hours, to reading till daybreak, to developing latent talents in music and art or their appreciation. In short, they can be individualists, free from society's shrill demands, existing outside the limits of conventional roles, and even outside the system itself. Withdrawal beckons enticingly.

But withdrawal is excruciatingly difficult to achieve and even when successful carries a very high price tag. For one thing, the outside world will not go away. It continually intrudes on the Xer's perimeter, requiring that rents and taxes be paid, demanding that the law, however inconvenient and unreasonable, be obeyed. It insistently knocks on the door with solicitations and enticing invitations. These importunities are difficult to rebuff. Alone and adrift, deprived of the stimulation that mingling with others of a different bent of mind ordinarily provides, isolated Xers lose the skill to evaluate and resist the enticements of the outside world—the very thing they most desperately wanted to avoid in the first place.

For another thing, there is a serious psychological cost attached to isolation: paranoia. Perhaps some paranoia was there to begin with. Xers who opt out of the system tend to believe the world treats them badly and holds them in less respect than they deserve. Even if this were true (as it may be: who gets as much approval as they want?), isolation will only aggravate feelings of rejection. Alone with their thoughts, Xers develop excessive senses of threat and injury. Without interaction with the outside world to test the legitimacy of grievances, paranoia will grow unrestrained, populating the Xer's world with enemies, producing a state of mind crippling in its effects. If it is peace of mind that Xers seek, they will not find it in fear-drenched isolation.

To sum up, the new information system—which promotes chameleonism in some Xers, frantic hedonism in others, or fantasies about drifting away to a world of their choosing where conflict is minimal and self-fulfillment more than a dream in still others—is one few Xers can escape, and then only at great cost. But why seek escape? After all, elite Xers have flourished in the information society. And yet, as already noted, many of them feel uncomfortable and inadequately esteemed. Living in a time of tumultuous change when old identities are coming unglued, some Xers feel lost, out of place, unwanted, and unloved. They feel unsafe, under too much pressure, left out. Some of them are fighting mad and eager to strike back at the people who control the new system, who torment them—if only they could figure out how.

The problem is that their tormentors are fellow Americans, who dress and speak like Americans, though sometimes with curious accents. Their foes are armed not with assult rifles but with computers, college degrees, and valuable skills. They are denizens of the techno-service society, products of the third great transformation that pushed services into the forefront of the economy and made the information economy paramount. The Xers and their antagonists are part of the same new era, only now being born, and birthing is not a pretty sight. Like a bawling babe, raw and noisy and unpredictable, the emerging era holds great promise.

Fighting has erupted over who is to control the newcomer, direct its growth, and benefit from its development. Such bickering between interested parties at a birthing is not uncommon, of course. But the fighting today is uncommonly fierce and unrelenting, nasty and serious, because it is between people with different personalities, values, and goals.

Still, America has been through birthing periods before. In the past, most people survived and many prospered, as will the Xer elite once it accepts the fact that the world it helped create is not always a comfortable place to live in, and that it will never be perfect. Many Xers already understand this and have elected to stay in the competitive game, fighting for their shares of the prize and using for the most part above-board tactics to achieve their goals. Chameleon Xers are also staying in the game, even though the methods they use— dissimulation and deception—are misleading and ultimately self-defeating. Most of the remainder—the ones contemplating withdrawal—have not yet made up their minds. They may choose eventually to stay in the game but not as serious players, participating only reluctantly.

But whether or not Xers play the game openly and passionately, aggressively or submissively; whether or not they take part surreptitiously and with consummate guile; whether or not they seek escape through the frantic pursuit of pleasure or the dream of withdrawal, the fact remains that there is no way out. That's too bad, perhaps, but there it is. If they stay the course, however, Xers may take consolation in the fact that the game is intrinsically interesting and that for some players it can be exceptionally rewarding. In any event, most Xers may well conclude that they have no realistic choice: they must be participants. With or without them, the game will go on.

Notes

CHAPTER 1

1. Thorstein Veblen, *The Theory of the Leisure Class* (New York: Macmillan, 1899). Veblen was not the last to deplore the free-spending habits and self-indulgence of the very rich. For recent examples of this genre see Christoher Lasch, *The Culture of Narcissism* (New York: W. W. Norton, 1978); Lincoln Collier, *The Rise of Selfishness in America* (New York: Oxford University Press, 1991); Robert H. Frank, *Luxury Fever* (New York: Free Press, 1999).

2. For a glance at the life-styles of this new breed, see Alan Sloan, "The New Rich," *Newsweek*, August 4, 1997, pp. 48–59; Robert J. Samuelson, *The Good Life and Its Discontents* (New York: New York Times Books, 1995); David Brooks, *Bobos in Paradise* (New York: Simon and Schuster, 2000). In addition to their way of living, the origins and training of the new elite have also caught the attention of journalists. See, for example, Michael Lind, *The Next American* (New York: Free Press, 1995); Nicholas Lemann, *The Big Test: The Secret History of American Meritocracy* (New York: Farrar, Straus, Giroux, 1999). None of these books says much about Generation X, which they tend to combine indiscriminately with the Boomers, or anything at all about chameleonism.

3. See Peter Schwartz, Peter Leyden, and Joel Hyatt, *The Long Boom*, (Reading, Mass.: Perseus Books, 1999); John Cassidy, "No Satisfaction: The Trials of a Shopping Nation," *New Yorker*, January 25, 1999, pp. 88–92; Louis Uchitelle, "107 Months, and Counting," *New York Times*, January 30, 1999, Section 3, pp. 1 and 16; John M. Schlesinger and Nicholas Klish, "A Century of Booms, and How They Ended," *Wall Street Journal*, February 1,

2000, Section B, pp. 1 and 14; George J. Church, "The Good Bad News," *Time*, September 25, 2000, pp. B2–B4.

4. *New York Times*, December 26, 1999, Section 4, p. 1; Paul J. Lin and Mathew Benjamin, "The battle royal for your wallet," *U.S. News and World Report*, January 22, 2001, p. 58.

5. Neil Howe and William Straus, "The New Generation Gap," *Atlantic Monthly*, December 1992, pp. 67–89.

6. This is the estimate of Meredith Bagby. See her book, *Rational Exuberance* (New York: Dutton, 1998). Estimates of Xer numbers vary with the analyst and the temporal parameters used to define the Xer generation. Steven Dunphy, in "Generation X: The Infopreneurs of Tomorrow?" *Technological Forecasting and Social Change*, February 1999, p. 200 uses the time frame 1963–1980 and puts Generation X at 45 million. Neil Howe and William Strauss, in "The New Generation Gap," p. 68, use the time frame 1961–1981 and put the Xer generation at 80 million. Karen Ritchie, *Marketing to Generation X* (New York: Lexington Books, 1995, p. 27) also uses the parameters 1961–81 and arrives at the figure 79.4 million. My own examination of the data in the *Statistical Abstract of the United States* leads me to agree with Bagby's time frame and numbers. See also chapter 5 of the present book.

7. Joseph Nocera, "The Arriviste Has Arrived," *New York Times Magazine*, November 15, 1998, p. 68; Chris Taylor, "In Search of Google," *Time*, August 21, 2000, p. 66.

8. John Cassidy, "The Firm," *New Yorker*, March 8, 1999, p. 30.

CHAPTER 2

1. Erich Fromm, *Man for Himself* (New York: Holt, Rinehart and Winston, 1947), pp. 67–78; Richard Stengel,*You're Too Kind* (New York: Simon and Schuster, 2000), p. 16. See also Erich Fromm, *The Sane Society* (New York: Rinehart, 1950); Ruth L. Munroe, *Schools of Psychoanalytic Thought* (New York: Henry Holt, 1955, pp. 470–472).

2. H. L. Havell, *Republican Rome* (New York: Frederick A. Stokes, 1914, p. 475). The comment by Pico delle Mirandola on man's chameleon nature can be found in Jacques Barzun, *From Dawn To Decadence* (New York: HarperCollins, 2000), p. 60; For more about Lord Chesterfield and chameleonism, see Richard Stengel, p. 230.

3. See L. A. Festinger, *A Theory of Cognitive Dissonance* (Stanford: Stanford University Press, 1957).

4. Quoted in Neal Gabler, *Life the Movie* (New York: Knopf, 1998), p. 219.

5. A discussion of theories of anxiety can be found in Rollo May, *The Meaning of Anxiety* (New York: Ronald Press, 1950), p. 349; Calvin S. Hall and Gardner Lindzey, *Theories of Personality* (New York: John Wiley and

Sons, 1957); Christopher F. Monte, *Beneath the Mask* (New York: Praeger, 1977); Salvatore R. Maddi, *Personality Theories* (Homewood, Ill.: Dorsey Press, 1980).

6. Sigmund Freud, *Civilization and Its Discontents* (New York: W. W. Norton, 1930).

7. Harry Stack Sullivan, *The Interpersonal Theory of Psychiatry* (New York: W. W. Norton, 1953).

8. Alfred Adler, *The Practice and Theory of Individual Psychology* (New York: Humanities Press, 1951); Karen Horney, *Our Inner Conflicts* (New York: W. W. Norton, 1945); also see her magisterial summation, *Neurosis and Human Growth* (New York: W. W. Norton, 1950).

9. Karen Horney, *The Neurotic Personality of Our Time* (New York: W. W. Norton, 1937).

10. Ibid.

11. David Riesman, Nathan Glazer, and Reuel Denney, *The Lonely Crowd* (New York: Doubleday, 1953).

12. Ibid. p. 103.

13. Ibid. p. 271.

CHAPTER 3

1. J. Walker Smith and Ann Clurman, *Rocking the Ages* (New York: HarperBusiness, 1997), p. 101. Notwithstanding their large numbers and their influence on society, the Xer mind set has received surprisingly little attention from social analysts. Glimpses of what Xers are thinking can be found in Claire Raines, *Beyond Generation X* (Menlo Park, Calif.: Crisp, 1997); Michael Wexler and John Hulme, *Voices of the Xiled* (New York: Doubleday, 1994); Tom Beaudoin, *Virtual Faith* (San Francisco: Jossey-Bass, 1998.)

2. I have taken a stab at this. See Bernard Carl Rosen, *Winners and Losers of the Information Revolution* (Westport, Conn.: Praeger, 1998.)

3. See Daniel Bell, "The Social Framework of the Information Society," in Michael Dertouzos and Joel Moses, *The Computer Age* (Cambridge, Mass.: M.I.T. Press, 1979); M. Porat and M. Rubin, *The Information Economy* (Washington D.C.: U.S. Commerce Dept., 1977); Stephen Saxby, *The Age of Information* (New York: New York University Press, 1990); Michael Dertouzos, *What Will Be* (San Francisco: Harper Edge, 1997).

4. This is a common theme in descriptions of Xer life. See, for example, Douglas Rushkoff, *Playing the Future* (New York: HarperCollins, 1996).

5. Malcolm Gladwell, "Running from Ritalin," *New Yorker*, February 15, 1999, p. 80. Ritalin is often used to quiet hyperactive children, but it can have the opposite effect.

6. James Gleick, *Faster: The Acceleration of Just About Everything* (New York: Pantheon Books, 1999). Also Malcom Gladwell, *The Tipping Point: How Little Things Make a Big Difference* (New York: Little, Brown, 2000).

7. George Beard, *American Nervousness: Its Causes and Consequences* (New York: Putnam's, 1881), p. 104.

8. Ibid., p. 105.

9. See Bernard C. Rosen, *The Industrial Connection* (New York: Aldine, 1982) for a review of early responses to technological change. A good book on this topic, and one that I have made much use of, is by Samuel P. Hays, *The Response to Industrialism, 1885–1914* (Chicago: University of Chicago Press, 1957).

10. Andrew Sullivan, "What We Look Up to Now," *New York Times Magazine*, November 15, 1998, pp. 19–20.

11. Tom Maguire, "Conflicting Signals," *American Demographics*, November 15, 1998, p. 60.

12. Smith and Clurman, p. 130.

13. David Lipsky and Alexander Abrams, *Late Bloomers* (New York: Times Books, 1994), p. 28.

14. This has been called Carter's "malaise" speech, although the term appears nowhere in his address. It may have crept into popular use as a result of a book by Christopher Lasch that was popular at the time. See his *The Culture of Narcissism* (New York: W. W. Norton, 1978). The oil crisis is described in Robert Hargreaves, *Superpower: A Portrait of America in the 1970s* (New York: St. Martin's Press, 1973); and Daniel Yergin, *The Prize* (New York: Simon and Schuster, 1991).

15. The Long Term Capital Management debacle is described in Michael Lewis, "How Eggheads Crashed," *New York Times Magazine*, January 24, 1999, pp. 24–31. The firm survived its crisis and is today a smaller, more careful replica of its former self. Hedging and speculation, however, never lost its appeal to the get-rich-quick crowd, which continues to include some Xers.

16. For a description of the plight of Xers when financial markets fall apart, see Elizabeth Bumiller, "Free Fall in the Financial District," *New York Times Magazine*, November 15, 1998, p. 74. A more detailed analysis of why markets collapse can be found in Charles R. Hughes, *Money, Greed, and Risk* (New York: Random House, 1999).

17. Bruce Tulgan, *Managing Generation X* (Santa Monica, Calif.: Merritt, 1995), p. 31.

18. Lipsky and Abrams, p. 84.

19. For a detailed analysis of trends in divorce see J. Ross Eshlemann, *The Family* (Boston: Allyn and Bacon, 1985); Jessie Bernard, "The Adjustments of Married Mates," in Harold T. Christensen, *The Handbook of Marriage and the Family* (New York: Rand McNally, 1964); Ben J. Wattenberg, *The Birth Dearth* (New York: Pharos Books, 1987).

20. Lipsky and Abrams, p. 87.

21. Karen Ritchie, *Marketing to Generation X* (New York: Lexington Books, 1995), p. 40.

22. Ibid., p. 41.

23. Lipsky and Abrams, p. 86.

24. Ibid., p. 79.

25. Kristi Lockhart Keil, "An Intimate Portrait of Generation X," *American Enterprise*, January/February, 1998, pp. 49–55.

26. Susan Mitchell, *Generation X* (Ithaca, N.Y.: New Strategist, 1997), p. 17.

27. Lipsky and Abrams, p. 103.

28. Keil, p. 52.

CHAPTER 4

1. Descriptions of these great transformations can be found in the following sources: *Encyclopedia of American Economic History* (New York: Scribner's, 1980), pp. 413–426; Samuel P. Hays, *The Response to Industrialism, 1885–1914* (Chicago: University of Chicago Press, 1957); Ernest L. Bogart and Donald L. Kemmerer, *Economic History of the American People* (New York: Longmans, Green, 1947); George Soule and Vincent P. Caroso, *American Economic History* (New York: Dryden Press, 1957); Arthur Cecil Bining and Thomas C. Cochran, *The Rise of American Economic Life* (New York: Scribner's, 1964).

2. For a more detailed description of the putting-out system see Max Weber, *The Protestant Ethic and the Spirit of Capitalism* (New York: Charles Scribner's, 1948), pp. 66–67.

3. See Stephen S. Cohen and Joseph Zysman, *Manufacturing Matters* (New York: Basic Books, 1987). The title of this book is somewhat misleading. What the authors are arguing, with some effectiveness, is that manufacturing continues to be important to the overall health of the society, notwithstanding its replacement by services as the preeminent force in the economy.

4. Overviews of urban growth in the United States can be found in Philip M. Hauser and Leo F. Schnore, eds., *The Study of Urbanization* (New York: John Wiley and Sons, 1966); Raymond W. Mack and Calvin P. Bradford, *Transforming America* (New York: Random House, 1979).

5. For an analysis of the impact of industrialization on the family see William Goode, *World Revolution and Family Patterns* (New York: Free Press, 1963); Bernard C. Rosen, *The Industrial Connection* (New York: Aldine, 1982).

6. Quoted in Richard D. Thau and Jay S. Heflin, eds., *Generations Apart* (Amherst, N.Y.: Prometheus Books, 1997); see also Neil Howe and William Strauss, "The New Generation Gap," *Atlantic Monthly*, December 1992, p. 80.

7. The rise of the service economy is described in Thomas Weiss, "Service Sector," in Glen Porter, ed., *Encyclopedia of American Economic History* (New York: Scribner's 1980), pp. 413–426; Victor Fuchs, *The Service Economy* (New York: Columbia University Press, 1968). For recent changes in the composition of the workforce see Samuel M. Ehrenhalt, "Work-Force Shifts in the 80s," *New York Times*, August 15, 1986; *Newsweek*, November 27, 1995, p. 98.

8. *Economist*, February, 20, 1994, p. 63; March 19, 1994, pp. 91–92. *New York Times*, April 24, 1994, Business Section, p. 11.

9. This is the appraisal of J. Walker Smith and Ann Clurman, *Rocking the Ages* (New York: HarperCollins, 1997), p. 8.

10. Smith and Clurman, p. 46.

11. Howe and Strauss, p. 69.

12. Ibid, p. 69.

13. Rob Owen, *Gen X TV: The Brady Bunch to Melrose Park* (Syracuse, N.Y.: Syracuse University Press, 1997).

14. Karen Ritchie, *Marketing to Generation X* (New York: Lexington Books, 1995), p. 25.

CHAPTER 5

1. C. Russel, "The Baby Boomer Turns 50," *American Demographics*, December 1999.

2. *Statistical Abstract of the United States* (Washington, D.C.: Bureau of the Census, 1970, 1991, 1998).

3. Karen Ritchie, *Marketing to Generation X* (New York: Lexington Books, 1995), p. 21.

4. Neil Howe and William Strauss, *Generations* (New York: Morrow, 1991).

5. Ritchie, p. 27.

6. Ibid.

7. Ann Clurman, *Time*, June 9, 1997, p. 60.

8. Meredith Bagby, *Rational Exuberance* (New York: Dutton, 1998), p. 3.

9. Ibid, p. 24.

10. Clurman, *Time*, June 9, 1997, p. 62.

11. Suneel Ratan, "Why Busters Hate Boomers," *Fortune*, October 4, 1993, p. 56.

12. *New Republic*, March 21, 1994, p. 6.

13. *New York Times*, November 21, 1999, Business Section, p. 14.

14. Ritchie, p. 25.

15. Neil Howe and William Strauss, "The New Generation Gap,"*Atlantic Monthly*, December 1992, p. 69.

16. Jeff Shesol, "Fun in Politics? As If," in Richard D. Thau and Jay S. Heflin, *Generations Apart* (Amherst, N.Y.: Prometheus Books, 1997), p. 62.

For a closer look at the political attitudes of Xers see Stephen C. Craig and Stephen Earl Bennett, eds., *After the Boom: The Politics of Generation X* (Lanham, Md. : Rowman and Littlefield, 1997).

17. Statistics on income inequality can be found in the Statistical Abstract of the United States, 1995, p. 478; Mickey Kaus, *The End of Equality* (New York: Basic Books, 1992) pp. 29–30; "Inequality," *Economist*, May 5, 1994, pp. 19–21; Christopher Jencks, *Inequality* (New York: Basic Books, 1972); Sheldon Danziger and Peter G. Gottschalk, *America Unequal* (Cambridge, Mass.: Harvard University Press, 1995).

18. *Time*, June 9, 1997, p. 66.

19. Ibid., p. 62.

20. Ibid., p. 63.

CHAPTER 6

1. My discussion of perfectionism draws upon the work of Karen Horney, *The Neurotic Personality of Our Time* (New York: W. W. Norton, 1937), and on Alfred Adler, who also placed much emphasis on the striving for perfection in his analysis of personality. See H. L. Ansbacher and R. R. Ansbacher, eds., *The Individual Psychology of Alfred Adler* (New York: Harper, 1956). It is not clear how much Horney and Adler directly influenced each other. At any rate, to my way of thinking, Horney's explication is clearer on the subject of perfectionism. The stability of the self, in which perfectionism is embedded, is much disputed. Unlike Horney and Adler, who stress the self's resistance to change, some theorists emphasize the mutability of the self. Perhaps Erving Goffman is the most noted exemplar of this position. See his *Presentation of Self in Everyday Life* (Edinburgh: University of Edinburgh Press, 1956). See also Louis A. Zurcher, Jr., *The Mutable Self* (Beverly Hills; Calif.: Sage, 1977).

2. Margery Wolf, *Women and the Family in Rural Taiwan* (Stanford, Calif.: Stanford University Press, 1972); W. F. Nydegger and C. Nydegger, "Tarong: An Illocos Bario in the Philippines," in Beatrice B. Whiting, ed., *Six Cultures* (New York: John Wiley, and Sons 1963); T. W. Maretzki and H. Maretzki, "Taira: An Okinawan Village," in Whiting; David Landy, *Tropical Childhood* (Chapel Hill: University of North Carolina Press, 1959); Bernard C. Rosen, *The Industrial Connection* (New York: Aldine, 1982).

3. Neil Howe and William Strauss, The New Generation Gap *Atlantic Monthly*, December 1992, p. 77.

4. Several self-fulfillment theories in psychology are examined in Salvadore Maddi, *Personality Theories* (Homewood, Ill.: Dorsey Press, 1980). Inexplicably, Maddi leaves out Horney in his discussion of major self-fulfillment theorists. See also Erich Fromm, *Man for Himself* (New York: Rinehart, 1947); Abraham H. Maslow, *Toward a Psychology of Being* (New York: Van Nostrand, 1962); Carl R. Rogers, *On Becoming a Person* (Boston: Houghton Mifflin, 1961).

5. Howe and Strauss, "The New Generation Gap," *Atlantic Monthly*, p. 74.

6. J. Walker Smith and Ann Clurman, *Rocking the Ages* (New York: Harper Business, 1997), pp. 49–51.

7. Ibid., p. 84.

8. Ritchie, p. 135.

CHAPTER 7

1. Erich Fromm, *Escape from Freedom* (New York: Rinehart, 1941).

2. Quote is from Samuel Eliot Morison and Henry Steele Commager, *The Growth of the American Republic* (New York: Oxford University Press, 1937).

3. Bettina Berch, *The Endless Day: The Political Economy of Women and Work* (New York: Harcourt Brace Jovanovich, 1982), p. 42.

4. Sources of statistics about female participation in the paid workforce in the past are as follows: Alice Kessler-Harris, *Out to Work* (New York: Oxford University Press, 1982); Julie A. Matthaei, *An Economic History of Women in America* (New York: Schocken, 1982); Alba M. Edwards, *Comparative Occupational Statistics for the United States, 1870–1940* (Washington, D.C.: U.S. Bureau of the Census, 1943); Elyce J. Rotella, *From Home to Office* (Ann Arbor, Mich.: UMI Research Press, 1981).

5. Walter Karp, *New York Times*, Book Review Section, August 17, 1986, p. 24.

6. Quoted by Robert A. Benett, *New York Times*, June 20, 1986.

7. Bureau of Labor Statistics, cited by Willim Serrin, "Shifts in Work Put White Men in the Minority," *New York Times*, July 31, 1984.

8. Bureau of Labor Statistics "Women in the Workforce: An Overview," U.S. Department of Labor, July 1995.

9. Bernard Carl Rosen, *Women, Work and Achievement* (New York: St. Martin's Press, and London: Macmillan, 1989), p. 133; Bernard C. Rosen and Carol S. Aneshensel, "The Chameleon Syndrome: A Social Psychological Dimension of the Female Sex Role," *Journal of Marriage and the Family*, November 1976, pp. 605–17.

10. Cited by Cathy Young, *Ceasefire* (New York: Free Press, 1999), p. 40.

11. Helen Fisher, *The First Sex* (New York: Random House, 1999), p. 43.

12. Deborah Tannen, *You Just Don't Understand* (New York: Ballantine Books, 1990); Elinor Lenz and Barbara Myerhoff, *The Feminization of America* (Los Angeles: Tarcher, 1985), p. 223.

13. Helen Fisher, p. 84.

14. Ibid., p. 85.

15. Ibid., p. 102.

16. Young, p. 22.

17. Ibid., p. 15.

18. The literature on androgyny is large, though the concept itself has changed little over the past two decades. Much of the writing is devoted to measuring androgyny. The nonspecialist reader may find the following sources helpful. Ellen Piel Cook, *Psychological Androgyny* (New York: Pergamon Press, 1985); Karen Trew and John Kremer, eds., *Gender and Psychology* (New York: Oxford University Press, 1998); Sandra L. Bem "Probing the Promise of Androgyny" in A. G. Kaplan and J. P. Bean, eds., *Beyond Sex-Role Stereotypes* (Boston: Little, Brown, 1976); J. T. Spence and R. L. Helmreich, *Masculinity and Femininity* (Austin: University of Texas Press, 1978).

19. *New York Times Magazine*, February 27, 2000, pp. 19–20; Amy Dickinson, "What Boys Need," *Time*, August 7, 2000, p. 94; Christina Hoff Sommers, *The War against Boys* (New York: Simon and Schuster, 2000).

20. Olga Silverstein and Beth Rashbaum, *The Courage to Raise Good Men* (New York: Viking, 1994), p. 240. The media and entertainment industry have picked up this theme. Men are depicted in sitcoms aimed at boys as beer-guzzling, slacked-jawed dolts. In evening dramas aimed at women, the males are sensitive and willing to open up. See Anita Gates, *New York Times*, April 9, 2000, Section. 2, p. 1.

21. Christine Hoff Sommers, *Who Stole Feminism?* (New York: Simon and Schuster, 1994); For a recent view on the divisions within the women's movement see also Ruth Rosen, *The World Split Open* (New York: Viking, 2000).

22. Silverstein and Rashbaum, p. 38.

CHAPTER 8

1. Data on immigration are taken from the *Statistical Abstract of the United States*, 1995 and 1999; Peter Brimelow, *Alien Nation* (New York: Random House, 1995), especially Appendices, 1, 1B, and 2; Sam Roberts, *Who We Are* (New York: Times Books, 1993); Bill Bryson, *Made in America* (London: Secher and Warburg, 1994); *Congressional Quarterly Almanac*, 52, (1996); George J. Borjas, *Heaven's Door: Immigration Policy and the American Economy* (Princeton, N.J.: Princeton University Press, 1999).

2. *New York Times*, March 10, 1996.

3. Quote from Samuel P. Hays, *Responses to Industrialization, 1885–1914* (Chicago: University of Chicago Press, 1957), p. 99.

4. Hays, p. 99. A general account of late-nineteenth-century attitudes toward immigrants can be found on pp. 99–104.

5. George Madison Grant, *The Passing of the Great Race* (New York: Scribner's, 1922) cited in Hays, p. 102.

6. Irving Howe, *World of Our Fathers* (New York: Harcourt Brace Jovanovich, 1976), p. 76.

7. The statistics are taken from Howe, pp. 57–63. See also Eric Homberger, *Scenes from the Life of a City* (New Haven, Conn.: Yale University Press, 1995).

8. Howe, p. 67.

9. Ibid., p. 69.

10. Ibid., p. 72.

11. Ibid., p. 70.

12. My discussion of Lilian Wald draws upon Howe, pp. 90–94.

13. Howe, p. 90.

14. Ibid., p. 94.

15. See Borjas and Brimelow. Relevant statistics are scattered throughout these books. See especially Appendices 1, 2, and 3 in Brimelow.

16. Borjas, p. 39.

17. Statistics on the racial composition of the American population are taken from Brimelow, pp. 62–68, 116–117; also Jon Meacham, "The New Face of Race," *Newsweek*, September, 18, 2000, pp. 38–64.

18. Roberts, pp. 49–50, 80–82.

19. Ben J. Wattenberg, *The Birth Dearth* (New York: Pharos Books, 1987).

20. Borjas, pp. 11–12.

21. Ibid., pp. 20–21.

22. Reported by Daniel Akst, *New York Times*, May 7, 2000, Business Section, p. 4.

23. Michael Lewis, *The New New Thing* (New York: W. W. Norton, 1999); Anthony Spaeth, "The Golden Diaspora," *Time*, June 19, 2000, pp. B26–28.

24. Paul Krugman, *New York Times*, Week in Review, March 19, 2000 p. 15; also Karen Breslau, "Tomorrowland, Today," *Newsweek*, September 18, 2000, pp. 52–53. For further description of the Asian component in the new immigration wave see Peter I. Rose, *Tempest-Tost* (New York: Oxford University Press, 1997).

CHAPTER 9

1. Recently there has been a spate of books that use evolutionary theory in the interpretation of a wide variety of human behavior. See for example, Robert Wright, *The Moral Animal: Evolutionary Psychology and Everyday Life* (New York: Vintage Books, 1995); Randy Thornhill and Craig T. Palmer, *A Natural History of Rape* (Cambridge, Mass.: MIT Press, 2000); Stephanie Gutmann, *The Kinder, Gentler Military* (New York: Scribner's, 2000).

2. Readers who want a broad overview of theories of social change, without delving too deeply into the subject, may find the following books useful: Wilbert E. Moore, *Social Change* (Englewood Cliffs, N.J.: Prentice-Hall, 1974); Guy E. Swanson, *Social Change* (Glenview, Ill.: Scott, Foresman, 1971); Richard P. Applebaum, *Theories of Social Change* (Chicago: Markham, 1970).

3. Winston Churchill, *A Roving Commission* (London: Mandarin, 1930), quoted in Winston Weathers and Otis Winchester, *A New Strategy of Style* (New York: McGraw-Hill, 1978), p. 220.

4. Aristotle, *The Politics*, 1337a, trans. Ernest Barker (Oxford: Oxford University Press, 1948), p. 390.

5. Ibn Khaldun, *The Muqaddimah*, trans. F. Rosenthal (New York: Pantheon, 1958). For an example of how Ibn Khaldun's work has been used, see Daniel Bell, *The Cultural Contradictions of Capitalism* (New York: Basic Books, 1976) pp. 82– 83.

6. Felipe Fernandez-Armesto, *Millenium* (New York: Scribner's, 1996), p. 116.

7. Quoted in Robert H. Lauer, *Perspectives on Social Change* (Boston: Allyn and Bacon, 1977), p. 32.

8. Quoted in John Keegan, *A History of Warfare* (New York: Knopf, 1992), p. 189.

9. P. A. Sorokin, *Social and Cultural Dynamics* (New York: Bedminster Press, 1962); O. Spengler, *The Decline of the West* (New York: Knopf, 1926); A. J. Toynbee, *A Study of History* (New York: Oxford University Press, 1947).

10. Arthur M. Schlesinger, Jr., *The Cycles of History* (Boston: Houghton Mifflin, 1986), pp. 24, 45.

11. Business journalists are particularly inclined to cyclical theory. See, for example, Robert J. Samuelson, *Newsweek* , February 28, 1994, p. 67.

12. Schlesinger, Jr., ibid.

13. Comments on the attraction of the idea of progress to Americans appear, for example, in D. W. Brogan, *The American Character* (New York: Knopf, 1944); Margaret Mead, *And Keep Your Powder Dry* (New York: Morrow, 1943); David M. Potter, *People of Plenty* (Chicago: University of Chicago Press, 1954); Rupert Wilkinson, *The Pursuit of American Character* (New York: Harper and Row, 1988).

14. Francis Geis and Joseph Geis, *Cathedral, Forge and Waterwheel* (New York: HarperCollins, 1994); Lynn White, *Medieval Technology and Social Change* (Oxford: Clarendon Press, 1962); Peter James and Nick Thrope, *Ancient Inventions* (New York: Ballantine Books, 1994), p. 13.

15. Fernand Braudel, *Civilization and Capitalism*, vol. 1 (New York: Harper and Row, 1979), pp. 215–220.

16. Paul Johnson, *Enemies of Society* (New York: Atheneum, 1977), p. 55.

17. A historical exploration of the idea of progress can be found in Robert Nisbet, *History of the Idea of Progress* (New York: Basic Books, 1980); and John Bagnell Bury, *The Idea of Progress* (New York: Macmillan Company, 1932).

18. See William W. Tarn, *Helenistic Civilization* (London: E. Arnold, 1930), for a classic description of the Hellenistic era.

19. Quoted in Joseph Epstein, *Ambition* (New York: E. P. Dutton, 1980), p. 8.

20. P. Boissonade, *Life and Work in Medieval Europe* (New York: Harper Torchbooks, 1964, p. 5).

21. Quoted in John Kenneth Galbraith, *The Affluent Society* (New York: Houghton Mifflin, 1958), p. 21.

22. Will Durant, *The Story of Philosophy* (New York: Simon and Schuster, 1926), pp. 431–432.

23. Richard Hofstadtler, *Social Darwinism in American Thought, 1860–1915* (Philadelphia: University of Pensylvania Press, 1944).

24. An examination of the Sumnerian position can be found in Robert Green McCloskey, *American Conservatism in the Age of Conservatism* (Cambridge, Mass.: Harvard University Press, 1951).

25. Epstein, p. 1.

CHAPTER 10

1. For incisive accounts of divisions and complaints in America today see Robert Hughes, *The Culture of Complaint* (New York: Oxford University Press, 1993) and Arthur M. Schlesinger, Jr., *The Disuniting of America* (New York: W. W. Norton, 1992).

2. Michael Lewis, "The Artist in the Gray Flannel Pajamas," *New York Times Magazine*, March 5, 2000, p. 46.

3. Nina Munk, "The Price of Freedom," *New York Times Magazine*, March 5, 2000, p. 52.

4. Max Frankel, "Free Agents Unite," *New York Times Magazine*, March 5, 2000, p. 54.

5. Munk, p. 54.

6. Ibid.

7. For an overview of utopian communities in the United States see Laurence Veysey, *The Communal Experience* (New York: Harper and Row, 1973); Donald E. Pitzer, ed. *America's Communal Utopias* (Chapel Hill: University of North Carolina Press, 1997). For a history of the Oneida Community see Spencer Klaw, *Without Sin: The Life and Death of the Oneida Community* (New York: Penguin Press, 1993), and Mary Lockwood Carden, Oneida: *Utopian Community to Modern Corporation* (Baltimore: Johns Hopkins Press, 1969). A valuable description of the commune's demise can be found in a book by Constance Noyes Robertson, a granddaughter of John Noyes. See her *Oneida Community: The Breakup, 1876–1881* (Syracuse, N.Y.: Syracuse University Press, 1972).

Selected Bibliography

Abrams, Charles. *The City Is the Frontier*. New York: Harper Colophon Books, 1965.

Adler, Alfred. *The Practice and Theory of Individual Psychology*. New York: Humanities Press, 1951.

Anton, Ted. *Bold Science*. New York: W. H. Freeman, 2000.

Anzias, Arno. *Ideas and Information*. New York: Simon and Schuster, 1989. Applebaum, Richard P. *Theories of Social Change*. Chicago: Markham, 1970.

Aristotle, *The Politics*,1337a. Translated by Ernest Barker. Oxford: Oxford University Press, 1948.

Bagby, Meredith. *Rational Exuberance*. New York: Dutton, 1998.

Barzun, Jacques. *From Dawn To Decadence*. New York: HarperCollins, 2000.

Beard, George M. *American Nervousness: Its Causes and Consequences*. New York: Putnam's, 1881.

Beaudoin, Tom. *Virtual Faith*. San Francisco: Jossey-Bass, 1998.

Bell, Daniel. *The Comming of the Post-Industrial Society*. New York: Basic Books, 1973.

———. *The Cultural Contradictions of Capitalism*. New York: Basic Books, 1976.

Bennis, Warren, and Phillip E. Slater. *The Temporary Society*. New York: Harper and Row, 1968.

Berch, Bettina. *The Endless Day: The Political Economy of Women and Work*. New York: Harcourt Brace Jovanovich, 1982.

Bernstein, Richard. *Dictatorship of Virtue*. New York: Knopf, 1994.

Bining, Arthur Cecil and Thomas C. Cochran. *The Rise of American Economic Life*. New York: Scribner's Sons, 1964.

Bloch, Marc. *The Medieval Society*. Chicago: University of Chicago Press, Pheonix Edition, 1964.

Bluestone, Barry, and Bennett Harrison. *The Deindustrialization of America*. New York: Basic Books, 1982.

Bogart, Ernest L., and Donald L. Kemmerer. *Economic History of the American People*. New York: Longmans, Green 1947.

Boisonnade, P. *Life and Work in Medieval Europe*. New York: Harper Torchbooks, 1964.

Borjas, J. *Heaven's Door: Immigration Policy and the American Economy*. Princeton, N.J.: Princeton University Press, 1999.

Bowra, C. M. *The Greek Experience*. New York: World, 1957.

Brands, H. W. *The Reckless Decade*. New York: St. Martin's Press, 1995.

Braudel, Fernand. *Civilization and Capitalism*. New York: Harper and Row, 1979.

Brimelow, Peter. *Alien Nation*. New York: Random House, 1995.

Brogan, Dennis W. *The American Character*. New York: Knopf, 1944.

Brooks, David. *Bobos in Paradise*. New York: Simon and Schuster, 2000.

Bryson, Bill. *Made In America*. London: Secker and Warburg, 1994.

Bury, John Bagnell. *The Idea of Progress*. New York: Macmillan, 1932.

Catton, Bruce. *The Civil War*. New York: American Heritage Books, 1960.

Christensen, Harold T. *The Handbook of Marriage and the Family*. New York: Rand McNally, 1964.

Churchill, Winston, *A Roving Commission*. London: Mandarin, 1930.

Clark, Kenneth. *Civilization*. New York: Harper and Row, 1969.

Clecak, Peter. *America's Quest for the Ideal Self*. New York: Oxford University Press, 1983.

Cohen, Stephen S., and Joseph Zysman. *Manufacturing Matters*. New York: Basic Books, 1987.

Collier, James Lincoln. *The Rise of Selfishness in America*. New York: Oxford University Press, 1991.

Cook, Ellen Piel. *Psychological Androgyny*. New York: Pergamon Press, 1985.

Craig, Stephen C., and Stephen Earl Bennett, eds. *After the Boom: The Politics of Generation X*. Lanham Md. : Rowman & Littlefield, 1997.

Croly, Herbert J. *Promise of American Life*. Hamden, Conn.: Archon Books, 1963, originally published 1903.

Danziger, Sheldon, and Peter G. Gottschalk. *American Unequal*. Cambridge, Mass.: Harvard University Press, 1995.

Derber, Charles, William A. Schwartz, and Yale R. Magrass. *Power in the Highest Degree*. New York: Oxford University Press, 1990.

Dertouzos, Michael. *What Will Be*. San Francisco: Harper Edge, 1997.

Dertouzos, Michael, and Joel Moses. *The Computer Age*. Cambridge, Mass.: M.I.T. Press, 1979.

Dordick, Herbert, and Georgette Wang. *The Information Society*. Newbury Park, Calif.: Sage, 1993.

D'souza, Dinesh. *Illiberal Education*. New York: Free Press, 1991.

Durant, Will. *The Story of Philosophy*. New York: Simon and Schuster, 1926.

Epstein, Joseph. *Ambition*. New York: Dutton, 1980.

Edwards, Alba M. *Comparative Occupational Statistics for the United States, 1870–1940*. Washington, D.C.: U.S. Bureau of the Census, 1943.

Eshlemann, J. Ross. *The Family*. Boston: Allyn and Bacon, 1985.

Fernandez-Armesto, Felipe. *Millenium*. New York: Scribner's, 1996.

Festinger, L.A. *A Theory of Cognitive Dissonance*. Stanford, Calif.: Stanford University Press, 1957.

Finley, Moses I. *The Ancient Economy*. Berkeley: University of California Press, 1973.

Fisher, Helen. *The First Sex*. New York: Random House, 1999.

Frank, Robert H. *Luxury Fever*. New York: Free Press, 1999.

Freud, Sigmund. *Civilization And Its Discontents*. New York: W. W. Norton, 1930.

———. *Works of Sigmund Freud: Standard Edition*, Vol. 9. London: Hogarth Press, 1957.

Fromm, Erich. *Escape from Freedom*, New York: Rinehart, 1941.

———. *Man for Himself*. New York: Holt, Rinehart and Winston, 1947.

———. *The Sane Society*. New York: Rinehart, 1950.

Fuchs,Victor. *The Service Ecconomy*. New York: Columbia University Press, 1968.

Gabler, Neal. *Life the Movie*. New York: Knopf, 1998.

Galbraith, John Kenneth. *The Affluent Society*. New York: Houghton Mifflin, 1958.

Garraty, John A. *The New Commonwealth, 1977–1890*. New York: Harper and Row, 1968.

Gartner, Alan, and Frank Riessman. *The Service Economy and the Consumer Vanguard*. New York: Harper and Row, 1974.

Geis, Francis, and Joseph Geis. *Cathedral, Forge and Watermill*. New York: HarperCollins, 1994.

Gilder, George. *Wealth and Poverty*. New York: Basic Books, 1981.

Gitlin, Todd. *The Twilight of Common Dreams*. New York: Metropolitan Books, 1995.

Gladwell, Malcom. *The Tipping Point: How Little Things Make a Big Difference*. New York: Little Brown, 2000.

Gleick, James. *Faster: The Acceleration of Just About Everything*. New York: Pantheon Books, 1999.

Goffman, Erving. *Presentation of Self in Everyday Life*. Edinburgh: University of Edinburgh Press, 1956.

Goode, William. *World Revolution and Family Change*. New York: Free Press, 1963.

Gorer, Geoffrey. *The American People*. New York: W. W. Norton, 1948.

Graña, Cesar. *Bohemians versus Bourgeoisie*. New York: Basic Books, 1973.

Grant, George Madison. *The Passing of the Great Race*. New York: Scribner's, 1922.

Green, Robert McCloskey. *American Conservatism in the Age of Conservatism*. Cambridge, Mass.: Harvard University Press, 1951.

Greenberg, Stanley. *Middle Class Dreams*. New York: Time Books, 1995.

Grenier, Richard. *Capturing the Culture*. Washington, D.C.: Ethics and Public Policy Center, 1991.

Gutmann, Stephanie. *The Kinder, Gentler Military*. New York: Scribner's, 2000.

Hall, Calvin S., and Gardner Lindzey. *Theories of Personality*. New York: John Wiley and Sons, 1957.

Hamilton, Edith. *The Greek Way*. New York: W. W. Norton, 1942.

———. *Mythology*. New York: Mentor Books, 1953.

Hargreaves, Robert. *Superpower: A Portrait of America in the 1970s*. New York: St. Martin's Press, 1973.

Hauser, Arnold. *The Social History of Art*, vol. 1. New York: Vintage Books, 1957.

Hauser, Philip M., and Leo F. Schnore, eds. *The Study of Urbanization*. New York: John Wiley and Sons, 1966.

Havell, H. L. *Republican Rome*. New York: Frederick A. Stokes Company, 1914

Hays, Samuel P. *The Response to Industrialism, 1885–1914*. Chicago: University of Chicago Press, 1957.

Heer, Friedrich. *The Medieval World*. New York: Mentor Books, 1963.

Henry, William A. *In Defense of Elitism*. New York: Doubleday, 1994.

Herrnstein, Richard J., and Charles Murray. *The Bell Curve*. New York: Free Press, 1994.

Hoffman, Martin L. and Lois Wladis Hoffman, eds. *Review of Child Development Research*. New York: Russell Sage Foundation, 1964.

Hofstadtler, Richard. *Social Darwinism in American Thought, 1860–1915*. Philadelphia: University of Pennsylvania Press, 1944.

Homberger, Eric. *Scenes from the Life of a City*. New Haven, Conn.: Yale University Press, 1995.

Horney, Karen. *Neurosis and Human Growth*. New York: W. W. Norton, 1950.

———. *The Neurotic Personality of Our Time*. New York: W. W. Norton, 1937.

———. *Our Inner Conflicts*. New York: W. W. Norton, 1945.

Howe, Irving. *World of Our Fathers*. New York: Harcourt Brace Jovanovich, 1976.

Howe, Neil, and William Strauss. *Generations*. New York: Morrow, 1991.

Hughes, Charles R. *Money, Greed, and Risk*. New York: Random House, 1999.

Hughes, Robert. *The Culture of Complaint*. New York: Oxford University Press, 1993.

———. *The Shock of the New*. New York: Knopf, 1981.

Ibn Khaldun, *The Muqaddimah*. Translated by F. Rosenthal. New York: Pantheon, 1958.

James, Peter, and Nick Thrope. *Ancient Inventions*. New York: Ballantine Books, 1994.

Jencks, Christopher. *The Homeless*. Cambridge, Mass.: Harvard University Press, 1994.

Johnson, Paul. *Enemies of Society*. New York: Atheneum, 1977.

Kaplan, A. G. and J. P. Bean, eds. *Beyond Sex-role Stereotypes*. Boston: Little, Brown, 1976.

Kaus, Mickey. *The End of Equality*. New York: Basic Books, 1992.

Keegan, John. *A History of Warfare*. New York: Knopf, 1992.

Kerkhoff, Alan C. *Socialization and Social Class*. Englewood Cliffs, N.J.: Prentice-Hall, 1972.

Kessler-Harris, Alice. *Out to Work*. New York: Oxford University Press, 1982.

Klaw, Spencer. *Without Sin: The Life and Death of the Oneida Community*. New York: Penguin Press, 1993.

Kraut, Alan M. *The Huddled Masses*. Arlington Heights, Ill.: Harlan Davidson, 1982.

Krugman, Paul. *Peddling Prosperity*. New York: W. W. Norton, 1994.

Landy, David. *Tropical Childhood*. Chapel Hill: University of North Carolina Press, 1959.

Lapham, Lewis. *Money and Class*. New York: Heidenfeld and Nicolson, 1988.

Lasch, Christopher. *The Culture of Narcissism*. New York: W. W. Norton, 1978.

———. *Haven in a Heartless World*. New York: Basic Books, 1977.

———. *The Revolt of the Elite and the Betrayal of Democracy*. New York: W. W. Norton, 1995.

Lauer, Robert H. *Perspectives on Social Change*. Boston: Allyn and Bacon, 1977.

Lebergott, Stanley. *Pursuing Happiness*. Princeton, N.J.: Princeton University Press, 1993.

Lemann, Nicholas. *The Big Test: The Secret History of American Meritocracy*. New York: Farrar, Straus, Giroux, 1999.

Lenz, Elinor, and Barbara Myerhoff. *The Feminization of America*. Los Angeles: Tarcher, 1985.

Le Vine, Robert A. *Culture, Behavior and Personality*. Chicago: Aldine, 1974.

Lewis, Michael. *The New New Thing*. New York: W. W. Norton, 1999.

Lind, Michael. *The Next American Nation*. New York: Free Press, 1995.

Lipman-Blumen, Jean. *Gender Roles and Power*. Englewood Cliffs, N.J.: Prentice-Hall, 1984.

Lipset, Seymour Martin. *The First New Nation*. New York: Basic Books, 1963.

Lipsky, David, and Alexander Abrams. *Late Bloomers*. New York: Times Books, 1994.

Lutz, Tom. *American Nervousness, 1903*. Ithaca, N.Y.: Cornell University Press, 1991.

Lynd, Robert S., and Helen M. Lynd. *Middletown*. New York: Harcourt, Brace, 1929.

———. *Middletown in Transition*. New York: Harcourt, Brace. 1937.

Mack, Raymond W., and Calvin P. Bradford. *Transforming America*. New York: Random House, 1979.

Maddi, Salvatore. *Personality Theories*. Homewood, Ill.: The Dorsey Press, 1980.

Madrick, Jeffrey. *The End of Affluence*. New York: Random House, 1995.

Magnet, Myron.*The Dream and the Nightmare*. New York: Morrow, 1993.

Maslow, Abraham H. *Toward A Psychology of Being*. New York: Van Nostrand, 1962.

Matthaei, Julie A. *An Economic History of Women in America*. New York: Schocken, 1982.

May, Rollo. *The Meaning of Anxiety*. New York: Ronald Press, 1950.

Mazels, Alfred. *Industrial Growth and World Trade*. Cambridge: Cambridge University Press, 1963.

McKenna, Elizabeth P. *When Work Doesn't Work Anymore*. New York: Delacorte Press, 1997.

McLean, George M. *The Rise of Anarchy in America*. Chicago: R. G. Badoux, 1890.

McLoughlin, William G. *Revivals, Awakenings and Reform*. Chicago: University of Chicago Press, 1978.

Mead, Margaret. *And Keep Your Powder Dry*. New York: Morrow, 1943.

Mills, C. Wright. *The Power Elite*. New York: Oxford University Press, 1956.

Mitchell, Susan. *Generation X*. Ithaca, N.Y.: New Strategist, 1997.

Monte, Christopher. *Beneath the Mask*. New York: Praeger, 1977.

Moore, Wilbert E. *Social Change*. Englewood Cliffs, N.J. : Prentice-Hall, 1974.

Morison, Samuel Eliot, and Henry Steele Commager. *The Growth of the American Republic*. New York: Oxford University Press, 1937.

Morris, Charles R. *A Time of Passion*. New York: Harper and Row, 1984.

Munroe, Ruth L. *Schools of Psychoanalytic Thought*. New York: Henry Holt, 1955.

Nisbet, Robert. *History of the Idea of Progress*. New York: Basic Books, 1980.

Novak, Michael. *The Rise of the Unmeltable Ethnics*. New York: Macmillan, 1992.

Osborne, John W. *The Silent Revolution*. New York: Scribner's, 1970.

Owen, Rob. *Gen X TV: The Brady Bunch to Melrose Place*. Syracuse, N.Y.: Syracuse University Press, 1997.

Parks, Henry Bamford. *The American Experience*. New York: Random House, 1947.

Parsons, Talcott. *The Social System*. Glencoe, Ill.: The Free Press, 1951.

Pirenne, Henri. *Economic and Social History of Medieval Europe*. New York: Harcourt, Brace, 1937.

Pitzer, Donald E., ed. *America's Communal Utopias*. Chapel Hill: University of North Carolina Press, 1997.

Plumb, J. D. *England in the Eighteenth Century*. London: Penguin Books, 1950.

Polyani, Karl. *The Great Transformation*. New York: Rinehart, 1944.

Porat, M., and M. Rubin. *The Information Economy*.Washington D.C.: U.S. Commerce Dept., 1977.

Potter, David M. *People of Plenty*. Chicago: University of Chicago Press, 1954.

Porter, Glen, ed. *Encyclopedia of American Economic History*. New York: Scribner's, 1980.

Raines, Claire. *Beyond Generation X*. Menlo Park, Calif.: Crisp, 1997.

Reich, Robert B. *The Work of Nations*. New York: Knopf, 1991.

Riesman, David, Nathan Glazer, and Reuel Denney. *The Lonely Crowd*. New York: Doubleday, 1953.

Ritchie, Karen. *Marketing to Generation X*. New York: Lexington Books, 1995.

Roberts, Sam. *Who We Are*. New York: Times Books, 1993.

Robertson, Constance Noyes. *Oneida Community: The Breakup, 1876–1881*. Syracuse, N.Y.: Syracuse University Press, 1972.

Rogers, Carl R. *On Becoming a Person*. Boston: Houghton Mifflin, 1961.

Rose, Peter I. *Tempest-Tost*. New York: Oxford University Press, 1997.

Rosen, Bernard C. *The Industrial Connection*. New York: Aldine, 1982.

———. *Winners and Losers of the Information Revolution*. Westport, Conn.: Praeger, 1998.

———. *Women, Work and Achievement*. New York: St. Martin's Press and London: Macmillan, 1989.

Rosen, Ruth. *The World Split Open*. New York: Viking, 2000.

Rotella, Elyce J. *From Home to Office*. Ann Arbor, Mich.: UMI Research Press, 1981.

Rushkoff, Douglas. *Playing the Future*. New York: HarperCollins, 1996.

Samuelson, Robert J. *The Good Life and Its Discontents*. New York: Times Books, 1995.

Saxby, Stephen. *The Age of Information*. New York: New York University Press, 1990.

Schlesinger, Arthur. *Political and Social History of the United States, 1829–1925*. New York: Macmillian, 1925.

Schlesinger, Arthur M., Jr. *The Cycles of History*. Boston: Houghton Mifflin, 1986.

———. *The Disuniting of America*. New York: W.W. Norton, 1992.

Schneider, Wolf. *Babylon Is Everywhere*. New York: McGraw-Hill, 1963.

Schwartz, Peter, Peter Leyden, and Joel Hyatt. *The Long Boom*. Reading, Mass.: Perseus Books, 1999.

Silverstein, Olga, and Beth Rashbaum. *The Courage to Raise Good Men*. New York: Viking, 1994.

Smith, J. Walker, and Ann Clurman. *Rocking the Ages*. New York: HarperBusiness, 1997.

Sommers, Christina Hoff. *The War against Boys*. New York: Simon and Schuster, 2000.

————. *Who Stole Feminism?* New York: Simon and Schuster, 1994.

Sorokin, P. A. *Social and Cultural Dynamics*. New York: Bedminster Press, 1962.

Soule, George, and Vincent P. Caroso. *American Economic History*. New York: Dryden Press, 1957.

Spence, J. T., and R. L. Helmreich. *Masculinity and Femininity*. Austin: University of Texas Press, 1978.

Spengler, O. *The Decline of the West*. New York: Knopf, 1926.

Statistical Abstract of the United States. Washington, D.C.: Bureau of the Census, 1970, 1991, 1998.

Stengel, Richard. *You're Too Kind*. New York: Simon and Schuster, 2000.

Stephenson, Jane. *Men Are Not Cost Effective*. New York: HarperCollins, 1995.

Sullivan, Harry Stack. *The Interpersonal Theory of Psychiatry*. New York: W. W. Norton, 1953.

Swanson, Guy E. *Social Change*. Glenview, Ill.: Scott, Foresman, 1971.

Tannen, Deborah. *You Just Don't Understand*. New York: Ballantine Books, 1990.

Tarn, William W. *Hellenistic Civilization*. London: E. Arnold, 1930.

Tawney, Richard H. *Religion and the Rise of Capitalism*. New York: Harcourt, Brace, 1926.

Thau, Richard D., and Jay S. Heflin, eds. *Generations Apart*. Amherst, N.Y.: Prometheus Books, 1997.

Thornhill, Randy, and Craig T. Palmer. *A Natural History of Rape*. Cambridge, Mass.: MIT Press, 2000.

Tocqueville, Alexis de. *Democracy in America*. New York: Vintage Books, 1954.

Toynbee, A. J. *A Study of History*. New York: Oxford University Press, 1947.

Trew, Karen, and John Kremer, eds. *Gender and Psychology*. New York: Oxford University Press, 1998.

Tulgan, Bruce. *Managing Generation X*. Santa Monica, Calif.: Merritt Publishing, 1995.

Veblen, Thorstein. *The Theory of the Leisure Class*. New York: Macmillan, 1899.

Veyne, Paul. *A History of Private Life, vol. 1*. Cambridge, Mass.: Belknap Press, 1987.

Veysey, Laurence. *The Communal Experience*. New York: Harper and Row, 1973.

Wattenberg, Ben J. *The Birth Dearth*. New York: Pharos Books, 1987.

Weathers, Winston, and Otis Winchester. *A New Strategy of Style*. New York: McGraw-Hill, 1978.

Weber, Adna. *The Growth of Cities in the Nineteenth Century*. Ithaca, N.Y.: Cornell University Press, 1965.

Weber, Max. *The Protestant Ethic and the Spirit of Capitalism*. New York: Scribner's, 1948.

Wexler, Michael, and John Hulme. *Voices of the Xiled*. New York: Doubleday, 1994.

White, Lynn. *Medieval Technology and Social Change*. Oxford: Clarendon Press, 1962.

Whiting, Beatrice. *Six Cultures*. New York: John Wiley and Sons, 1963.

Wilkinson, Rupert. *The Pursuit of American Character*. New York: Harper and Row, 1988.

Williams, Rhys M. *Cultural Wars in American Politics*. Hawthorne, N.Y.: Aldine de Gruyter, 1997.

Wilson, William Julius. *The Truly Disadvantaged*. Chicago: University of Chicago Press, 1987.

Wolf, Margery. *Women and the Family in Rural Taiwan*. Stanford, Calif.: Stanford University Press, 1972.

Wood, Gordon S. *The Radicalism of the American Revolution*. New York: Vintage, 1993.

Wright, Robert. *The Moral Animal: Evolutionary Psychology and Everyday Life*. New York: Vintage Books, 1995.

Wrong, Dennis. *The Problem of Order*. New York: Free Press, 1994.

Wyllie, Irwin G. *The Self-Made Man in America*. New Brunswick, N.J.: Rutgers University Press, 1954.

Yergin, Daniel. *The Prize*. New York: Simon and Schuster, 1991.

Young, Cathy. *Ceasefire*. New York: Free Press, 1999.

Young, Michael. *The Rise of the Meritocracy*. London: Thames and Hudson, 1958.

Zurcher, Louis A., Jr. *The Mutable Self*. Beverly Hills, Calif.: Publications, 1977.

Index

About the Author

BERNARD CARL ROSEN is Emeritus Professor of Sociology at Cornell University. He has been director of research projects on the causes and effects of social change in five countries and three continents and a visiting professor to several foreign universities, including the London School of Economics and the University of Padua. He has published six books, including *Winners and Losers of the Information Revolution* (Praeger, 1998) and *The Industrial Connection*, as well as numerous articles in a wide variety of journals.